IN THE SHADOW
OF THE HAN

IN THE SHADOW OF THE HAN

LITERATI THOUGHT AND SOCIETY AT THE BEGINNING OF THE SOUTHERN DYNASTIES

CHARLES HOLCOMBE

UNIVERSITY OF HAWAII PRESS, HONOLULU

94 95 96 97 98 99   5 4 3 2 1

Library of Congress Cataloging-in-Publication Data
Holcombe, Charles, 1956–
In the shadow of the Han : literati thought and society at the
beginning of the Southern dynasties / Charles Holcombe.
p.   cm.
Includes bibliographical references and index.
ISBN 0–8248–1592–0 (acid-free paper)
1. China—History—Northern and Southern dynasties, 386–589.
I.   Title.
DS748.6.H65   1994
931'.03—dc20   94–28355
CIP

University of Hawaii Press books are printed on acid-free paper
and meet the guidelines for permanence and durability of
the Council on Library Resources.

Book design by Kenneth Miyamoto

For Andrea,
my daughter

Veritas et fortitudo

CONTENTS

ACKNOWLEDGEMENTS

My involvement with China's great age of northern and southern division began innocently enough with a graduate research
project at the University of Michigan in the winter of 1980. How
little I knew then! The subject proved to be rich—exhausting and
inexhaustible as well as maddeningly difficult to piece together
into a satisfactorily coherent pattern.

The research that eventually led to the writing of this book
took place mostly in the Michigan Library in the years since 1980.
My research in Ann Arbor was supplemented by travel to Kyoto
University in 1984–1985, the Library of Congress during the summer of 1988, Shaanxi Teachers College in Sian (Xian) during the
summer of 1992, and the University of Iowa, periodically. My Chinese language skills were also sharpened by a stint at Taiwan
National Normal University in 1980–1981 and through the constant education provided by my wife Jen (née Li Yü-chen).

Research in Japan was made possible through the mediation of
Kenneth DeWoskin and was conducted under the direction of
Professor Kominami Ichirō. In Kyoto, Professor Tonami Mamoru
kindly allowed me to observe, as a silent participant, the impressive seminar on Chinese Aristocratic Society bequeathed to him
by the late Kawakatsu Yoshio. My debt to Kyoto's Research Institute for Humanistic Affairs is large, and my all too brief stay in
Kyoto instilled in me an abiding love for that ancient city nestled
between the mountains.

Research in Washington was supported by a Summer Faculty

Research Grant from Northeast Missouri State University. It is thanks to Northeast Missouri, and former President Charles McClain in particular, that I even have an academic career.

My research in Sian benefited from the generous assistance of Professor He Qinggu (Ho Ch'ing-ku). The trip was made possible by an exchange program with the University of Northern Iowa coordinated by Dr. Robert Leestamper.

As a graduate student at the University of Michigan, I found myself under the special care of Professor Chun-shu Chang. I could not have been more fortunate. Professor Chang together with his wife and colleague Shelley Hsueh-lun Chang set standards of erudition that I may aspire to but never hope to match. I am grateful to them both.

Of my many teachers at Michigan over the years, I also wish to thank in particular (in alphabetical order) Kenneth DeWoskin, Albert Feuerwerker, Roger Hackett, Charles Hucker, Harriet Mills, Sam Nagara, and Ernest Young. Each, in his or her own way, made a singular contribution to my growth as a scholar and also as a human being.

I hammered out the first draft of this book during the summer of 1990. Some of its initial shortcomings were subsequently addressed by Roger Ames, Rafe de Crespigny, Albert Dien, Dennis Grafflin, and Richard Mather. My colleagues at Northern Iowa Jay Lees and Roy Sandstrom also guided me through the logic of some of the more tortured passages in my text. All of the these scholars, however, must be absolved of any complicity in the end product. Blame for all opinions expressed in this book and for any remaining factual errors must be mine alone.

Conference presentations relating to this research were made at the Mid-America Conference on History, Springfield, Missouri, in 1987 ("A State of the Mind: Ideology, Self-Cultivation and Power in Fourth-Century China"); the Midwest Conference on Asian Affairs at Madison, Wisconsin, in 1988 ("Southern Magnates: Land and Power in Early Six Dynasties South China"); and at Bloomington, Indiana, in 1990 ("A Perfect Gentleman: Chih Tun and the Horizons of Fourth-Century Chinese Thought"). A report on the work in progress was also made to the Early Medieval China Group, meeting in conjunction with the Association for Asian Studies annual conference in New Orleans in 1991 ("To Be and Not To Be: The Riddle of Neo-Taoism"). The report was subsequently reproduced in the group *Newsletter,* number 4 (1991).

Additional thanks go to Gregory Sterling for his cartographic assistance, Li Feng-mao, Jens Petersen, Alan Berkowitz, and Yuet Keung Lo for invaluable research suggestions, the staff of the University of Northern Iowa Interlibrary Loan Department, our indispensable departmental secretary Judith Dohlman, and the head of the History Department John Johnson for moral support when it really counted.

Finally, I owe a special debt of gratitude to the University of Hawaii Press and my editor there, Patricia Crosby.

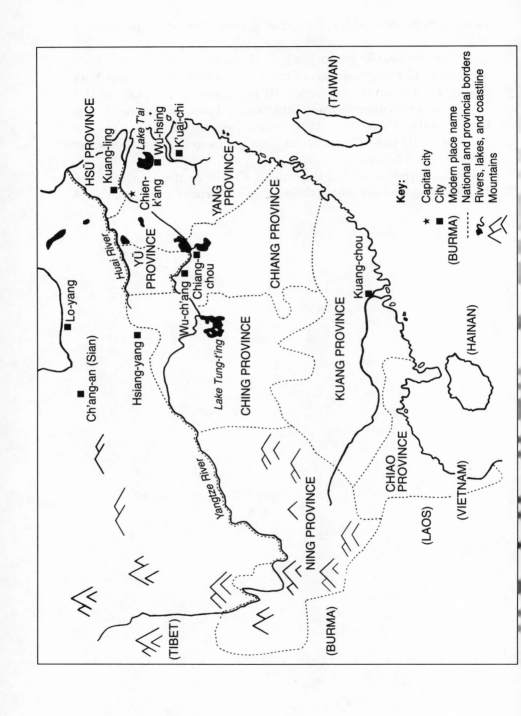

1

INTRODUCTION: REIMAGINING CHINA

> We reflect back upon the times of chaos, when the land was divided and states were founded, starting a pattern of contention. Wars were waged daily, spilling blood in the wilds. From its beginnings in hoary antiquity through countless generations down to the Five Emperors, none were able to prevent this. Now the [First] emperor has made one family of all under heaven. Soldiers will not rise again. Vexations and injuries have been done away with. The common people are settled in peace, the benefits of which are eternal.
>
> —First Emperor of Ch'in,
> I-shan Inscription, 219 B.C.

In the third month of A.D. 318, news of the death of the last emperor of the Western Chin dynasty reached Ssu-ma Jui, the Prince of Chin, at his court in the city known as Chien-k'ang (modern Nanking).[1] The prince went into mourning, and shortly thereafter ascended the throne to become the first emperor, Emperor Yüan (r. 318–323), of a dynasty in exile, the Eastern, or second half, of the Chin (318–420). Whereas his predecessors in the Western Chin (265–317) had "faced south" to rule over the vast expanses of a unified China, Emperor Yüan exercised a precarious sway only in the south, and his reign marks the beginning of what Chinese historians call the period of the Northern and Southern dynasties. For the next three centuries China was to be divided.

Reimagined Community

A relatively sophisticated civilization in southeast China—what may, broadly speaking, be referred to as Chiang-nan, the region south of the Yangtze River—dates back to antiquity, and large numbers of northern immigrants moved into the area as early as the late Han dynasty (206 B.C.–A.D. 220). However, the "cradle" of Chinese civilization was the Yellow River valley to the north, and

1

Chiang-nan still retained something of the flavor of a frontier zone when Ssu-ma Jui first moved there.[2] Soon afterward the remnants of the old regime were driven from their ancient northern homeland by foreign invaders.[3] The state that Ssu-ma Jui, as Emperor Yüan, then established in exile in the south became a haven for refugees who fled the strife-torn Central Plain in large numbers.[4] Together with the older residents of the south, they worked to restore the lost outlines of a Chinese imperial state.[5]

The emperor hastened to construct altars to the deities of soil and grain, to build an ancestral temple at the new court, and, after some debate, to conduct sacrifices to Heaven in the southern suburbs of the city in demonstration of the new regime's legitimacy.[6] Famous literati such as Tiao Hsieh (d. 322) and Ho Hsün (260–319), who were able to recall the vanished protocols of the northern court, were consulted in the restoration of a ritual appropriate to the Confucian monarchy.[7] In this reconstruction their gaze was not restricted to immediate precedent; they also cast their vision back past recent imperial dynasties to the distant Chou period—the classical font for Confucian legitimacy—in framing their vision of the ideal Chinese state.[8]

Nations, as Benedict Anderson suggests, are at their core all "imagined communities."[9] This suggests something of the process by which the Chinese state was reconstituted amid unfamiliar surroundings in Chiang-nan in the early fourth century. Without implying that fourth-century China experienced anything like the uniquely modern phenomenon we call nationalism, it may still be said that the Chinese elite did exhibit a somewhat similar mythicocultural sense of identification with the grand heritage of China.[10] The Eastern Chin court appealed to "traditionalism," in the sense that Theodore Bestor uses the word, as a "device for managing or responding to social change" and validating new arrangements by means of reference to supposedly venerable cultural norms.[11] In order to civilize the rough frontier world of fourth-century Chiang-nan—a land where ethnic "Han" Chinese might even have been a numerical minority—a Chinese nation had first to be reinvented there.[12]

When the Yellow River valley cradle of Chinese civilization fell to bands of marauding foreigners, "China" was recreated in the marshes of the lower Yangtze valley by a refugee literati elite according to the model carried south with them in their heads. Naturally, they got much of it wrong. "Traditionalism" shaped the emergence of the Southern dynasties, but faulty memories and new material and institutional conditions distorted that tradition into novel shapes. The China that took shape in exile in the fourth-century south was at the same time an unbroken development in the premodern tradition, which historians today like to set in contrast with China's modern transformation, and the product of a remarkable revolution that twisted that tradition into a new and distinctive form. Although it was undeniably a continuation of classic Chinese civilization and it was self-consciously intended to be a reproduction of past glories, a substantially new world emerged in fourth-century south China.[13]

The Significance of a Lesser Dynasty

To date, relatively little attention has been devoted to this medieval Chinese world by mainstream English-language scholarship. Because it was an age of political disorder and military weakness in the face of a foreign threat, there has been an inclination to disparage the Northern and Southern dynasties.[14] There are several reasons for reconsidering this traditional neglect now, however. For one thing, as Kuwahara Jitsuzō reported as early as 1927, the fourth-century exodus to Chiang-nan marks the beginning of that great shift in China's demographic center of gravity from north to south that figures so prominently in later eras.[15] Accompanying this influx of population into the south, also, came the first phases of the great commercial expansion of Chiang-nan, which underlay and made possible the astonishing "economic revolution" Mark Elvin ascribed to the Sung (960–1279).[16]

In addition, the Southern dynasties were "an age of brilliant aristocratic culture."[17] Art—calligraphy, painting, and sculpture —made great advances; and, in literature, there was exuberant activity in the fields of poetry and history—to say nothing of the first stirrings of an interest in fiction. This period was one of the most creative in Chinese history philosophically since the "Hundred Schools" of the late Chou, and the period also witnessed the maturation of China's two great religious systems: Buddhism and (religious) Taoism. Indeed, together with the Sui and T'ang dynasties (589–906), this period could be called the golden age of religion in China.

It was only in the realm of politics that the Southern dynasties could be labeled "dark ages," comparable to the troubled times of early medieval Europe. From the final years of the Han, wars and invasions convulsed China, and dynasty after dynasty slipped from the throne with numbing regularity. Although nothing can mitigate the real human tragedy of these conflicts, even this political instability can be said to have had a positive dimension. The Northern and Southern dynasties became the only extended period since the founding of the first empire by Ch'in Shih-huang in 221 B.C. when the role of the central government did not overshadow and sometimes choke off aspects of Chinese private life.

As Mori Mikisaburō observes, the early imperial dynasties of Ch'in and Han had been "typical absolutist bureaucratic states." During the Northern and Southern dynasties, however, imperial civil servants gained largely hereditary control over appointment to office, and a substantial measure of financial independence, becoming "free men whose source of livelihood was under their own control."[18] Freed now from subservience to autocratic imperial masters, members of the Southern dynasty elite were released to pursue individual self-realization through religion, art, music, poetry, and social activities, and were not obliged to concentrate narrowly on advancement through the ranks of the bureaucracy, as might be the case under more effective absolute imperial supervision.

The third and fourth centuries thus became China's great age of the "discovery of humanity" *(ningen no hakken)* in Mori Mikisaburō's words, or the age of what Yü Ying-shih has labeled "the discovery of the individual."[19] In comparison with other periods of imperial Chinese history, the age of division might even have witnessed a degree of intellectual and social emancipation for women.[20] It was a rare time in Chinese history when the exploration of a person's soul, for members of the elite, took precedence over court intrigue and bureaucratic career building.

This process of individual self-realization is illustrated by Yano Chikara's study of third-century written evaluations of candidates for government office. In the first half of the third century, the Wei dynasty had tried to restore centralized imperial power and implemented a policy that "only talent be promoted" *(wei-ts'ai shih-chü)*. Under this regime administrative efficiency and bureaucratic service were given priority in evaluating candidates for office, but after the usurpation of the throne by the Ssu-ma family in 265, evaluations for office lost much of their interest in administrative considerations and took on an increasing concern for the artistic, musical, and conversational ability of the candidates.[21] This transformation simultaneously illustrates both the increasing weakness and inefficiency of the central government and the dawning of a cultural interest in the world beyond politics.

The political disarray that was left behind after the collapse of the Han imperial order provided an atmosphere tense with uncertainty, but this uncertainty might have contributed to the artistic and philosophical freshness of the age. A time of strife may also be a time of creative competition. And the very fact that the Northern and Southern dynasties form the longest period of political division in imperial Chinese history makes this a "counternormal" *(fan-ch'ang)* episode.[22] As a singularity in the enduring edifice of imperial power in China, the Northern and Southern dynasties demand closer inspection.

Only twice in Chinese history, since the beginning of the empire in 221 B.C., has the very foundation of the Chinese world order been challenged.[23] The most recent of these challenges has been posed by the modern West, in the nineteenth and twentieth centuries. The other great cultural challenge took place during the era of division, after the fall of the Han dynasty in A.D. 184–220, when the entire imperial system was radically confronted by sustained political collapse and, before long, the loss of much of the north to foreign invaders.

One significant difference between the modern Chinese crisis and the medieval one, however, is that modern Chinese intellectuals could not avoid absorbing certain elements of Western culture, whereas (apart from accepting Indian Buddhism) medieval intellectuals could only turn inward to a reformulation of tradition itself to resolve their crisis. None of the invading foreigners of the period of division presented China with an attractive alternative to China's own civilization. The medieval Chinese, therefore, could turn only to fading memories of their own past glories to support them as they faced the specter of decline.

Acutely conscious of its fall from the imperial heights of the Han dynasty, the Chinese court called for a revitalization of the ancient ideals, as best they could be reconstructed from the imperfect records of the day. This call for restoration, in turn, then became a powerful force for change that together with Buddhism and the weakness of the central state itself remade China in the Northern and Southern dynasties.

China's Middle Ages

Aside from the cultural achievements of the Northern and Southern dynasties, and their unique position in the otherwise scarcely interrupted chain of imperial Chinese history, a final reason for interest in this period is that it provides a way of testing certain theories about the universality of patterns of historical development. China entered its medieval era with a decentralized and aristocratic social and political system that bears striking superficial resemblance to the European Middle Ages. The fall of Han, like that of Rome, was attended by so-called barbarian invasions. As the Christian religion swept Europe, so too Buddhism conquered China. There was at least a temporary decline in commerce and an apparent reversion to a manorial economy, whose great estates were often tilled by dependent farmers bearing some resemblance to European serfs. And, most notably, both China and Europe experienced the rise of a new kind of aristocratic elite during their respective middle ages.

Like medieval Europe, Northern and Southern dynasties China was politically decentralized, with a blurring of the distinction between public and private authority. Although local authorities tried to govern as far as possible in the name of an imperial bureaucracy, they enjoyed a large measure of autonomy. Local society came to seem increasingly remote from the active attentions of the court, and the famous "rule of avoidance" (by means of which successive imperial Chinese regimes guaranteed the loyalty and limited the power of local officials by forbidding them assignments to their own home districts) lapsed.[24] The countryside came to be ruled as much by local men of substance as by the central government.

Even the court came to be dominated by private great families. In the early days of the Eastern Chin, Wang Tao's (276–339) prestige and influence were nearly equal to that of Emperor Yüan.[25] Later, toward the end of the dynasty in the early fifth century, when a man who had fled north in revolt against the Eastern Chin was asked about conditions at the Chin court, he supposedly replied: "Although the ruler of Chin has the honor of facing south [in the traditional posture of a ruler], he does not have the

reality of control. Prime ministers hold the government, governance issues from many portals, authority has left the imperial
family, and all this has become normal."[26]

A critical parallel between medieval Europe and China is that
both societies have been described as aristocratic. Jack L. Dull, for
example, classifies Northern and Southern dynasties society as
"aristocratic" in his essay on "The Evolution of Government in
China".[27] "Nobility" or "aristocracy" is a standard if nontechnical
English dictionary translation for such terms as *kuei-tsu* (Japanese
kizoku), which Asian scholars habitually use in reference to the
period. And yet, a number of English-language students of the
Northern and Southern dynasties are troubled by this constant
use of the English word "aristocracy."

David Johnson's book *The Medieval Chinese Oligarchy*, for example, took the question of whether or not the medieval Chinese
elite was an "aristocracy" as its central problematic. In the end,
Johnson concluded that, although it is undeniable that a few hundred great families did succeed in dominating medieval society
for centuries, they did not constitute a genuine aristocracy because they lacked any clear "juridical" basis and their titles were
not directly hereditary. Instead of "aristocratic" titles, Johnson
argues, the great families of medieval China relied for their status
on their virtual monopoly over the machinery of appointment to
government office. Johnson, therefore, regarded the term "oligarchy" to be a more appropriate designation for the early medieval Chinese elite.[28]

Although Yang Kuang-hui notes that hereditary titles actually
were common during this period and contributed significantly to
the ability of the medieval elite to perpetuate itself over multiple
generations, Johnson's critique is well-founded.[29] Despite the
increased personalization of the ruler-subject bond noted by Yü
Ying-shih, the medieval Chinese elite remained, in Albert Dien's
words, "members of lineages ... whose shared resource was
... privileged access to official appointment" and whose source of
power ultimately "derived from their capacity as officers of the
state."[30]

The early medieval Chinese great families might more accurately be described as hereditary or partially hereditary bureaucrats than as aristocrats. This was because medieval China failed
to develop (beyond a rudimentary and sporadic stage) the characteristic institutions of feudalism, familiar from European his-

tory, of vassalage and the fief. There were no channels of power for the medieval Chinese elite to occupy, apart from office in the central imperial state. Although access to office did become restricted to an essentially closed hereditary elite, office itself never became proprietary—the hereditary property of the office holder—thus sharply distinguishing it from the counties, duchies, and lesser fiefs of feudal Europe.[31] China's medieval elite was certainly "aristocratic," in Patricia Ebrey's sense of possessing "hereditary high social status, independent of full court control," but it did not constitute a *feudal* aristocracy and was therefore not at all what the term usually implies in a European context.[32]

During the period of division following the Han dynasty, China did not move from an imperial system to a feudal one. Government retained its imperial structure. The quasi-aristocratic privileges of the hereditary great families and the decentralized condition of government in Northern and Southern dynasties China were simple consequences of the weakness of the emperors and the relative strength of the great ministerial families, and did not signify that any fundamentally new system had taken the place of the old Ch'in-Han model.

The Feudalism Controversy

To be sure, Chinese scholars today do call this system "feudal," but they also call the Ch'in and Han empires "feudal" and all the other imperial dynasties down to the "semifeudal, semicolonial" nineteenth and twentieth centuries. In fact, it is striking that the very features of Northern and Southern dynasties society that seem to Western eyes most closely to resemble medieval European feudalism—political decentralization and the rise of private great family power—are viewed by many modern Chinese scholars as departures from the "feudal" norm.

For example, Chung Ch'i-chieh writes that early-sixth-century northern institutional reforms, which "restricted the political power of the great families and increased central authority, *strengthened feudal rule.*"[33] "Feudal" rule here means centralized rule or what Chien Po-tsan called "feudal autocracy with centralized authority" (*chung-yang chi-ch'üan te feng-chien chuan-chih chu-i*)[34]. That is, in contemporary mainland China "feudal rule" is identified with "imperial rule." Such centralized feudalism is essential to the modern Chinese understanding of "feudalism" and is what allowed Wang Chung-lo to come to the startling conclusion that medieval European feudalism was somehow "abnormal."[35]

Clearly, Chinese scholars on the mainland have formulated a definition of feudalism that is unrecognizable to many students of the European Middle Ages. An explanation for this phenomenon must begin with the adoption of Marxist criteria during the 1950s as the standards for Chinese historical scholarship. "Historical materialism" and an emphasis on the decisive role of class struggle in history were promoted at that time; and, in order to combat obscurantist theories about the uniqueness of China's Confucian civilization, the universality of the so-called scientific laws of historical development was proclaimed. The five successive stages of historical progress—primitive communism, slave society, feudalism, capitalism, and ultimately communism again—first introduced to China by Kuo Mo-jo in 1930, became established doctrine.[36]

It is true that, in the spirit of "seeking truth through facts" proclaimed by the Teng Hsiao-p'ing regime in the 1980s, some scholars have recently questioned the rigid applicability of this model.[37] Such doubts come at a time when the dissemination of the theory throughout China has become almost universal, however, and they clearly fall outside the mainstream of contemporary Chinese historiography.[38] The five-stage model is now an established doctrine on the mainland, and the principal question under debate by scholars of premodern history is simply when the transition from slave society to feudalism specifically took place. On this issue there has been much disagreement.[39]

A common solution, presented in a standard middle-school history text, has feudal society beginning in the Warring States period (475–221 B.C.), when the state ownership of land that typified slave society gave way to private ownership. Under the revolutionary legal changes introduced in the state of Ch'in in the fourth century B.C. and elsewhere, an efficient centralized national administrative system was established—undercutting, if not elimnating, the old hereditary aristocracy—and a feudal socioeconomic system solidified as the class structure gradually polarized into an opposition between wealthy landlords and poor peasants. Finally, in 221 B.C., Ch'in unified all under heaven into the first empire, and an enduring imperial system of "feudal autocracy" was established.[40]

Although feudal society therefore preceded the imperial system and is defined somewhat differently from it, both issued at
least in part from a common set of Warring States legal innovations, and their respective chronologies largely overlap. It should
be no surprise that the two systems are therefore closely linked in
the minds of many modern Chinese scholars. In the now es-
tranged, but certainly well-informed, opinion of a past director of
the Institute of Marxism-Leninism and Mao Tse-tung Thought at
the Chinese Academy of Social Sciences, "Chinese feudalism . . .
took the form of a highly concentrated unified empire in which
land could be bought and sold, but most of the land belonged to
the landlords, and the political, economic and other power was
concentrated in the hands of . . . the emperor."[41]

What makes this system feudal, in the Marxist sense, is the
socioeconomic class structure that pits great landlords against
poor peasants. Kao Min, for example, quotes Marx in saying that
"the great estate was the true foundation of feudal society in the
Middle Ages." But, in China, this socioeconomic definition of feudalism must still confront a twofold difficulty. On the one hand,
as Erich Pilz observes, in order to accommodate the changing
economic realities of two millennia of imperial rule—notably, the
late imperial system "of small, privately held farms that were
freely bought and sold"—Chinese scholars have been obliged to
apply their economic criteria so broadly as to make Chinese "feudalism" scarcely distinguishable from that of any other preindus-
trial agrarian society.[42] On the other hand, as Kao Min acknowledges, the feudal landlord class in China had to compete extensively with the state itself for ownership of land up until the
eighth century A.D.[43]

The contemporary Chinese model of imperial absolutism was
supposedly echoed in the words of the Japanese crown prince in
A.D. 646, at the high tide of early Chinese influence in Japan: "In
Heaven there are not two suns: in a country there are not two
rulers. It is therefore the Emperor alone who is supreme over all
the Empire, and who has a right to the services of the myriad people."[44] Under this Japanese understanding of the Chinese imperial model, both land and labor were the exclusive prerogatives of
the monarch. Citing Marx's theory of an "Asiatic mode of production," Hou Wai-lü in fact concluded in 1954 that land monopolization by the imperial family was the principal characteristic
of medieval Chinese "feudalism."[45] Since state ownership of the

"means of production" is decidedly difficult to reconcile with a
Marxist definition of feudalism, however, Hou came under predictably intense criticism, and a great historiographical debate
erupted in China in the late 1950s and early 1960s as to the essential nature of feudal land tenure.

Among Japanese Marxists, one leading historical school came
to the conclusion that the early imperial era, from Ch'in and Han
to Sui and T'ang, was not feudal at all, but a continuation of the
ancient Asiatic modes of production. It located the true beginning of China's "middle ages" in the Sung, in the tenth century
A.D.[46] Chinese Marxists, however, seem to have reached a compromise of sorts to the effect that whether actual landownership
lay in private or public hands, the defining characteristic of feudalism was that the landlord *class* controlled the land and its
tillers, on the basis of "special privilege" *(t'e-ch'üan)* rather than
purely economic considerations. Although, technically, some
state ownership of land is consistent with this definition of feudalism, most scholars choose to minimize its role and emphasize
instead the continued growth of large private estates under the
empire.[47]

The "feudalism" question, then, with special reference to the
issue of landownership, has been a major concern of Chinese historiography since the beginning of the People's Republic in
1949.[48] Scholars have been under considerable a priori pressure
to identify imperial China as "feudal," even if that entails some
departure from the original European model of feudalism. Any
suggestion that the empire was not "feudal" would be intolerable,
since it might call into question the orthodox paradigm of uniform, universal laws of historical development culminating in
socialism.[49] Within this "feudal" empire, then, the Northern and
Southern dynasties, far from constituting a medieval epicenter
for the feudal experience, form instead an irritating irregularity
in the normal course of centralized imperial "feudal autocracy."[50]

Servants of a Universal State

The intensity of the Chinese scholarly debate over feudalism was
a consequence of the adoption of a Marxist theoretical framework, but the reconceptualization of feudalism in terms of bureaucratic absolutism was simply a necessary adjustment to fit the
known facts of Chinese history. Patrimonial, autocratic, imperial

power has been an inescapable fact of life in China for two thousand years; this imperial prominence, in turn, directs the attention of historians toward strong dynasties and excludes the Northern and Southern dynasties from the mainstream of historical thought. Patriotic historians invariably insist that in Chinese history "unification is the inevitable direction; division is an occasional reverse course."[51] The long period of division between Han and Sui-T'ang thus becomes no more than an unfortunate digression.

This grand vision of national unity exerts tremendous attraction on the imagination of many Chinese and is commonly understood to be unambiguously desirable. As the middle-school text previously referred to instructs, Ch'in's unification in 221 B.C. "was beneficial to the security of people's lives and society's development of production, and met the common hopes of all peoples at that time."[52] The likelihood seems too great that, without the harmonizing influence of a stable center, there could only be great chaos under heaven. Without unity, society would descend to that primitive condition where life is if not short, at least solitary, poor, nasty, and brutish.[53] This was the classic argument of the First Emperor of Ch'in, who claimed to have put an end to civil strife and made "one family of all under heaven."

As Chia I (201–169 B.C.) described it, before the time of the First Emperor, in the Warring States period of late Chou,

> The feudal lords governed by force, the strong encroached upon the weak, the many abused the few, military coups were ceaseless, and the people were exhausted. Now Ch'in faces south and rules the empire. Thus there is a son of heaven on the throne. Since the hope of the people from the very beginning was to secure peace for their lives, there were none who did not humble their hearts and look up to the emperor.[54]

The other, cautionary, message of the danger of too much centralized power made explicit by Ch'in's sudden and horrible end could not, of course, be ignored; but an underlying assumption made by many Chinese intellectuals since the time of Confucius has always been that there should be some universal sovereign authority, a son of heaven, who will put the world in order and to whom true gentlemen should dedicate their lives in service.

Because of their tradition of public service and "deeply rooted Confucian assumptions about a scholar's [seeking] fulfillment through the offering of advice to the state," Chinese historians have often been puzzled by the indifference the Northern and Southern dynasties elite expressed toward holding government office.[55] Hung Mai (1123–1202) sought instinctively to cast Eastern Chin success in imperial bureaucratic terms, explaining that its emperors "handed over national affairs to a single minister and did not change his appointment, and entrusted external [affairs] to the governors and did not treat their authority lightly."[56] From a perspective of loyal and conscientious service to their imperial masters, however, the Eastern Chin and Southern dynasty literati fell spectacularly short of the ideal.

Disdain for practical administrative service was almost a hallmark of the early medieval Chinese elite. In office, they were notorious for neglecting their responsibilities. During the Eastern Chin dynasty Sun T'ung (mid–fourth century) was magistrate of Wu-ning. "In office he did not pay attention to trivial duties but gave vent to his wishes and roamed at ease. There were none of the famous mountains and scenic rivers that he did not exhaustively investigate."[57] Other literati simply refused to serve the state at all. Shen Ching (mid–fourth century) was admired by the great statesman Hsieh An (320–385), who offered him an appointment, but "Ching had enough independent wealth as one of the magnate-gentlemen of the Southeast; he had no intention to advance in office, and he retired claiming illness."[58] Those literati who did accept office, conversely, often did so only when they were in need of a sinecure.[59] Absorbed as they were with their own interests, many literati behaved the way Shan T'ao (205–283) did and "in service did not serve, in retirement did not retire."[60]

Such evident shirking of public responsibility provokes a reaction bordering on contempt from some patriotic modern scholars. "At this time the conception of the state was extremely slight, and they were naturally unaware of the great appropriateness of national unification, but they had also even forgotten the old custom of revering the royal house and expelling the barbarians," wrote Chang Chün-mai (1887–1969). "Thus we know what harm was done to China by the fashions" of that age.[61] In the Ch'ing dynasty, Chao I (1727–1814) marveled at the great southern gentlemen who accepted office only to protect their own families and who showed no dynastic loyalty whatsoever, but maintained their elevated social status while dynasties rose and fell around them.[62] Chao clearly disapproved of these useless fellows. In his view effective imperial leadership, such as it was, came mainly from men of common birth. One recent scholar even denies that the "confused government" of Wang Tao, in the Eastern Chin, and men like him had anything at all to do with the survival of the Southern dynasties, and credits their survival for three hundred years simply to the common people's willingness to endure corrupt and inefficient rule as preferable to the most likely alternative of devastation at the hands of northern invaders.[63]

Few Chinese intellectuals see the political indifference of the early medieval literati as anything other than selfish disregard of their political obligations and a possible reason for China's national humiliation at the hands of foreign invaders during the era of division. Huang Tsung-hsi (1610–1695) had a different perspective, however. He noted that "the order and disorder of the world does not consist in the rise or fall of one [imperial] family, but in the sadness or joy of all the people. Therefore . . . the rise and fall of Chin, Sung, Ch'i and Liang [the first four of the five Southern dynasties] had no relationship to their order or disorder."[64]

That all under heaven should be united into one big family is, without question, a noble aspiration. The great abiding unity of Chinese civilization over so many centuries is also rightfully a matter for pride and a splendid achievement—but it has not been accomplished without cost. The value of unity must, to some extent, be contingent upon the nature of the power that imposes it. In the dynastic state, citizens, ultimately, are reduced to the role of servants of a single royal family. The very strength of an autocratic central state, if it does not include adequate safeguards for the maintenance of individual liberties, may even be a measure of the subjection of its people. If absolute power, as they say, "corrupts absolutely," then a people (as individual human beings) may actually be fortunate not to find themselves under an effectively centralized universal state. As Rafe de Crespigny observes, "Though traditional historians of China may lament the division of the empire of Han . . . we should not assume that grand centralized authority was an advantage to the people or culture of China."[65]

The Impulse to Rebel

The Northern and Southern dynasties were an age of endemic warfare. There were battles between opposing courts in the north and south, and local conflicts within each of those regions. The period is also marked by a strikingly high frequency of "popular rebellions," which it would be convenient to understand in Marxist terms as indexes of the rise of an oppressive feudal landlord ruling class. It would be naive to suggest that these were "good times." But it may also assume too much to say that the numerous popular uprisings of the age are simply a reflection of landlord exploitation.

Popular rebellions, in fact, are a surprisingly ambiguous instrument with which to measure class conflict. Often, it is the children of the privileged who are first to rebel. American society was torn by popular unrest during the 1960s, yet questions of civil rights and political ideals were far more central to this social turmoil than was economically defined class war. In China there were numerous popular demonstrations and resistance movements in the 1980s that can only very awkwardly be explained in classic Marxist socioeconomic terms. In both cases, it was the yawning gap between unfulfilled popular ideals and reality that provoked social unrest.[66]

In Tokugawa Japan the class structure had been exceptionally rigid, yet Mikiso Hane writes that when the old feudal order was finally abolished in the early Meiji years, peasant disturbances ensued—and then began to subside after 1877, even as "the economic plight of the peasants continued to worsen."[67] Albert Feuerwerker has suggested "political exhaustion" as the primary variable determining the severity of popular rebellions in nineteenth-century China.[68] Prasenjit Duara is of the opinion that peasant violence under the Nationalist regime in the early twentieth century was motivated chiefly by protests against taxation.[69] In the case of the Southern dynasties, William Crowell has made a meticulous survey of popular rebellions, in which he found many instances of revolt against the state and government taxation but no examples of rebellion against private aristocratic "exploitation."[70] Indeed, local magnates sometimes sided with the poor farmers during the fourth-century rebellions.[71]

This scattering of evidence suggests that social unrest is more apt to be provoked by deeply felt grievances against the existing political order (a sense of disjunction between the realities of power and idealized expectations—or simply anger at taxation) than it is by the mere existence of social or economic inequality. It is the sense of injustice that triggers recourse to violence—and an injustice newly introduced is far more likely to touch off an explosive popular reaction than any long accustomed one, since what is perceived as just is often only what is customary.

Chinese scholars themselves generally deal with the evidence of popular uprisings during the Southern dynasties in a sophisticated manner, recognizing that government taxes and labor requirements were the immediate causes of much of the discontent, but arguing that the government here merely represented the interests of the economically ascendant landlord class.[72] It is precisely through the organs of the state that privileged social classes exercise their greatest influence. Wang Chung-lo, then, somewhat daringly acknowledged that Chinese popular rebellions, "from the very beginning of feudal [i.e., imperial] society until the finish, all were struggles against autocratic royal authority." Within the context of the Chinese Marxist "feudal" formula, however, he was still able to explain this in terms of class struggle, because "royal authority," after all, was merely "a concentrated expression of the strength of the feudal landlord class."[73]

Since a relative handful of great literati families did dominate the court during the Eastern Chin dynasty, it is often difficult to distinguish their private interests from the public concerns of the central government. Yet the power that these individuals wielded as agents of the state must be distinguished from the mere wealth and influence of ordinary private landowners. From the perspective of those who actually tilled the soil in early medieval China, moreover, the difference appears to have been perceptible.

That many commoners in the early fourth century took advantage of the prevailing confusion to evade registration on the empire's tax rolls by voluntarily submitting to great families as dependents is clear evidence of this perceived difference. It is humanly impossible for an emperor to be a mere distillation of any social class. By the very act of ascending the throne, an emperor (whatever his origin) takes on a new identity and a unique set of interests.[74] The institutional machinery of the state itself is capable at times of assuming an abstract and inhuman identity of its own, separate from the interests of its various human components. And, in office, a landlord's personal interests as an official may also be quite different even from his own class interests as a landlord.

In fourth-century Chiang-nan, small farmers might have thrust themselves into dependance on the landlord class because the exactions of the great families were more tolerable than the state tax and labor requirements; or, alternately, they might have done so simply because the great families were closer at hand and more unavoidable than remote emperors. In either case, competition between the state and the great families for control of land and labor—tax and rent—would seem to be a more immediately important theme of Southern dynasty history than the class struggle.

The Japanese Heresy

Apart from the Marxist paradigm for interpreting early medieval China, convincing systematic alternative visions have been slow to present themselves. Although Chinese scholarship on the period of division is not as extensive as it is for either the preceding Han (early imperial) or the subsequent Sui and T'ang (late medieval) periods, thousands of Chinese books and articles have nevertheless been published on the subject.[75] Not surprisingly, the Marxist viewpoint has been dominant among these. Beyond China's borders, the field of Northern and Southern dynasties studies is predictably less developed. Only in Japan has this period received truly appreciable attention, and, as Kao Min observes, even in Japan there has been a tendency for research to follow the Chinese lead. Japanese scholarship has made at least one distinctive contribution, however. This is the theme of the "local community," which unites local great families and commoners into a single community of interest.[76]

The medieval great families formed a bridge between court and countryside, and helped to provide stability both to the dynastic regime and to the village. Nakamura Keiji emphasizes this dual role of the medieval "aristocracy" in both the ideology of a centralized bureaucratic empire and in an idealized local society.[77] These great families thus occupied what Prasenjit Duara has called the "cultural nexus of power" at multiple levels of medieval Chinese society.[78] The combination of religious and family (lineage) leadership—identified by Duara as the two most outstanding devices for exercising rural authority in early twentieth-century China—with a near monopoly of high government office elevated the medieval great families to commanding heights in the Southern dynasties.

The Japanese concept of local community, with its attendant emphasis on culture and ideology, has proven highly controversial, however. Tanigawa Michio, in particular, has sometimes been accused of abandoning historical materialism in favor of some sort of mystical spiritualism.[79] In the eyes of Marxists, ideology can be little more than a reflection of and justification for the special interests of a society's dominant class.[80] Ideas are viewed as tools used by the socially privileged to mobilize others in their support. Their utility for that purpose was exploited by Chairman Mao, who relied extensively on thought reform in building his revolutionary new China.[81] The lurking suspicion that ideas can thus be easily manipulated for political ends merely reinforces our general modern distaste for ideology, however. "The purpose of ideological discourses, whether they deal with life or with work, is to prepare and organize the individual members of society into subjects on whom power can take hold."[82] If not a deception, then, ideology is, at best, a self-delusion, for which the only rational prescription is "revolt against the rule of thoughts."[83] But is escape from the rule of thoughts even possible?

Where does our modern suspicion of ideas come from? For René Descartes (1596–1650), in the seventeenth century, thought was the most self-evident of realities. It was the reality of those *res extensae* outside the mind that Descartes felt it necessary to prove.[84] To the post-Cartesian scientific community this seemed manifestly backward, however. Reality was physical matter. The mystery of human consciousness itself could be explained in physical terms as a product of electrochemical neural activity. It became easy for minds conditioned to this scientific approach to begin to disregard thought as some mere "phantom interposed between afferent and efferent impulses"—an insubstantial thing, "flitting vaporously amongst the cog-wheels, the pulleys, the steel castings of a relentless world-machine."[85] Classic Marxist economic determinism is merely an extreme example of this general modern process of materialist reduction, applied to the study of history.[86]

But notice that it is human minds themselves that have performed this reduction of the mind to material processes. The reconceptualization of thought in terms of physical patterns of neural activity no more disproves the reality of thought than does the reduction of heat to molecular motion eliminate the reality of the subjective sensation of heat.[87] A fire still feels hot, and still burns, and human minds still generate ideas. The scientific intent to perform this operation is, moreover, itself provided by the mind for purposes intelligible only to the mind.

Materialist reductionism illuminates, however, the fallacy of belief in universal, absolute, ideal truth. Historically, our loss of faith in ideology is also fed by the realization of how a variety of different ideological structures have evolved under differing historical circumstances, at different times, around the world. But the same scientific operation that removes ideals from the realm of the transcendent simultaneously also places them squarely here on earth, as potential actors in the historical process themselves. We may well disown our faith in transcendent ideals and call ourselves materialists, but we cannot honestly deny the central role of consciousness in the human experience. Ideas and beliefs are real historical forces, at least potentially as important to the study of history as patterns of landownership.

The Cultural Imperative

There can be no question but that two thousand years of Chinese imperial power were sustained, in part, by such Confucian ethical slogans as "humanity and righteousness." In Michel Foucault's analysis it is the very moral prestige of an ideological formulation like Confucianism that makes possible "the imposition of cultural and economic hegemonies."[88] Such symbols are the source of a power that compels submission and undermines resistance.[89] But, in the process, ideology is transformed into something more than just a smoke screen concealing the reality of power: it becomes the framework within which real power must operate. In the Foucaultian view the language a society chooses to frame its discourse influences not only its patterns of expression and modes of understanding, but ultimately also the disposition of power itself.[90]

The magic spell of an ideological formulation is cast over audience and speaker alike. Within any ideological system certain groups or individuals may be favored by the terms of discourse—they might even conceivably have consciously fabricated the system for their own benefit—but all are equally subject to it: culture is "a machine in which everyone is caught, those who exercise power just as much as those over whom it is exercised."[91] Within any society, leaders will (eventually) be held accountable to the standard set by the ideals they use to justify their leadership.[92] In China, therefore, Confucian ideals might at least sometimes have had the effect of "moderating the class opposition between the people and the rulers," if only for the purpose of preserving the privileged position of those same rulers.[93]

The histories record that Juan Fang (280–322)

> by nature was pure and restrained, and disregarded possessions. As a Gentleman [of the Board of Civil Office] he did not shun hunger and want. Because he was a famous gentleman, Wang Tao and Yü Liang [two of the most distinguished and powerful individuals of the time] gave him food and clothing, as a result of which Fang was "established."[94]

Juan might actually have owed the "establishment" of his career more to the prominence of his family than to virtuous behavior, and the historian is clearly more interested in teaching a moral lesson than in objectively recording facts, yet it would be a serious mistake simply to dismiss the huge number of such stories that fill medieval Chinese writings. Psychological factors figure prominently among the range of objective conditions that determine human behavior, and a shrewd calculation of individual self-interest at times may coincide with naive idealism.

Nor is this necessarily mere coincidence, either: in early China it was at least in part intentionally so. The rewards system was consciously adjusted to promote specific ideals. Thus, for example, Chang Chin-chih gained the tangible benefit of exemption from local labor service by imperial proclamation, shortly after the year 424, in recognition of his charitable acts of ostensibly selfless virtue.[95] Watanabe Yoshihiro observes that by late Han times the giving of relief to less fortunate kinsmen not only strengthened family cohesion, but also earned the generous donor favorable consideration within the bureaucratic selection system.[96]

The medieval Chinese ideology justified the privileged position of its elite class, but elite status also was acquired and maintained by means of satisfying the expectations of that ideology. Legitimacy thus became contingent upon conformity with accepted cultural ideals. Real material incentives therefore stood behind and reinforced the idealistic appeal to virtue that reverberates throughout the Chinese records.

Great wealth and military force are manifestations of power, but power itself is an idea—an intangible and protean abstraction that inheres in the ability to influence people and objects rather than in the material objects themselves. Within any society power resides in a "cultural nexus." We can learn as much about the real forces in operation in a society by inquiring into what it values and how it expresses those values as we can by emphasizing the enumeration of mere physical details. Such data as the dimensions and numbers of material objects, however fascinating and informative they may be, are of secondary importance. As Wilhelm Dilthey (1833–1911) once observed, "It is the task of historical analysis to discover the consensus which governs the concrete purposes, values and ways of thought of a period."[97]

Chinese Literati

If this formulation is true for history in general, it is especially apt for early medieval China, where, as Yü Ying-shih writes, "ideas and social realities were closely interlocked."[98] Early medieval China was peculiarly ideologically charged, in part because assignment to government office was explicitly based on elite cultural attainments through the mechanism of the Nine Ranks system (to be discussed in greater detail later). Through it, the distribution of political power, which generated both prestige and wealth, was linked to the prevailing ideological system.

This ideological connection resulted in the ostentatious "cultural" orientation that was one of the most pronounced characteristics of the Southern dynasty elite. Because the early medieval elite drew so much of its self-conception from the prevailing Buddho-Taoist-Confucian cultural complex (in early medieval China it is seldom useful, and sometimes impossible, to try to separate these three ideological strands), I prefer to label it a "literati" class rather than use the disputed and perhaps misleading term "aristocracy" or the more cumbersome and uninformative "great families." The term "literati" conveys something of the cultural flavor of the generic Chinese appellation *shih-ta-fu* and is intended here as an approximate translation of that term, although it does not begin to suggest the prestige and political stature implicit in the Chinese.

The Eastern Chin elite sprang increasingly from well-established families and usually owned at least some land (but not always vast estates). They occasionally held command over independent military forces, and they sometimes enjoyed great stature in a specific local community—but they nearly always had the opportunity to serve in central government office and manifested at least the pretension to cultural achievement, through scholarship, Confucian virtue, philosophic brilliance, wit, and artistic or literary ability. If we exclude the qualities that were not universally applicable to the elite at the national level (as opposed to families with purely local influence), we may conclude that the Eastern Chin national literati were an (increasingly closed and hereditary) official class, boasting an aura of extreme cultural refinement.

In China, Benjamin Schwartz reminds us, "the notion that the normative 'objective' sociopolitical order depends on the inner virtues of kings and officials" and "the idea that men of virtue...prove their right to authority by the possession of virtue" antedate even Confucius.[99] This ancient and fundamental faith that the essence of leadership lies in the cultivation of personal virtue was magnified in early imperial times by the pervasive spread of Confucianism in the Han dynasty and the elaboration of certain theories of cosmic correspondences. It induced Ssu-ma Jui, as Emperor Yüan of the Eastern Chin, to proclaim in 318 that if only he himself "were pure and quiet, others would be correct naturally."[100] When such ideas were promoted and reinforced by the imperial selection system, a "cultural nexus" emerged that explains the rise to power of an ideologically oriented literati class in early medieval China.

English-Language Scholarship: The State of the Field

If the principal contributions of Japanese-language scholarship to early medieval Chinese studies have been the controversial themes of the local community and the role of ideology, English-language scholarship has thus far added less. Although individual works of English-language scholarship are sometimes of exquisite quality, scholarship remains scattered and isolated. The field remains disproportionately underdeveloped.

A brief review of the most noteworthy English-language books in the field illustrates how diffused English-language scholarship is, by period, region, and discipline.[101] The appearance of a collection of Etienne Balazs' pathbreaking sinological essays—notably the piece titled "Nihilistic Revolt or Mystical Escapism: Currents of Thought in China during the Third Century A.D." (first published in French in 1948)—in a fine English edition in 1964 is remarkable not only for its excellence, but also for the manner in which it continues to tower over the field some forty years after many of the essays were written.[102]

In the discipline of history, Rafe de Crespigny has recently delivered a spritely narrative account of the early years of the third-century southern kingdom of Wu.[103] In *The Aristocratic Families of Early Imperial China*, Patricia Ebrey traced the progress of a single, northern, "aristocratic" family through a thousand years of history, exploring along the way the nature of elite kinship groupings and the relationship between aristocracy and bureaucracy. David Johnson used modern social science techniques in *The Medieval Chinese Oligarchy* to study systematically the composition of the medieval elite, and Aat Vervoorn located the Confucian origins of the early medieval inclination toward eremitism in the Han and earlier periods.[104]

Some of the most outstanding contributions to knowledge of early medieval history have been made by scholars outside the discipline of history. Indeed, students of philosophy, literature, and art sometimes seem to be more excited by the medieval period than are historians. Donald Holzman found hidden political significance in a close reading of the poetry of one notorious third-century northern "libertine."[105] Richard Mather capped his prolific career with a nuanced literary biography of the fifth-century poet, historian, and man of affairs Shen Yüeh, through which he nicely captured the spirit of the southern court.[106] Although Martin Powers' important new book *Art and Political Expression in Early China* is concerned exclusively with the earlier Han dynasty, like Aat Vervoorn's work on eremitism it establishes a critical framework for understanding post-Han history—in this case by tracing the rise of a middle-income bureaucratic elite, meritocratically selected in consideration of public opinion, from evidence in late Han provincial tomb art.[107] Audrey Spiro, similarly, found evidence of changing social values in fourth- and fifth-century tomb relief-mural portraits.[108] And attention has been lavished on the period, as the formative age of Buddhism in China, by students of philosophy and religion. In this domain Erik Zürcher's *The Buddhist Conquest of China* remains a cornerstone of scholarship in English.[109]

Much of the best English-language work has taken the form of articles in scholarly journals rather than full-length monographs. A considerable number of primary sources from the medieval period have also been translated into English, with consequent advantage in making that world more accessible to an English-speaking audience.[110] Many of these translations contain valuable introductions, setting the texts squarely in their historical environments.

English-language scholarship on the period of division between the Han and the Sui and T'ang periods has thus begun well, but it is only a bare beginning. This period remains perhaps the least understood major period of Chinese history. We need fresh approaches to reconcile the many apparent contradictions in our understanding of early medieval history and a new theoretical framework in which to locate the Northern and Southern dynasties. The present volume seeks to approach these questions tentatively, through a sympathetic exploration of what medieval Chinese literati actually said about themselves, in the hope of reconstructing a balanced, multileveled portrait of literati society in the fourth-century south. To borrow a phrase from Carol Gluck, "the subject under consideration here is the interpretation of the political and social world as the articulate elite lived it—or imagined they lived it" in fourth-century south China.[111]

2

REFUGEE STATE:
A BRIEF CHRONICLE OF
THE EASTERN CHIN

"The House of Chin is in decline, skulking far away beyond the River," said one northerner disparagingly of the Eastern Chin dynasty in the middle of the fourth century.[1] His words were intended to absolve his rough northern ruler of any sense of disloyalty to the legitimate former Western Chin dynasty, as he assumed the title of founding emperor of a new northern one. Although the Eastern Chin remained the most stable and successful of all fourth-century regimes, it was a regime in exile. However ephemeral the fourth-century stream of petty northern semibarbarian kingdoms were—known to the history books as the "Sixteen Kingdoms"—they proudly occupied what had always been considered the center of Chinese civilization: the Yellow River basin and the Central Plain of northern China. The Eastern Chin dynasty, to save itself, had fled into exile in the south, beyond the natural defenses of the Long (Yangtze) River. There it and the other Southern dynasties that followed presided over an empire that was greatly diminished in size.

The Eastern Chin empire was confined, with some variation over time, to territory south of a line drawn by the river Huai roughly through the geographic center of modern China. Since much of the far south and west remained sparsely populated and underdeveloped at this time, the zone of effective Eastern Chin jurisdiction was largely concentrated in the twin Yangtze River provinces of Yang-chou in the east and Ching-chou in the west.[2] Yang-chou included parts of modern Kiangsu, Anhwei, and near-

ly all of modern Chekiang. Its territory encompassed the capital
at Chien-k'ang (modern Nanking), the fertile Lake T'ai region,
and much of the lower Yangtze River drainage basin. Yang-chou
formed the economic and cultural base of the Southern dynasties. Ching-chou covered vast stretches of land in the middle
Yangtze region, embracing much of modern Hupeh and Hunan.
It had formerly also been an important cultural center in the
Later Han, but it had now become the principal theater of ongoing military operations between the opposing Northern and
Southern dynasties, and it was reduced to the status of an embat-
tled but strategically important borderland.

Conditions highly favorable to rice cultivation have made
Chiang-nan the most populous and prosperous region of China
at least since Sung times (960–1279), but in the fourth century
it was still regarded as an exotic alien land by many Chinese literati, and its humid climate was an object of dread. The Buddhist
monk Shih Tao-an (312–385) warned a northern monarch in the
mid–fourth century that "the land in the southeast is low and the
atmosphere is unhealthy" and gave him examples of ancient rulers who ventured into Chiang-nan never to return alive.[3] The
famous calligrapher Wang Hsi-chih (309–c. 365), who served the
Eastern Chin regime in exile in Chiang-nan and lived most of his
life in the south, nonetheless complained repeatedly of the ail-
ments caused by the dampness of the region.[4] Even centuries
later in the T'ang dynasty (618–906), as Edward Schafer has
shown, the south was still viewed by many Chinese as a strange
land, half threatening and half romantically alluring.[5]

This exoticism of the land south of the Yangtze River should
not be exaggerated, however. Even in high antiquity the Ch'u,
Wu, and Yüeh kingdoms of the south had made important contributions to Chinese civilization. T'an Ch'i-hsiang has estimated
that as early as the Later Han dynasty nearly half (4.30 million out
of a total 9.33 million) of the households in China resided south
of the Huai River line of demarcation.[6] Chiang-nan had already
witnessed extensive development and heavy settlement by the
fourth century and was hardly the tenuous frontier outpost sometimes suggested by literary descriptions of the period. Nonetheless, the northern Yellow River valley had been the traditional seat
of Chinese civilization—the "Central States" (or, more quaintly,
Middle Kingdoms) from which modern China (Chung-kuo) takes
its name—and, as recently as the Western Chin regime (265–316)

in the third century, Chiang-nan still appeared culturally insignificant viewed from the capital in the north at Loyang.[7]

After the chaos surrounding the fall of the Han, which began with the outburst of rebellion by the Yellow Turbans in 184 and was finally consummated by the abdication of the last Han emperor in 220, Emperor Wu (r. 265–290) of the Western Chin dynasty succeeded in briefly unifying all China under his sway for a generation of peace in the late third century. From about 280 until the end of the century, "oxen and horses covered the countryside, and surplus grain was left in the fields."[8] But after Emperor Wu's death, the same contemporary author reports, "the governance of the state fell upon reckless men."[9] The new century began with the Ssu-ma ruling family consumed by fratricidal civil wars, known as the "disturbances of the eight princes," which lasted from 300 to 306. This disintegration of dynastic control, in turn, provided an opportunity for non-Chinese tribes, referred to collectively as the "five Hu" peoples *(wu-hu),* to begin marauding across the Central Plain during the Yung-chia era (307–313). By 317 these alien conquerors, together with their Chinese confederates, had chased the scattered remnants of the Chin government south into Chiang-nan.

Large numbers of Chinese citizens were either killed or driven from their homes during the wars at the beginning of the fourth century. It is impossible to ascertain exactly how many, but the *Chin-shu,* a dynastic history compiled in the seventh century drawing extensively on contemporary documents, estimated that between 80 and 90 percent of the Western Chin officials either died or fled into exile at this time.[10] The percentage of commoners affected would have been much smaller, but the aggregate total must have been significant. During these years north China was stripped of a good part of its population, and the south was burdened by an influx of refugees.

To accommodate the new arrivals in the south administratively, a system of commanderies and counties in exile *(ch' iao chün hsien chih-tu)* was established, beginning with Southern Lang-yeh Commandery in 335. Altogether, the Eastern Chin regime established no fewer than eighty-one commanderies in exile and 236 counties. This proliferation of administrative units vastly increased the complexity of local administration during the Southern dynasties and gave impetus to the runaway expansion of office holding that was also a hallmark of the age.[11]

Okawa Fujio has demonstrated that much of the actual growth in the registered population that occurred during the early Southern dynasties took place in the old established commanderies of Wu and Wu-hsing, near Lake T'ai; but it was in the previously underdeveloped region of northern Chekiang, in K'uai-chi Commandery, where the great émigré literati congregated and began to carve out estates for themselves.[12] These three commanderies, then, together with the capital Chien-k'ang itself constituted the economic and cultural heart of the Eastern Chin regime.

As the situation in north China deteriorated, top Western Chin officials made preparations to secure their retreat to Chiang-nan. The notoriously nihilistic chief minister of the failing dynasty, Wang Yen (256–311), sent his younger brother Wang Ch'eng to garrison Ching-chou and dispatched his cousin Wang Tun (266–324) to Ch'ing-chou in modern Kiangsu.[13] Although Tun then murdered the brother in Ching-chou in 312, Tun's rapidly swelling military power guaranteed continued Wang family influence into the early years of the new dynasty.

In the meantime, in 307, the ruling Ssu-ma family sent one of its members, the Prince of Lang-yeh, Ssu-ma Jui, to establish a dynastic base in the southeast, conferring upon him the title General Pacifying the East.[14] There the prince found a realm scarcely more stable than the collapsing northern heartland. Chiang-nan was torn by armed conflict between unruly magnate coalitions in the early years of the fourth century. By gaining the critical military support of Wang Tun and with the advice of Tun's accomplished literati cousin Wang Tao, Ssu-ma Jui was able to win the allegiance of a significant majority of the southern elite and to effect a successful restoration of the House of Chin in exile in Chiang-nan. Then, after the fall of the last Chin dynasty capital in the north, Ssu-ma Jui took for himself the title Prince of Chin in 317 and in 318 was proclaimed Emperor Yüan of the restored Eastern Chin dynasty.

Emperor Yüan staffed his administration predominantly, although not exclusively, with émigré literati who, like himself, had escaped disaster in the Central Plain by fleeing south to Chiang-nan. The prominence of these émigrés at the court was a source of understandable frustration for some of the older southern families. The resulting friction between the new arrivals and the established southern families is illustrated by the case of Chou Chi (256–313), a great southern magnate who personally helped suppress three rebellions in Chiang-nan between 303 and 310, preserving control of the region for the House of Chin. For this very substantial achievement, Chou Chi was rewarded with appointment as grand administrator of Wu-hsing, but the emperor reportedly remained uncomfortable with Chou's independent military power, and Chou soon found himself unable to blend in with fashionable émigré society. In exasperation, after having loyally suppressed so many rebellions on behalf of the dynasty, Chou finally plotted rebellion himself and died swearing his son to vengeance against the "rascal" *(ts'eng-tzu)* northern literati. Ironically, however, instead of offering unwavering opposition to the émigré court, Chou's grandson went on to play an important role on behalf of the refugee court in putting down further southern rebellions.[15]

This sequence of events illustrates the peculiar mixture of frustration and acceptance with which the native southern elite greeted the arrival of the northern émigré literati. Japanese scholars theorize that the somewhat puzzling success of the northern émigrés in dominating southern society in the early fourth century was due to a lack of cohesion among the native southern elite, their inability to respond effectively to the rapid social and political change of the times, and their sense of awe and inferiority at the superior ideological and cultural pretensions of the northern literati.[16]

In the early years of the Eastern Chin much military power was concentrated in the hands of Wang Tun. From his base at Wu-ch'ang, on the upper Yangtze River not far from modern Wuhan, Wang constituted both the principal bastion of the dynasty against further invasion from the north and an ever-present threat. This threat was realized in 322 when Wang Tun went into rebellion, making accusations against one of the emperor's favorites as his excuse. He quickly captured the capital, and by 323 he had gained almost total control of the southern empire. Wang Tun's cousin Wang Tao remained loyal to the House of Chin and helped draw up plans, together with the emperor and others, to oppose Tun.[17] It was for this reason that the Wang family was able to retain much of its influence after Wang Tun died in 324 and was posthumously condemned by the court.

Wang Tun's rebellion is important because it established a precedent for antagonism between the western military command and the court. This conflict would continue to plague the Eastern

Chin for the duration of its existence. Emperor Yüan had died while Wang Tun was still ascendant in 323, and his successor, the capable Emperor Ming (r. 323–326), lived for only three more years. He was followed on the throne by Emperor Ch'eng (r. 326–343), who became monarch at the tender age of five in 326. Until Emperor Ch'eng reached maturity, the direction of the state fell upon a coalition of senior ministers, in which Wang Tao's influence, tarnished now by the recent rebellion of his cousin, was eclipsed by the rise of the new emperor's uncle, Yü Liang (289–340).[18]

After weathering yet another disastrous rebellion in 327–328, prompted by the resentment of an émigré military leader at Yü family domination of the court, Yü Liang was appointed in 334 to Wang Tun's old military command over the six provinces of the west.[19] From his garrison in the west, Yü Liang was then able to intimidate the dynasty in much the same way that Wang Tun had. According to the *Chin-shu:*"Although Liang was stationed at an external garrison, he grasped the authority of the court. Since he was based on the upper reaches [of the Yangtze] and had strong troops, those who adhered to him were numerous. [Wang] Tao, from within, was unable to subdue him."[20]

At Yü Liang's death in 340, control of the western military forces was retained by his family, but when Yü Liang's younger brother died five years later, the court was finally able to intervene in the succession. In 345 a court conference made the fateful decision to transfer military command in the west to a rising young general named Huan Wen (312–373).[21] This act ended Yü family domination of the court, but it opened the door to an even greater danger. Huan Wen was exceedingly ambitious, and, after a successful expedition to conquer the region of modern-day Szechuan in 347, "the court shook in awe of him."[22]

In 354 Huan launched an expedition to realize the long-cherished goal of recapturing the north, and in 356 he succeeded in retaking the old Western Chin capital at Loyang. There he repaired the long-neglected imperial tombs, and in that same year he proposed restoring the dynastic capital to the north.[23] This was a considerable propaganda coup, and, although the capital was not moved and Loyang was eventually lost again in 365, Huan Wen's military accomplishments by this time had brought domination of the court nearly within his reach.

In 371 Huan Wen acted to realize his ambition, deposing the

reigning emperor and setting up the youngest son of the first Eastern Chin ruler, Ssu-ma Yü (320–372), as the puppet emperor Chien-wen (r. 371–372).[24] Ssu-ma Yü had been the actual leader of the court faction ever since the death of Emperor K'ang in 345, and he was the first Eastern Chin monarch since Emperor Yüan to take the throne as a mature adult. His position now that he had finally reached the throne, however, was weak. At the time of his coronation Huan Wen deployed troops in the imperial palace, and, although these were soon withdrawn, there was no question but that Ssu-ma Yü's coronation was actually a coup d'état elevating Huan Wen to the threshold of the monarchy.[25] After Ssu-ma Yü died the next year, then, Huan Wen demanded the "Nine Gifts" of imperial favor, indicating his clear intention to usurp the throne. It was only the delaying tactics of Hsieh An (320–385) and other loyal Eastern Chin officials that ultimately prevented Huan Wen from realizing this ambition before his own death nine months later.[26]

Huan Wen's death bought the dynasty a temporary reprieve, and for a generation the court was spared the menace of its own western armies. It was not long before a new threat emerged to take their place, however. During most of the fourth century, north China had been torn by rival armies and divided among numerous petty kingdoms, but in 370 the Former Ch'in kingdom managed briefly to unify the entire north. This vigorous new state soon turned its attention to the south and embarked on an attempted conquest of the Eastern Chin. This attempt led to a climactic confrontation between northern and southern forces; and in 383, according to the traditional version of the story, at least, a much smaller Eastern Chin army successfully defeated the Former Ch'in invasion force in one of the most important battles of all Chinese history, the battle of the Fei River.[27] This battle saved the dynasty, preserved ethnic Chinese control over south China, effectively destroyed the Former Ch'in state in the north, and brought the outstanding Eastern Chin statesman Hsieh An to the pinnacle of his prestige and power.

The Eastern Chin troops that won the battle of the Fei River were known as the Northern Palace Army (Pei-fu ping). They had been organized by Hsieh An's nephew around the nucleus provided by a refugee military band that had fled from the north and settled in the Ching-k'ou area, just down river from the capital, at the turn of the century. It was these men who saved the dynasty from northern conquest, and these same soldiers were destined to save the dynasty one more time in the early fifth century—but also from the ranks of this army emerged the man who would finally bring the Eastern Chin dynasty to an end in 420, Liu Yü (356–422). In the end this new military organization, the Northern Palace Army, formed yet another center of military power to compete with the civilian authority at the court in Chien-k'ang.

In the same year that Hsieh An's masterful defense of the dynasty and the great victory at the Fei River brought Hsieh to the pinnacle of his influence, in 383, the young Emperor Hsiao-wu (r. 373–396) entrusted control over the government to his brother, the Prince of K'uai-chi, Ssu-ma Tao-tzu (364–402). Hsieh An had been too successful, and the emperor was suspicious. Hsieh's influence thus went into decline at the very moment of his triumph, and after Hsieh's death in 385 no individual remained at court with sufficient authority to check Ssu-ma Tao-tzu's faction. Ssu-ma Tao-tzu and his son were thus able to dominate the court through the final years of the century, until their deaths in 402. The murder of Emperor Hsiao-wu in 396 only confirmed Ssu-ma Tao-tzu's grip on the government, since he was made regent for Emperor Hsiao-wu's incompetent heir.

This turn of events was unfortunate for the House of Chin, since Prince Tao-tzu was (reportedly) given to drink and not noticeably conscientious in the performance of his duties.[28] "Treacherous flatterers plotted among themselves" under his lax administration, reports the official history of his dynasty.[29] Writing a millennium and a half later, in the eighteenth century, Chao I concluded that the Eastern Chin dynasty survived as long as it did, in spite of the youth and feebleness of nearly all of its monarchs, because of its great good fortune in being blessed with a succession of able and public-spirited ministers such as Wang Tao and Hsieh An. But "when Prince Tao-tzu of K'uai-chi represented the nation with mediocrity and [his son] Yüan-hsien confused the government with wild stupidity, it was engulfed and drowned."[30]

In 399 the Taoist rebel Sun En (d. 402) swept out of his lair in the sea to ravage K'uai-chi Commandery. His victories can be read as an index of the misrule in the imperial government by Ssu-ma Tao-tzu and his faction. This devastating rebellion in the heart of the Eastern Chin dominion provided the militarists on both the northern and western frontiers with an opportunity to gain leverage against the court. Huan Wen's son Hsüan (369–

404) benefited first. He seized control of his father's old west-ern command, cut off supplies to the court, and rose up in arms against the Eastern Chin, killing Ssu-ma Tao-tzu and his son, deposing the emperor, and in 403 installing himself as the found-ing emperor of a new dynasty.

Huan Hsüan's hour of triumph was short, however. His rise had been based on the military strength of the upper, western, reaches of the Yangtze River, and while he had temporarily neu-tralized the rival power of the newer Northern Palace Army by killing off its top leaders, he had failed thoroughly to eliminate that competing source of military power. In 404 and 405, Liu Yü, using the Northern Palace Army as a springboard, defeated Huan Hsüan on behalf of the Eastern Chin ruling house.[31]

Although Liu's campaign restored Chin dynastic rule, this res-toration was a formality that deceived no one. The real authority was the military power of Liu Yü, and the last Eastern Chin em-peror himself is reported to have acknowledged when he relin-quished the throne to Liu Yü in 420 that "at the time of Huan Hsüan the mandate of heaven had already changed."[32] In this way the Eastern Chin dynasty finally came to an end with the usurpa-tion of a general from the Northern Palace Army. From this time forward military coups were to characterize the series of South-ern dynasties that ruled in Chiang-nan down to its final absorp-tion by the north in 589.

The political history of the Eastern Chin dynasty thus appears to be a story of unrelenting combat, between old southern fami-lies and the émigré literati, between the court and warlord armies on the frontiers, and not least between the Eastern Chin regime itself and the various non-Chinese kingdoms north of the Huai River. One comes away from reading the standard chronicles of these years, such as the *Tzu-chih t'ung-chien* or the dynastic histo-ries, with a picture of the Northern and Southern dynasties as a time of ceaseless warfare and tireless struggle for political and military supremacy. As accurate as this impression may be, it is only one side of Southern dynasty history.

THE SOCIOECONOMIC
ORDER

3

John Fairbank has observed that one of the most essential distinctions between Western history and Chinese history is that Europe "saw the growth of dominant social classes which were originally outside the framework of government and were based on private property."[1] China did not. Early medieval China threatened to become an exception to this generalization, however. During the centuries after the fall of the Han dynasty, a powerful and independent-spirited literati class emerged if not directly to challenge, at least to undercut the authority of autocratic emperors.

This new literati class was hardly unconnected to the central government, however. The class materialized around its monopolization of the civil service appointment system, and office holding continued to provide it with critical prestige and financial support until its final dissolution at the end of the T'ang. During this period private property never supplanted official stipends and perquisites as a source of wealth and power, and the literati class remained bound to the fortunes of the central state. Instead of feudal territorial lords, medieval China had literati.

For a time in the fourth-century south, the balance of real power may have briefly shifted away from the centralized monarchy to the great literati families. The lingering entanglement of those great families with the central state, however, eventually made possible an imperial restoration and led ultimately even to the extinction of the class itself. In the late imperial period, these

34

literati great families were replaced by a new mandarin class of professionalized public servants whose basic loyalty to the imperial state would never again be in question.

Writing in the eighth century, when the cycle was well on its way to completion and autocratic imperial authority had already been restored, Liu Fang looked back on the earlier breakdown of imperial control and discerned three distinct stages in it. During the age of imperial order in the Han dynasty, citizens "knew the prohibitions," government was uniform, and the rulers were true "kings." But by Wei and Chin times the empire had descended to an age of brute "force," when, thanks to the Nine Ranks system, "the regions had different governments, and families had contentious hearts." Then, after the fall of north China in the early fourth century, both north and south dissolved into anarchy, and China (meaning the centralized imperial state) suffered through an even more deeply troubled age of "weakness."[2]

Liu's description is correct in its bare outlines but can be sharpened with a few minor refinements.[3] First, after Han fell, there was an initial period when it was generally assumed that Han-style imperial unity would soon be restored under a new dynastic ruling house, and an assortment of pretenders fought among themselves for that honor. The two Chin dynasties that followed in the late third, fourth, and early fifth centuries, were the high age of aristocratic triumph when, as Mori Mikisaburō writes, "the royal family themselves were lords holding aristocratic characteristics."[4] During the Eastern Chin in particular, great *shih-ta-fu* families towered over the land. This was the period when the medieval literati crystallized as a distinct class. When Eastern Chin was succeeded by Sung in 420, literati social prestige continued to climb, but literati political domination over the court weakened, and the long road to imperial resurgence began.

Literati Independence

During the Three Kingdoms period in the early third century, Ts'ao Ts'ao and the Wei dynasty came close to imposing Han-style imperial control over all of China. But Wei imperial power had to yield to a Ssu-ma coup d'état as early as 249, and the Ssu-ma usurpation of the throne in 265 marks the definitive end of these early attempts to restore the reality of Han-style imperial authority. In that year the new emperor of Western Chin enfeoffed some twenty-seven of his own relatives as princes, giving units of the old imperial state to them for kingdoms. Although these "princes did not go to their kingdoms, but [lived as] officials in the capital," and the Western Chin state had no deliberate intention of ceasing to be a centralized imperial government, the enfeoffments were a clear sign of what we might now call "feudalization" (in the sense of decentralization and privatization of government) at the very top.[5]

Northern and Southern dynasties society in China never quite attained the dimensions of classic Western-style feudalism, because no equivalent to the fundamental European feudal military bond between lords and vassals ever emerged, but early medieval China did exhibit some striking parallels to developments in Europe after the fall of Rome.[6] In particular, there was a pronounced process of decentralization and privatization of authority. For example, in 282 Liu I complained that Emperor Wu (r. 265–290) was worse than even the bad last emperors of Han, since when they "sold offices the proceeds went into their official treasury; when your majesty sells offices the proceeds go in your own private door."[7]

Such privatization of interests is anathema to Confucian ideology. The conventional Confucian position was underscored in the third century by Emperor Wu's contemporary Fu Hsüan, who admonished his readers to remember: "Government consists in doing away with the private.... Doing away with the private is how to establish the just [*kung*] Tao, and only by being just can you rectify the empire."[8] Despite this Confucian ideal, by the third century the authority of the central government had been extensively dismembered by the great *shih-ta-fu*. Even emperors, during this period, exercised their residual power only in the capacity of first private family among equals. And, despite the unequivocal message of Confucian ideology, it was even possible to rationalize this decentralization of authority as being more in the interest of the "public."

The old Chinese word that we conventionally translate into English as "feudal," *feng-chien*, originally referred, before it was diverted by Marxist historians to distinctly different purposes, to the royal act of enfeoffing great nobles as lords in their own quasi-independent territories.[9] This usage corresponds rather closely to the classic formula of medieval European feudalism, although in this case it derives from the system that prevailed in

China during the lengthy preimperial Chou dynasty (c. 1027–256 B.C.).[10] After the replacement of the *feng-chien* system by a central-ized bureaucratic empire in the third century B.C., a prolonged debate—still ongoing in the twentieth century—ensued among Chinese scholars regarding the relative merits of the two systems: decentralized feudalism and centralized empire. Not too surpris-ingly, in view of the Confucian context, this debate tended to be couched in terms of which system was more just, in the deeply entrenched moral sense of benefiting public rather than private interests.[11]

In the third century B.C., at the court shortly to become that of the First Emperor of Ch'in (and of China), one writer opined: "There is no greater disorder than the absence of a son of heaven [ruler]. Without a son of heaven the strong subdue the weak, the many abuse the few, and mutual destruction through the deploy-ment of troops cannot cease."[12] Thus a strong central govern-ment was viewed as necessary to save the people from themselves. This dark, Hobbesian vision of humanity helped justify the estab-lishment of a centralized authoritarian regime by the First Em-peror of Ch'in in 221 B.C.

In the eyes of many subsequent Confucian moralists, however, Ch'in succeeded in releasing the common people from bondage to the old feudal nobility only at the price of reducing everyone to subservience to a single tyrant. Thus a member of the third century A.D. ruling house of Wei, Ts'ao Chiung, explained the rapid collapse of Ch'in power by saying: "The Ch'in kings ruled their people autocratically. Therefore, when they were in danger, there was no rescue. . . . [In contrast, the wise] former kings [of antiquity] knew that autocratic government could not last; there-fore they shared their government with others."[13] In this way *feng-chien,* or feudalism, was reinterpreted as a public sharing of au-thority in contrast to its private concentration in the hands of the ruler of a centralized empire. Such an interpretation was under-standably especially popular among the *shih-ta-fu* of early medi-eval China, since it did not envision the sharing of power among the entire population of China through representative self-gov-ernment, but rather authorized a broad *shih-ta-fu* class to exercise power on the public behalf.

Autocratic imperial power probably reached its nadir with the Eastern Chin dynasty in the fourth century. After that, following the coronation of Liu Yü as first emperor of the new Sung dynasty in 420, none of first emperors of any of the succeeding Southern dynasties came from established great families.[14] The plebeian emperors showed a reinvigorated interest in restricting great family privilege and restoring imperial power. Success came only in small increments, however, in part because the new people brought to power by Liu Yü's usurpation were often more interested in attaining great family status for themselves than they were in undercutting great family influence.[15] As Chao I notes, "The aristocratic view of that age had, through custom, become a matter of course, which even emperors and princes could not change."[16]

The Southern dynasty *shih-ta-fu,* as one contemporary remarked, were "not those whom the son of heaven could command." Wang Seng-ta (423–458), for example, repeatedly offended the imperial family by such actions as refusing to do obeisance during an audience, and the emperor was left to explain personally to his empress that Wang could not be punished because he was a great noble.[17] Although in imperial China, as in ancient Rome, law was whatever the emperors decided it should be, the independent authority of the Southern dynasty *shih-ta-fu* was temporarily sufficient to curb the autocratic exercise of imperial will.[18] It would not be until 589 that all of China would once again be united under a resurgent imperial dynasty; and even then, for some centuries, emperors would continue to confront the entrenched privileges of sometimes intractable great families.

Aristocratic independence peaked in the fourth century, however. At that time the retreat of the Chin court south behind the defensive barrier of the Yangtze left the imperial court temporarily vulnerable and dependent on the support of great literati. Even before this time, during the Three Kingdoms era, Chiang-nan had already been more radically "feudalized" than the north. Great private estates flourished in the third-century south, and Three Kingdoms Wu allegedly even saw the establishment of a veritable system of fiefs.[19] When the Eastern Chin set up its court-in-exile at Chien-k'ang in 318, the weakened court temporarily lacked even the resources to build an imperial palace, contenting itself with only the most important symbols of imperial rule, such as an ancestral temple and altars to the deities of the soil and grain.[20] Mao Han-kuang estimates that real military authority as well as most key government positions were in the hands of great families at this time, and Okazaki Fumio adds that at the start of the Eastern Chin, the court could not even restrict the private minting of currency.[21] Despite the material weakness of the Eastern Chin position, however, the literati as a class, somewhat remarkably, rallied to the defense of the dynasty.

The Eastern Chin dynasty managed to survive for a little more than a century in the face of unrelenting military challenges from both within and without. In the view of Kawakatsu Yoshio, the Eastern Chin survival was made possible largely because of the potency of its "ideological control."[22] While the great families each had their own private interests to pursue, a continued ideological commitment to the Confucian imperial system remained vital to each. The survival of the (weakened) empire was also vital to the material interests of the literati as officials; the very weakness of the throne made it all the easier for great families to support it, since they could be confident that the dynasty lacked the means to infringe significantly upon their own prerogatives. Only strongmen who themselves aspired to usurp the throne had any motivation to challenge the idea of royal Ssu-ma family legitimacy, and such would-be emperors would naturally, at the same time, have been anxious to affirm the basic principle of imperial rule.

The Eastern Chin appeal to the ideology of empire was apparent from the beginning. In the summer of 318, just months after ascending the throne, the first Eastern Chin emperor issued a proclamation that exemplifies his allegiance to the Confucian value system: "Magistrates must only serve the old regulations and with correct persons illustrate the laws, hold in check the powerful, seek and relieve the solitary, shelter the populace, and encourage agriculture and sericulture. Provincial governors and inspectors must investigate each other and may not look after their private [interests] at the expense of the public."[23] No literati could quarrel with such a mandate to uphold traditional virtue, and as long as the Eastern Chin court limited itself to such idealistic appeals, it had no need to fear opposition from the literati.

The problem was that a direct challenge to the literati was also explicit in this ideological appeal. The *shih-ta-fu*, after all, were often among the "powerful" persons that magistrates were enjoined to restrain. A contradiction therefore existed in the relationship of these literati to the state, and when the imperial government seriously attempted to recover some of its lost administrative authority, the reaction of the literati was ambivalent.

During the course of the Eastern Chin dynasty, a number of attempts were made to restore effective central administration. The most significant of these were the so-called *t'u-tuan,* or residence determination, drives that came in 326 to 334, 341, 364, and 412 to 413.[24] These *t'u-tuan* were efforts on the part of the central government to bring the population of the empire, especially the displaced persons who had fled south at the end of the Western Chin, back onto the tax rolls.

> After the collapse of the Central Plain, people left their native regions and made a new beginning left [i.e., south] of the River. Powerful families made annexations and did not establish registrations for some of the guests living there as refugees. The worthy leaders of an entire generation all undertook the enclosure of households.[25]

In the confusion following the loss of the north in the second decade of the century, large numbers of commoners as well as literati had escaped from the traditional Chinese homeland in the north and gravitated to Chiang-nan. The government was too feeble and the population too unsettled at that time to register the refugee peasants accurately at permanent locations, and powerful local families took advantage of the situation to conscript this untaxed farm labor as dependent households. As the confusion began to dissipate, however, the government wished to restore these citizens to imperial jurisdiction. The *t'u-tuan* measures were designed to achieve this goal.

Since antiquity the Chinese had supposedly kept careful census lists of the population for official use.[26] In the Chin dynasties these were called *huang-chi,* or "yellow registers." The registers recorded name, age, native place, family composition, health and labor-service status, office, title, local pure criticism *(ch' ing-i),* and eventually status as literatus or commoner for every family in a district.[27] As a concession to the hopes of refugees eventually to return to their original homes in the north, in the Eastern Chin dynasty displaced persons were initially allowed to remain listed under their original northern administrative units, which were then recorded on separate "white registers."[28] The superior ability of great families to stay on these separate white registers in the face of later government efforts to consolidate the registries might have contributed to the eventual distinction in registration between gentlemen and commoners.

The Eastern Chin government's various *t'u-tuan* drives met with some success at disclosing the dependent households of great magnates. During either the first or the second effort, for example,

> Shan Hsia [fl. 317–343] was magistrate of Yü-yao [in modern Chek-iang]. At the time they were just beginning to establish a base left [i.e., south] of the River, and the law forbade leniency. Powerful families often concealed the population for their personal depen-dents. Hsia used the stern law as a guideline, and within eighty days of his arrival in the county, he had disclosed more than ten thou-sand people.[29]

The best known and perhaps the most effective of all the East-ern Chin *t'u-tuan* efforts was the third one, conducted in 364 by the great general Huan Wen. It was in connection with this *t'u-tuan* that Wang Piao-chih (305–377) uncovered some thirty thou-sand unregistered persons in K'uai-chi Commandery (Cheki-ang).[30] Ironically, Wang was not only one of the most efficient administrators of Huan Wen's *t'u-tuan,* but he was also one of the few gentlemen of the period who remained unintimidated by Huan Wen's military power, refusing to the end to divert his trib-ute from the emperor to Huan.[31]

These periodic *t'u-tuan* were not the only efforts by the central government to tighten its grip over the population. The inten-tion, at least, to do so was continual, although the means were often lacking. In the early 380s, for example, as the dynasty braced for invasion from the north, "to strengthen the basis of external defense a review of the people and provisions was made, and the region of the three Wu [the Eastern Chin tax base] was greatly clarified."[32] The tension between the interests of the great families to conceal households for dependent labor, on the one hand, and the desire of the court to register those families in order to tax and mobilize them for defense and other purposes, on the other, was a permanent fixture of the period. The ordinary people were pawns caught between the powers of the state and the great families.

The significance of the fact that the two most effective *t'u-tuan* efforts, those of 364 and 412 to 423, were conducted by usurpers or would-be usurpers (Huan Wen and Liu Yü) should not be over-looked. In the contest between centralized imperial authority and great family autonomy, the court found itself a relative loser in the fourth century. Only especially powerful warlords who hoped to usurp the throne for themselves, like Huan Wen or Liu Yü, had both the means and the incentive to force people back onto the yellow registers. If the *t'u-tuan* programs at least temporarily brought some displaced commoners back onto the government tax rolls, their more lasting effects would have been simply to eliminate the possibility of evasion of registration by individual small farmers and to drive increasing numbers of commoners into the arms of those great magnates who did hold the power to disregard the imperial registration laws.

Despite the independent private authority of many medieval great families, however, the real foundation for the towering prestige of the nationwide literati class, ironically, lay in its automatic hereditary *right* to "serve" the central state as high officials. As Nakamura Keiji has demonstrated, this right appears, in turn, to have been based to some extent on literati domination of the local community, since admission to the national bureaucracy was supposedly determined by evaluations of the candidates conducted at the local level.[33] The "cultural nexus" in the local community provides a partial explanation of the rise of the medieval literati class.

The Local Community

The invasions that destroyed the Western Chin at the start of the fourth century compelled Chinese throughout the north to seek safety wherever they could find it. Many ordinary citizens took shelter under the protection of great local leaders whose private civil and military authority now sometimes approached the dimensions of classic Western feudalism. Three such figures are particularly noteworthy: Su Chün (d. 328), Ch'ih Chien (269–339), and Tsu T'i (266–321), each of whom led a particularly large band of armed followers south in submission to the new Eastern Chin regime. The biographies of all three men, extreme examples of independent power rooted in the local community, have characteristic features in common.

Su Chün's biography in the *Chin-shu* records:

During the disturbances of the Yung-chia era [307–313], the common people fled or gathered into camps where they were. Chün banded together several thousand families and erected fortifications in his home county. Of the local camps of strongmen at that time, Chün's was the strongest. He dispatched his senior secretary Hsü Wei to display the call to arms in all the camps, making known the royal influence. He also collected the bleached bones [of the dead] and buried them. Those far and near were affected by his kindness and righteousness, and elected Chün as master.[34]

Some of the more surprising elements of this story (in which the moralizing hand of the historian no doubt has been applied heavily) include the emphasis on Chün's "kindness and righteousness," his bow in the direction of royal authority, and the clear statement that he was popularly "elected."

The account of Ch'ih Chien is similar:

> At the time there was a famine in the area. Among the gentlemen of the province there were commonly some who were moved by his [Ch'ih Chien's] kindness and righteousness, and they provided him with aid. Chien redistributed what he obtained to comfort the orphans and aged of his lineage and native place. Those who trusted to him and were completely relieved were very numerous. They all said to each other: "Today the son of heaven is in exile and the Central Plain is without a lord. We must put our confidence in [his] humanity and virtue, which we can follow to escape." They then collectively elected Chien as master, and, raising more than a thousand families, they all fled to I-shan in Lu.[35]

In this account Ch'ih Chien displays the same "kindness and righteousness" noted in the case of Su Chün, except that here it looms even larger—perhaps because Ch'ih Chien was a loyal servant of the Eastern Chin, famous for his Confucian accomplishments, whereas Su Chün ended life as a rebel and a villain, as far as the historian was concerned. Of note also is the same emphasis as in the case of Su Chün on voluntary popular submission to Ch'ih's leadership.

It is not to be supposed that Ch'ih Chien actually was a poor farmer of humble birth who, as a result of his impeccable moral conduct, won the affection of his neighbors and was "elected" in some democratic fashion to lead the community. Although Ch'ih was, allegedly, poor in his youth, he sprang from a distinguished family and had already attained national recognition by the time he gained power.[36] What is significant in this story is not any implication of upward social mobility, opportunities for which were limited in the aristocratic society of early medieval China, but rather the demonstration of the terms under which viable social and political power had to be deployed in the local community. Without his appearance of "kindness and righteousness," whether sincere or cynically manipulative, people would not have accepted Ch'ih Chien's authority.

The historian is at pains to show that Ch'ih Chien did not impose himself by force upon a helpless population, despite the military emergency and the military character of his authority, but that he was willingly accepted as leader by the community because he adhered to the expected code of elite behavior. What "really happened" is a different question from what the historian chose to report, but there is no reason to doubt that Ch'ih Chien had as much desire to appear legitimate in his own time as the historian had to depict him that way.

Praise for such characteristics as "kindness and righteousness" is a recurrent topos in biographies of early medieval China.[37] Such statements should therefore be treated with caution as purported descriptions of actual individual personalities. However, the stereotypical formulation takes on significance as an example of the demeanor that contemporaries expected and valued in a leader. It is appropriate to wonder if Ch'ih Chien was really such a paragon of virtue as this biographical passage claims, but there is no doubt that this was the behavioral model against which he was judged by his local community.

As for Tsu T'i,

> When the capital was in chaos, T'i led several hundred families of relatives and villagers to safety at the Huai and Ssu rivers. He used the carriage and horse that he was riding to convey the aged and infirm who were marching with him, and he personally went on foot. He shared medicine, clothing, and provisions with the group. He had, moreover, numerous stratagems for dealing with emergencies, and so young and old all honored him and elected T'i master of the march.[38]

Here and in the previous account of Ch'ih Chien, new elements creep into the story. Tsu T'i is not only acclaimed by the people as their leader, but he shares his possessions, and their hardships, with them. The "people," as in the case of Ch'ih Chien, are specified to be members of his own lineage and fellow villagers. This last point is perhaps most significant, for the local power base of the medieval Chinese elite often had a strong family coloration—although, as Jennifer Holmgren has shown in a convincing study of local society in the fifth-century Northeast, affinal connections through marriage, dependence, and sheer physical proximity were often as significant in medieval Chinese local society as membership in a direct patrilineal descent group.[39] Patricia Ebrey notes also that, despite the apparent continuity of terminology employed by Chinese sources, the actual structure of medieval kinship arrangements varied greatly over time.[40]

In the happiest of eras effective direct central government in China (at least in the late imperial period) rarely extended below the level of the county magistrate. In times of dynastic weakness, the Chinese people were thrust even further back on the resources of their independent local communities. Japanese scholars of the so-called Kyoto school, accordingly, view this community organization, which they call *kyōdōtai*, as a critical element in Chinese history.[41] Their approach has met with considerable suspicion, however. Its depiction of "communitarian" bonds transcending class and personal interests is reminiscent of the utopian medieval romanticism familiar in the West through the works of William Morris and others.[42] Marxists are offended by the theory's apparent denial of the centrality of class struggle in history, and skeptical social scientists are inclined to suspect that people are rarely really motivated by such noble-sounding communitarian ideals.[43] The concept is also tainted by its association with Japanese aggression during the Second World War, when ideologues in the Shōwa Research Association such as Miki Kiyoshi (1895–1945) used the idea of such a "cooperative body" to justify the imposition of a New Order in East Asia.[44]

It is difficult to believe that any community of interest between the peasantry and the local elite could override their natural antagonism. As Tanigawa Michio writes:

> Is there not a contradiction in such a class [the local magnates], which has interests opposite to those of the people, leading the people. . . ? In my description of magnate *kyōdōtai*, because I emphasized the distinguished families' pose of suppressing their private interests, aiding the people, and working for family and friends, I was immediately exposed to furious criticism in the academic world.

Skepticism is natural, but evidence for the *kyōdōtai* phenomenon is overwhelming to anyone who takes the trouble to read extensively in the primary sources. As Tanigawa goes on to say, "Speaking for myself, because I was in the midst of diligently reading the dynastic histories of the Six Dynasties [i.e., Southern dynasties] period, the appearance of magnate *kyōdōtai* floated up naturally."[45]

Apart from the conventional analysis rooted in socioeconomic class distinctions, a wide variety of other conceivable theoretical approaches could be taken to describe patterns of social relations. Much evidence suggests that in China, even today, some of the most significant fracture lines separating competing from cooperating groups fall vertically along hierarchical networks of patron-client relationships rather than horizontally between socioeconomic classes.[46] In one sense such relations still represent class exploitation of the client by the patron, but in another sense this approach explains why the relationship need not be exclusively antagonistic. While a great magnate and his array of dependents are far from being equally privileged (by definition), the arrangement may nonetheless be mutually beneficial (to some extent they both need each other), and poor dependents may enjoy a greater commonality of real material interests with their rich or politically privileged patrons than they do with their counterparts in other, possibly rival, bands. How clients feel about their patrons—whether they resent or admire them—is a separate issue.

From still another perspective, as Lucian Pye observes, in a traditional culture like early medieval China, where status itself is the most highly coveted "end value," someone with aspirations to high status could actually be inhibited from exploiting his position for his own material gain and encouraged by "the politics of status" to make grand gestures on behalf of the community, in order to legitimate his own status and win acclaim.[47] The possibility of such alignments and interests taking precedence in people's lives often acts in practice to suppress overt manifestations of class struggle.

When it comes to ideal patterns of social behavior, there can be no doubt what image was projected by the early medieval Chinese texts themselves. In the fifth century T'ao Ch'ien (365–427) commended to his sons the example of an outstanding Chin dynasty Confucian who "shared his wealth with seven generations, and in his family there was no appearance of resentment."[48]

T'ao Ch'ien's exemplar is a shadowy figure who may represent a composite ideal rather than a real historical person, but countless other examples of sharing wealth, not just with the immediate family but with the extended lineage as well, can be unearthed from the historical record. The Han dynasty Fan family, for example, "reached the myriads in wealth, but they gave to their lineage and graced the village with their favor."[49] When the Han dynasty finally fell, Yang Chün (fl. early third century) led a band of over a hundred families out of central China, "relieved the destitute, and shared all his possessions" with his lineage.[50] In the fifth century, when Wang Hung's avaricious father died, Hung "burned all his contracts, not receiving any debts. The remaining old possessions were all entrusted to his younger brothers."[51] Such examples of distribution of wealth among the lineage and immediate community are countless. In the Six Dynasties era, "examples of such things as burning contracts or bonds and renouncing claims (voucher burning), or giving up private property to relieve starving people (charity) can even be said to have been rather stereotypical."[52]

The reason stories such as these should command attention today and not simply be dismissed as so much empty Confucian propaganda is that redistribution of property in medieval China was far more than a simple act of selfless idealism: it was a critical step in the assumption of a leadership role over the local community. A posture of paternalistic benevolence became a quasi-essential prerequisite to the exercise of effective leadership. By the act of "selfless" giving, the patriarch asserted power over his community. Thus, in the Kyoto school interpretation summarized by Joshua Fogel, "the link between the generic moral-intellectual character of the *shih-ta-fu* and control of the local populace . . . is not a facade but a real facet of class control."[53]

The lineage formed the spine of the early medieval Chinese social system, and networks of reciprocal obligations radiated outward from the core family to the entire clan and beyond.[54] Within the hierarchy of the medieval local community, the local magnate played the role of paterfamilias: protector and provider, with heavy moral connotations of Confucian benevolence. A splendid example of this kind of familistic ideal is provided by one third-century gentleman:

His brothers all died early, and he reared their orphans. His compassion was known throughout the district. Fields, homes, and slaves were all handed over to him. If there was someone in the neighborhood who died, he put on mourning, ceased agricultural work, and helped in the building of caskets. If one of his students

died in his home, he would lay him out in the lecture hall. He was
summoned to office but never went.[55]

The story illustrates several significant themes. One of these is
the pose of reluctance to accept appointment to office in the central government, which became almost stereotypical behavior in
the immediate post-Han era. Even people who actually accepted
office in the government were routinely expected to make a gesture of refusal. Once a position in the government was accepted,
moreover, a leader of the local community was transformed into a
representative of the central power structure. Until such office
was accepted, however, the bond was primarily between the local
leader and his community, whose interests he might even be said
to represent.

Other themes to note in this story include the expression of
concern for the entire extended family community, exemplary
moral leadership as "teacher" rather than as warrior or economic
manager, and the suggestion that people would requite such leadership by entrusting it with their property. As Tanigawa writes, "A
relationship of trust between the leader and people who admired
his character formed the axis for the group" in medieval *kyōdōtai*.[56]

In considering this ideal of local community leadership it is
important to keep two points in mind. First, it was an *ideal,* and
no one ever seriously expected it to be fully realized. Second,
despite some apparent egalitarian implications, this communal
ideal could be used by the local elite to justify its ascendance,
much as Theodore Bestor says that appeals to communal identity
and egalitarian ideals have been used to justify local hierarchies
in late-twentieth-century Tokyo.[57] From a skeptical Marxist perspective Kao Min writes that "using lineage blood relations to
conceal the reality of class exploitation" had been typical behavior during the Han dynasty.[58]

Michel Foucault instructs that "power is tolerable only on condition that it mask a substantial part of itself."[59] If the disguise is
what wins acceptance, however, and becomes the basis for the
legitimacy of a certain distribution of power, then it can reasonably be viewed as a kind of superior reality to which the supposed
underlying "reality" beneath the mask is effectively subordinate.
Power becomes a prisoner of its own disguise. As Prasenjit Duara
discovered for early-twentieth-century China, a complex "cultural

nexus" established "the *matrix* within which legitimacy and authority were produced, represented, and reproduced."[60]

The ideological basis for the local authority of the medieval Chinese great families was the idealized memory of an ancient golden age. In that splendid but hazily remembered era, land was equitably distributed among the villagers according to the so-called Well Field system, so that the people "could acquire feelings and become affectionate, and acquire produce and share it equally," and village elders "knew the people who were good and bad, making them do labor service sooner or later, and knew the people who were poor and rich, making their taxes more or less."[61]

An example of how the communitarian ideal of the village elder's benevolent paternalism converts in practice to the exercise of administrative power is provided by Yü Kun, who led a group of kinsmen to refuge in the mountains around the turn of the fourth century. "In this high and dangerous defile, he blocked the footpaths, erected fortifications, planted [defensive] hedges, examined merit, made measurements, equalized labor and rest, shared possessions, repaired implements, measured strength and employed the able, making all things correspond to what they should. He caused villages to promote their leaders and neighborhoods to promote their worthy, and he personally led them."[62]

The Kyoto school's concept of *kyōdōtai* is useful in approaching medieval Chinese social history. It does not necessarily postulate dreamy utopian selflessness, nor does it deny the intensity of class or other competition within the boundaries of the local community. It is, in short, not really incompatible with either standard Marxist or skeptical social-scientific analysis, each of which undoubtedly contributes its own perspective on the truth. *Kyōdōtai* theory merely adds a new perspective to the common fund of understanding. In spite of the possibility of bitter internal animosities within the local community, *kyōdōtai* theory asserts that the cohesiveness of the community remained an inescapable fact of life and the primary social reality for many Chinese. With the disintegration of imperial state power at the end of the second century, moreover, conditions were ripe for a renewal of strong lineage and community bonds.[63]

Already, during the Han dynasty, the typical Chinese lineage included members of widely varying fortune. Rich subfamilies had a customary obligation to succor the poor within their own lineage, but this obligation simultaneously placed the poor in a position of dependence on their wealthier kinsmen and converted the lineage into a local power base for the rich.[64] The direction of relationships in this typical local community, therefore, was vertical. What happened at the end of the Han to transform local strongmen of this type into the by now familiar medieval great family was the weakening of the old imperial system of central control, which gave many of these preexisting local communities a new measure of independence.

Modern scholars are skeptical of the extent to which any premodern central government ever actually exercised administrative control over society at the local level. Robert Somers writes, for example, that "the premodern empire was extensive but not intensive; it ruled but it did not administer the affairs of society at-large."[65] Significantly, however, all of his Chinese examples are drawn from the late imperial period. There is no doubt that his statement accurately describes the situation in the last imperial dynasty, the Ch'ing, but does it apply equally to the first imperial dynasty, the Ch'in?

Recent archeological discoveries—especially the invaluable recovery of Ch'in dynasty documents from a grave at Yün-meng in 1975—confirm the impression presented by the traditional histories that the early empire actually did make a serious effort to apply fairly close direct official supervision over local society.[66] A meticulous study of the Yün-meng legal texts inspired A. F. P. Hulsewé to conclude that "in the 3rd century B.C. the state of Ch'in aimed at extending its influence over all spheres of the life of its inhabitants."[67] Ch'in seems to have aspired to and actually achieved an exceptionally high level of direct administrative control. It was only in the mid–T'ang dynasty, then, that this pattern was reversed: "A long-term secular trend beginning in the T'ang" has been identified "whereby the degree of official involvement in local affairs—not only in marketing and commerce but also in social regulation . . . and administration itself—steadily declined."[68]

Well before the T'ang, however, during the period of weak imperial governments following the collapse of the Han, a gap had already opened between the government's continued desire to regulate local society and its ability to do so. In antiquity, for example, the classics depict an exceedingly precise system of local communities, even the smallest of which were walled and carefully supervised.[69] As Miyazaki Ichisada observes, these presented ideal opportunities for the imposition of control from above. Such tightly walled communities made evasion of taxes and labor service almost impossible.[70] Following the collapse of the Han state, however, and in conjunction with the popular migrations that attended the early medieval period, this classical system of habitation was disrupted, and more spontaneous and informal assemblies of people led by local great families sprang up in its place. This process allegedly constituted the origin of the modern Chinese village *(ts'un)*.[71]

Anecdotal evidence for both the expectation of the classical imperial pattern of local residential supervision and the difficulties encountered trying to maintain the system amid the ruins of the Han is provided by the story of the hermit Chiao Hsien. In 211 a disturbance in his region caused Chiao to

> become lost from his family, and he hid alone among the islets in the [Yellow] River, eating grass and drinking water, without clothing or shoes. At that time Chu Nan, the head of Ta-yang, observed him, and, remarking that he [must be] an absconded soldier, wanted to send a boat to arrest him. [Hou] Wu-yang informed the county that "he is just a crazy person," and this was noted in his registration. He was given a stipend of five pints [of rice] per day.[72]

Although this story should be treated with the same caution as any other anecdote—it is not necessarily statistically significant, or even true—the unconscious assumptions of the author of the story that all persons (even those in hiding) must be carefully registered by the government and participate in the state tax or welfare system are worthy of attention.

The Yün-meng legal texts also suggest that in Ch'in times Confucian scholars led local community opposition to Ch'in imperial centralization.[73] In the third century A.D., as the tide of imperial centralization began to recede, great family leadership expanded to fill the vacuum at the local level. The relationship of these local great families to the new villages that began to dot the post-Han landscape is suggested by Miyazaki's comment that the villages were, in many cases, identical to the aristocratic "estates" *(chuang-yüan)* that also made their appearance at this time.[74] There was, furthermore, little hope now of any immediate restoration of the former degree of direct imperial control over the now widely scattered villages.

The imperial government deplored these developments, and

as soon as a measure of order was restored, it began to clamor for
a resumption of the old system. As Wei Kuan (220–291), an official at the Western Chin court, memorialized:

> Today the Nine Regions [of the empire] share the same regula-
> tions, and the great transformation [i.e., reunification] has finally
> begun. This minister and others believe we should clear away the
> latter laws [which deviate from venetable precedent], and, with the
> same intent as in the old system, make judgments concerning the
> land. From the dukes and nobles on down, everyone should be cor-
> rected according to where they [actually] live. There should never
> again be those who are distant guests living far away in strange
> lands. In this way [people who live in] the same district, neighbor-
> hood, or association will all form [real] communities. The gover-
> nors of commanderies and counties, because of long residence,
> can completely eliminate the Arbiters and Nine Ranks system and
> cause the virtuous to be raised up and talent promoted, each on
> the basis of local opinion.[75]

Although the Western Chin had succeeded in temporarily re-
unifying the entire empire, and settlement patterns might indeed
have stabilized somewhat at the time Wei Kuan wrote this proposal, Wei's memorial represents an imperial fantasy that ran counter to the direction of actual historical development. The Western
Chin court was itself highly privatized, and the independent
authority of the literati class was just then coming into flood tide.
With the utter collapse of the northern half of the empire early in
the fourth century, popular settlement patterns became more
fluid than ever before, and the state then lost many of its last
shreds of control over local society.

In the forests of Chiang-nan, at a time when land was relatively
abundant and population (for China) relatively sparse, Eastern
Chin great families concentrated their efforts on appropriating
the labor of the common farmers by reducing them to dependency. It goes without saying that no such relationship of dependence is ever a desirable condition and what great magnates call
"protection" (yin-pi) is a familiar euphemism for abuse and exploitation. But in the early-fourth-century south this condition was to
some extent voluntarily entered into. Poor farmers had the op-
tion of claiming registration by the government and paying
taxes.[76] Since this was a time of relative physical mobility, moreover, the very conditions that made it so easy for magnates to hide
their dependents from the central government also made it rela-

tively easy for poor farmers to move away from particularly oppressive private overlords if they chose to do so. At least to a certain extent, then, landlords and peasants alike must have conspired together to reconstitute local society beyond the purview of the state.

According to one contemporary,

> Because of the evil practices of the Ch'in and Chin [dynasties], the common people repeatedly conceal each other. Either a hundred houses join their doors, or a thousand adult males register together [as one, to deceive the census]. They entrust themselves to walled companies, fear neither smoke nor fire, publicly evade taxes and labor service, and dare to be disloyal and hateful. This injurious fashion destroys the regulations and is not to be permitted by the law.[77]

The passage is all the more interesting because it speaks with the outraged voice of the injured imperial government, not the suspect special interests of the great families.

It was the great families who benefited most from these developments. It is quite conceivable that conditions for the common farmer sharply deteriorated as a result of these changes; but the historical record, prejudiced as it certainly was, presents dependency upon the great families as the lesser of two evils when compared to continued subjection to the imperial state. One contemporary, Lu Chi (261–303), even argued that true feudal lords, like those of the ancient Chou dynasty, made better stewards of the land than bureaucratic imperial appointees, since they were stimulated to rule their lands well by self-interest, while officials appointed by a central government were only concerned with pleasing their imperial masters and seeking bureaucratic advancement.[78]

As a distinguished literatus and great landowner, Lu Chi certainly had his own self-interest in mind when he wrote this. Still, even at the peak of early centralized power under the Ch'in dynasty, a careful reading of the legal documents found at Yünmeng makes it clear that the state had a persistent problem with citizens attempting to flee to avoid labor requirements.[79] The great weakening of imperial power during the centuries of division made it significantly easier to evade unwelcome state obligations and magnified this tendency.

Since this was an age of constant warfare, when the state's tax

base was continually shrinking owing to both declining population and rampant tax evasion, "the court's taxes and labor requirements were numerous and heavy."[80] In the mid–fourth century, sometime between 351 and 355, Wang Hsi-chih wrote to his
friend Hsieh An that the state's heavy labor requirements in his
jurisdiction at K'uai-chi were driving the people either into hiding or into rebellion.[81] As a Sung dynasty emperor acknowledged
in an edict dated 458, "In the past, because there were many
deserters from the army, sometimes they spread disobedience
across the mountains and feared the application of military regulations, and sometimes they shirked labor service and avoided
punishment."[82] The plaintive outcry of Fan Ning (339–401),
tinged though it must be with hyperbole, is suggestive of what the
attitude of many medieval farmers toward the central state might
have been:

> Today the four frontiers are at peace, and beacon fires are not
> raised, yet the [state] granaries are depleted and the treasury is
> empty. The ancients, in using men [for labor service], did not go
> beyond three days a year, but today's labor requirements hardly
> allow three days of rest. It has reached the point that there are
> those who disfigure themselves and cut their hair, demanding to be
> released from service, who give birth to a son but do not raise him,
> and who when widowed do not dare remarry. How could it not be
> that resentment unites men and ghosts, disturbing the harmonious
> atmosphere?[83]

When these tensions finally burst forth in a bloody uprising,
that of Sun En in 399, the popular fury was directed primarily at
the government and those literati who held positions in its administration, not at the independent local landlord. As the *Chin-
shu* records, "When [Ssu-ma] Yüan-hsien [a leader of the imperial
faction that dominated the court after 385] was tyrannizing Wu
and K'uai-chi, the common people were unsettled. [Sun] En
accordingly stirred them up and attacked Shang-yü [county,
in K'uai-chi] from the sea, killing the magistrate."[84]

When a modern Marxist historian, seeking to illustrate the
principle of class struggle in third-century China, observes that
"the [independent] small farmers who, for the time being, had
not yet been totally ruined [by the rise of the great landlords]
were made to bear a heavy burden of land taxes, household taxes,
military service, labor service, and so on," eventually driving them

into the shelter provided by submission to a great landlord, one has to wonder who the worst exploiters really were—the landlords or the state?[85]

Indeed, recent scholarship from the People's Republic has asked much the same question. While emphasizing that the cruel exploitation of labor on great private estates should not be forgotten, Chu Shao-hou adds:

> It should not be supposed that the exploitation and oppression of the peasants on [great private] farms during the period of the Eastern Chin, Sixteen Kingdoms, and Northern and Southern dynasties was any greater or any crueler than that suffered by the [small] independent farmers [at the hands of the state]. On the contrary, in a certain sense, and under certain conditions, the exploitation and oppression suffered by peasants in [great private] farms was somewhat lighter than that of the independent farmers.[86]

The orthodox Marxist assumption is that the state simply represented the interests of the landlord class. Presumably, therefore, government oppression would merely be landlord exploitation in another guise. It requires but a moment's reflection to realize, however, that the state had a natural predisposition to favor taxpaying, labor-serving, independent small farmers over the tax- and labor-exempt dependents of magnates. It is true that in medieval China great family members were often able to infiltrate the highest ranks of the bureaucracy and win for their families and their dependents a significant degree of immunity from government demands, turning the machinery of state to their own advantage; but that the central government was weakened—in a sense, subverted—in the process merely underscores the extent to which it is fallacious to posit an automatic identity of interest between the central government and the landlord class. That members of local communities, including potentially even the leading local landowners, might have had interests quite at variance with those of the central state is nicely suggested by the utopian communal ideal of total independence from any imperial dynasty depicted in T'ao Ch'ien's (365–427) well-known story "Peach Blossom Spring."[87]

It was not the landowners, as a class, who identified with the central state, but rather the bureaucrats who did so; and it was the literati class who, increasingly, staffed that bureaucracy. Watanabe Yoshihiro has shown that the bureaucratic selection process had become detached from any local economic base by the early third century and dependent instead on cooptation by the national-level literati elite—the coterie of "famous scholars."[88] This new selection system interposed a barrier between local public opinion and the machinery of appointment. Subsequently, the flight to Chiang-nan at the start of the Eastern Chin dynasty (in the early fourth century) physically detached many of the most influential émigré literati from their native communities. Thereafter, it was the stratum of the "famous scholars," now unconnected with any real local community base, who were politically and socially ascendant at the national level.

Military Power

It is to be expected that the rise of the medieval Chinese great families would have had a military component. As the ability of the Han-style imperial state to maintain order decayed, local great families played a critical role in organizing the community for self-defense. Such camp masters as Su Chün, Ch'ih Chien, and Tsu T'i all commanded defensive bands early in the fourth century and all later served the Eastern Chin court in a military capacity. At his peak Su Chün, for example, had "ten thousand well drilled troops, very well equipped."[89] When he rose up in rebellion in 327, his military strength was sufficient to seize the capital from loyalist forces, and propelled him to the brink of capturing the throne before his death the next year. It was only the countervailing military power of other great private houses that, in the end, stood between Su Chün and a successful usurpation.

It comes as something of a surprise to learn, therefore, that Naitō Torajirō, Kawakatsu Yoshio, and the Kyoto school of Japanese scholarship consider the absence of a military aristocracy in China to be one of the chief distinctions between the European and the Chinese middle ages.[90] To understand what they mean, it is important to realize that the oft-repeated story of the rise of private armies—known as *pu-ch'ü*—in the post-Han period tends to exaggerate the actual state of militarization in medieval China. In fact, private militarization was largely an ephemeral response to temporary emergencies rather than a permanent and characteristic condition.

During the interregnum between the Former and Later Han dynasties (A.D. 9–25), effective central control over large parts of

China slipped from the hands of the state, and local inhabitants had no choice but to mobilize for their own protection. In Wu-k'ang County, for example, "at the time of the Red Eyebrows disturbance, villagers piled up stones beneath the mountain for a [defensive] wall."[91] Such local militarization ceased to be necessary as soon as Han rule was restored, however, and it quickly subsided.

During the prolonged disorder that attended the final agonies of the Han, the need for local self-defense was greater and more sustained. Local great families did organize private armies then, not merely to defend their homes but also to participate actively in the military struggle for local and national ascendancy that the fall of the Han precipitated. In the north the great strongman Ts'ao Ts'ao rose to power in just this fashion. Yet, as the Ts'ao family consolidated its hold over north China in the early third century, it acted vigorously to suppress other private armies.[92]

The Ts'ao Wei Kingdom was not entirely successful in this effort; after the Chin usurpation and the subsequent splintering of Western Chin power early in the fourth century, private local militarization for self-defense reached new heights. The history of the fourth century in north China is one of seemingly endless combat between petty militarized kingdoms, while the situation in the south, where the Eastern Chin grip on power was threatened by a continuous string of powerful warlords, was only a little better.[93] Still, except for the handful of great generals vying for the dubious privilege of usurping the throne, the literati class as a whole was usually content to surrender its military responsibilities to the central government whenever it was even marginally fit to assume them. A more significant development than the rise of private militarization in medieval China may actually be the tendency of these private military forces, once organized, to be converted into dependent labor for work in the fields in times of peace.[94]

The reason Japanese scholars, quite correctly, deny that medieval China witnessed the rise of a military aristocracy is that in China the military aspect of elite activity, though undeniable, was as limited as possible. Government must always perform certain basic military tasks, and when the central imperial state was inadequate to meet those responsibilities, the literati sometimes privately rose to fill the vacuum. The literati did not always do so gladly, however. No one could mistake the medieval Chinese lite-

rati for warriors like those of feudal Europe or Japan. At best they
were generals: civilian managers of armies. As a whole the Chinese literati boasted a profoundly antimilitary bias and a healthy
distrust of the profession of arms. As one Chin dynasty writer put
it, "A warrior managing affairs of state is like letting a wolf tend
sheep."[95]

For many literati, military affairs were of little interest. It is in-
structive to contrast the great martial hero of feudal Europe, Ro-
land, with a late-third-century Chinese gentleman like Fan Wei,
whose "family had loved scholarship for generations and possessed more than seven thousand *chüan* of books. Those who
came from far and near to read them were regularly more than a
hundred people, and Wei provided them with food and cloth-
ing."[96] If the Chinese literati class sometimes displayed its leadership through the mobilization of private armies, a (possibly)
more characteristic Chinese form of "vassalage" was the assem-
blage of large followings of dependent students—the so-called
men-sheng.[97]

The Struggle for the Land

Far more central to the definition of the medieval Chinese great
family than militarization and the appearance of private armies
was the rise of the private landed estate. In the eyes of some historians this feature is, indeed, one of the most characteristic of the
entire post-Han era. In the words of Chairman Mao, "Culture
. . . is a reflection of the politics and economics of a given society,"
and politics itself, in the end, is nothing more than "the concentrated expression of economics."[98] For Marxists, control over the
means of production is fundamental, and even many non-Marxist
scholars would echo this claim for the crucial importance of economic forces in history. The rise of great private estates during
the Northern and Southern dynasties is therefore widely viewed
as having been a determining characteristic of the period.

The first appearance of private landownership in China is associated with the rise of the Ch'in imperial state, beginning with
Shang Yang's land reforms in the mid–fourth century B.C. and
culminating under Ch'in Shih-huang's unified empire at the end
of the third century B.C.[99] Even under this new dispensation, state
supervision of the land remained conspicuous. Of the Ch'in
period legal texts found at Yün-meng, all six of the items involv-

ing land relate to the management of state land.[100] Beneath the continuing system of public land administration, however, lay an economy increasingly based on the individual farm family, which was given legal recognition in Ch'in by the taxing of agricultural produce beginning in 408 B.C. and the formation of household registration blocks in 375 B.C.[101] Under the Ch'in system, furthermore, once land was initially allocated by the state, it did not ordinarily revert to the government for redistribution, and it tended to become de facto private property.[102] Therefore, such public land as still existed in Ch'in times was largely of a supplemental or transitional nature and, apart from mountains, streams, and park lands, consisted mostly of fields not yet under cultivation.[103]

During the first imperial dynasties of Ch'in and Han, the argument goes, some fortunate families were able to exploit the opportunities provided by a relatively free market in land to accumulate substantial private holdings, so that by the early Western Han poor tenant farmers had reputedly often been reduced to renting the land of great landlords and paying half of their crop as rent.[104] According to the conventional wisdom, "The Han was unable to regulate land to settle the people, therefore . . . the fields of rich people sometimes covered an entire province, while the poor did not have the land on which to stand an awl."[105]

It is clear that by the Han period land was traded in what amounted to a free market, which certain prosperous families were able to corner to their own advantage. By the end of the Han dynasty, Hsün Yüeh (148–209) complained that while the central government only collected a tax of 1 percent from the peasantry, great magnates collected more than half their crops as rent, and enormous landholdings—which Hsün claimed (almost certainly with some exaggeration) sometimes ran into millions of acres—were permitting these great families to encroach upon the very prerogatives of the state.[106]

It is often claimed, then, that from the end of the Han on into the period of division, a system of large-estate building gradually superseded the supposedly relatively small-scale private farming of the Han. This progression is symbolized by the appearance of the word "estate" (chuang-yüan) early in the Southern dynasties.[107] By the late third century the Western Chin dynasty was the scene of ostentatious displays of wealth, some of which are collected into a chapter devoted to the subject in the Shih-shuo hsin-yü.[108] Wang Jung (234–305), for example, who was perhaps the least

savory member of the fabled Seven Worthies of the Bamboo
Grove, "was extensively endowed with fields and water mills in the
eight regions, embracing the entire empire. His stores and accu-
mulated cash were beyond count."[109] It is, incidentally, significant
that Wang Jung's wealth was by no means limited to land. Com-
mercialization is an important subtheme in early medieval economic history, which I shall return to later.

The civil wars and invasions that devastated the Western Chin
dynasty early in the fourth century brought a close to this well-
known period of extravagance, and the great families who fled
south to dominate the new Eastern Chin court in Chiang-nan
were obliged to begin afresh. At this, it must be said, they were
quickly successful. By the end of the century the notorious Tiao
family enjoyed "ten thousand *ch' ing* of fields, several thousand
slaves, and other [forms of] wealth equivalent to this."[110] Since
one Chin dynasty *ch' ing* converts into approximately 12.1 English
acres, the Tiao estate must have reached the proportions of some
121,000 acres.[111] Interestingly enough, this almost incomprehen-
sibly large figure is dwarfed by the figure of millions of acres
attributed to magnates in the late Han by Hsün Yüeh. The Tiao
family was by no means typical, but they were perhaps an extreme
example of a common tendency; they may in that sense be considered symbolic of the age.

More truly typical of the large aristocratic estates of the Southern dynasties was that of K'ung Ling-fu (fl. 460). In the mid–fifth
century he built a villa in Chekiang that was "thirty-three *li* [about
eleven miles] in circumference, with 265 *ch' ing* of water and dry
land, containing two mountains and also nine fruit orchards." It
is a significant indication of the state's approach toward such lav-
ish private landowning, incidentally, that an official accusation
was brought against K'ung because of this very estate, and the
majority of his biography in the *Sung-shu* is devoted to a discussion of K'ung's own administrative proposal to alleviate crowding
in Shan-yin by the state-imposed relocation of propertyless families to newly reclaimed polders in the region of modern
Ningpo.[112] Clearly, despite the existence of large private estates,
the central government continued to take an active interest in
land administration during this period.

K'ung Ling-fu's more than three-thousand-acre estate, it is important to note, was not entirely under cultivation, but also included mountains and lakes, and presumably stretches of forest

as well. The *chuang-yüan* of Southern dynasty China characteristi-
cally included large tracts of undeveloped park land, which the
literati apparently exploited to indulge their newly discovered
aesthetic appreciation for natural scenic beauty. Even assuming
that only a small percentage of K'ung Ling-fu's acreage was actually used for agriculture, however, the intensive labor demands of
wet-field rice cultivation, which already characterized southern
farming in this period, implies that he must have had ready access
to an abundant supply of dependent labor. This availability of
labor, in fact, was a major consideration in great family power and
influence in the post-Han era.

To put these figures into some kind of perspective, note that in
1987 there were 66,786 farms (3.2 percent of the total) in the
United States of two thousand or more acres in expanse. In that
year the average American farm covered 462 acres.[113] Such figures are almost meaningless, however, for purposes of comparison with medieval China, because of the modern American me-
chanization of agriculture. By the same token, any comparison to
the sizes of farms in twentieth-century China would also be meaningless, because of a population pressure today that would have
been inconceivable during the Southern dynasties. A more apt
comparison might be with the large estates of mid-eighteenth-
century New York, several of which ran into the hundreds of
thousands of acres and one of which was reportedly over a million.[114] In colonial America, as in medieval China, there occurred
an aristocratic carving up of what, from the point of view of the
aristocrats at any rate, was largely wilderness, for the purposes of
gradual development and cultivation using premodern technology. The medieval Chinese appropriation of land for estates in
Chiang-nan, then, was a scarcely noteworthy example of a fairly
typical premodern pattern of land development.

One important and extremely puzzling paradox remains, however. When we narrow our focus to observe only the Northern
and Southern dynasties, the rise of great estates at that time
seems to be unmistakable; but when we draw back for a more
panoramic view of Chinese history, scholars begin to speak of the
rise of great estates not during this period, but in the late T'ang
instead. In contrast to the late T'ang, the Northern and Southern
dynasties period seems to be characterized not so much by great
private estates as by notable government efforts to prevent
them.[115]

What happened in the middle of the eighth century to mark the beginning of a new age in Chinese economic history was the final termination of efforts by the central government at close supervision of the land. Such efforts had not only survived throughout the Northern and Southern dynasties, but are actually uniquely characteristic of that period, extending on through the Sui and early T'ang. To some extent these were not even futile, last-ditch efforts to preserve an ancient system of public land-ownership in the face of inexorable privatization, but rather entirely new systems inspired by appeals to a fondly imagined antique ideal.

Land regulation in early medieval China was inspired by the perhaps somewhat fanciful memory of the ancient Chou Well Field system, under the terms of which each household was supposedly allotted equal one-hundred-*mu* plots of land to cultivate. Despite Kuo Mo-jo's confident assertion that "ancient China without a doubt put into practice the Well Field system," Derk Bodde doubts that "such a checker-board pattern could ever have been laid out over wide areas with the mathematical exactness described by Mencius." Bodde does acknowledge, however, that the Well Field ideal may have had some basis in Chou administrative practice.[116]

In that ideal golden age of antiquity, the Chou had supposedly formed an "imperial household state" in which the entire realm belonged to the king personally. As patriarch of the national family, the monarch then personally attended to the needs of all his people as though they were his own children.[117] This paternalistic vision of the perfect state was enshrined in Confucian ideology, and later Confucians, beginning with Tung Chung-shu in the early Han, repeatedly urged that the principles (at least) of the old Well Field system be revived.[118] The disruptions to the existing pattern of landholding that attended the wars at the end of the Han dynasty, then, provided an opportune moment to experiment with Confucian-inspired land reform. After the revolt of the Yellow Turbans in 184, one contemporary argued, "the people are scattered, landed property is without masters, and all are public fields. At this time we should restore it [the Well Field ideal]."[119]

The series of government measures that followed over the next several centuries, intended to implement portions of the Well Field ideal, were partially facilitated by population decline, which left substantial amounts of formerly cultivated land at the government's disposal. It was not just the opportunity presented by vacant fields that stimulated these measures, however. Their inspiration and impulse also came from both the administrative interests of the state and the simultaneous triumph of a new literati class that conceived of itself through the Confucian ideological lenses of the classics. It is critical to an understanding of the medieval literati class to realize that its sense of identity—its self-image— was deeply affected by its reading of the ancient books.

The first significant government program for the administration of state land emerged out of the crisis situation in the third century. This was the *t'un-t' ien,* or agricultural colony system, of Three Kingdoms Wei.[120] The idea for these colonies originated with the military colonies that had been used in the past to help settle frontier regions.[121] In the Wei this system was also employed domestically, as internal colonies that were both military and civil in composition. Farmers on these colonies became, in effect, agricultural servants of the state.[122] The intention of the Wei government in promoting *t'un-t' ien* was to consolidate imperial control over at least a part of its citizenry and simultaneously to increase the state's revenue by stimulating agricultural production.

The agricultural colonies of Wei did not long outlive that dynasty, however. They were abolished in conjunction with the Ssu-ma usurpation of the throne between 266 and 280. The subsequent Western Chin dynasty witnessed a renewed assault by the landed great families on the state's claim to supreme title to all land in the empire. Even so, the Western Chin emperors did not lightly relinquish their claim to authority over the land. The so-called *chan-t' ien* land law they promulgated in 280 is one of the landmarks of Northern and Southern dynasties property control legislation.[123]

This law differed from its predecessor in being, at least in theory, universal in application. The Wei agricultural colonies had constituted, after all, little more than pockets of special imperial authority amid the surrounding power of the great families. Another critical innovation of the *chan-t' ien* system was that it made no effort to assert actual imperial ownership and administration over the land, but merely regulated and restricted privately owned land.[124]

For a system that concedes so much to the claims of private property, however, this *chan-t' ien* law also contained ambitious provisions for the government-supervised distribution of land to farmers and imposed limitations on the special exemptions for officials (a category almost synonymous now with the new *shih-ta-fu* class). Under this system each adult male was supposedly allowed seventy *mu* of land to cultivate, with fifty *mu* in some unclear fashion to be taxed by the state.[125] The details of this law are unfortunately obscure, and Kao Min argues that the seventy-*mu* figure was merely intended as the maximum amount of land a single adult male commoner could privately possess, whereas fifty *mu* was the amount of land each was required to pay taxes on.[126] It may be, furthermore, that the fifty-*mu* figure was never intended as anything more than a statistical average, since households also continued to be evaluated on the basis of their individual wealth during the Western Chin and assessed taxes accordingly.[127]

The *chan-t' ien* law was never intended to impose rigid equality on the entire farming population. No matter how the law is interpreted, however, it does seem to have required some degree of forced relative equalization of landholdings by the government, with the implication that those who held too much would have some confiscated, and those who held too little would have some allocated to them by the state.

After the retreat to the south in the fourth century, this Western Chin land law was maintained with some revision. As Yoshida Fudōmaro points out, however, the increased provisions for great family privileges made by these later revisions are symptoms of the continued erosion of imperial power during the Southern dynasties.[128] Despite this gradual withdrawal of imperial prerogatives, the state remained anxious to assert its claims to the land. An imperial edict of 336, for example, threatened death to offenders: "To occupy a mountain or to shelter a swamp is a violation of the statutes. All who steal a single *chang* [ten feet] or more will be publicly executed."[129]

The most famous example of all medieval Chinese land distribution laws, the "equal fields," or *chün-t' ien*, system of the Northern Wei, was enacted in north China in 485. When this system, which was continued during the Sui and early T'ang dynasties, disintegrated during the eighth century, Chinese attempts at state regulation of landholding finally came to an end and were not effectively renewed (despite recurrent proposals) until the communism of the twentieth century. Therefore, although there can be no denying that great private aristocratic estates do present a striking subtheme for the era, one of the most distinctive features of the entire Northern and Southern dynasties period was nonetheless a strong imperial resolve to regulate land distribution.[130]

The effectiveness of the original Western Chin law of 280 is difficult to evaluate, but the opinion of Ma Tuan-lin in the thirteenth century was that because of this law, for a generation at least at the end of the third century, "there were no households without [their own] fields."[131] Of course, Ma Tuan-lin was writing a thousand years after the event, and modern scholars are right to approach this question with caution. Etienne Balazs' conclusion in 1953 that the Chin land law "did no more than voice a vague Utopian idea, and could never have been carried out" voices the standard of much modern critical scholarship.[132]

The evidence for simply dismissing the Chin land law is rather thin, however.[133] The standard histories do provide abundant anecdotal testimony to abuses in the system—the illegal occupation of land and acquisition of dependents—but such evidence of violations of the law does not justify an immediate conclusion that the entire law must therefore have been a mere "legal fiction." Complaints of abuses can even be, in a perverse way, proof that someone, at least, took the law seriously. Elsewhere in Chinese history, moreover, when tangible new physical evidence has become available through the modern science of archeology or the discovery of long-lost archival records, there has been a disconcerting tendency for the new data to substantiate traditional Chinese accounts. Those traditional histories, therefore, should not lightly be dismissed.

The most dramatic and best-known example of this process of scientific verification of traditional records was undoubtedly provided by the excavation of a Shang dynasty (circa eighteenth to twelfth centuries B.C.) city at An-yang beginning in 1928.[134] More pertinently, Ikeda On believes that fragments of household registers found among the collection of manuscripts discovered at Tun-huang early in this century prove that for the late Northern dynasties and early T'ang, "the household, personal status, age-category, and land allocation systems that are described in contemporary historical sources were in fact put into operation."[135]

The correct interpretation of this new evidence from Tun-huang is still in dispute, however.[136] For the earlier Western Chin *chan-t' ien* system, even less information is available. The evidence remains little more than the classical description of the law in the *Chin-shu* and anecdotes scattered throughout the standard histories. Interpretation of the law, therefore, must hinge upon a general picture of state and society in early medieval China. It is surely inconceivable that the *chan-t' ien* system was ever rigidly implemented in any methodically perfect manner, but is it equally implausible that the spirit of the law might have been enforced in some approximate fashion? Might not the reality of land tenure during the period in question, in practice, have been some kind of balance between observation of the law and flagrant abuse?

The most persuasive argument for doubting the efficacy of any state-imposed land regulation in early medieval China is that no regime during this period was ever strong enough to enforce such a system against the wishes of the dominant literati class. Such reasoning is not only circular, however, it also depends on unproven assumptions about the basic interests of the literati class. The reason Balazs gives for his dismissal of the *chan-t' ien* law is that "those whose task it was to apply the law would have had to despoil themselves in doing so, being at the same time officials and large landed proprietors."[137] Is this assumption of the basic interests of the literati class an accurate one, however? Balazs himself concluded, with regard to the later equal fields system, that "it was the very provisions of the law that did the most to favor the formation of large landed estates."[138] Could it be that government officials had not the most to lose but rather the most to gain from enforcement of the law? In addition, if there was any contradiction in literati interests arising from their dual role as officials and landowners, is it clear that their identity as landlords would prevail?

Kao Min has shown that the *chan-t' ien* law of 280 approved and regularized the tax-exempt status of officials and the literati class as a whole.[139] To the extent that the literati class remained a hybrid bureaucratic-aristocracy, it actually had a vested interest in the *chan-t' ien* system. Under the terms of this law, generous provision was made for government officials on the basis of their rank. The *chan-t' ien* law specified, for example: "Those holding official rank from the first to the ninth occupy land according to their position. Those holding the first rank occupy 50 *ch' ing* [about 600 acres], rank two 45 *ch' ing*, rank three 40 *ch' ing*" and so on down to the ninth rank and 10 *ch' ing*. In addition, officials were entitled to protect their families for up to nine generations and to have servants in proportion to their rank up to a maximum of three personal attendants and fifty households of agricultural servants.[140] Such special official privileges would have constituted, moreover, a significant component of the whole land regulation system, since it has recently been estimated that there might have been as many as 150,000 households of legal official dependents in the fourth-century south alone—as much as one-quarter of the entire population.[141]

Such provisions have led Wu Tse to conclude that, far from imposing unwelcome restraints upon elite interests, "the *chant' ien* system was a feudal-rank landholding system by which the government protected the interests of the great families." Wu goes so far as to write that the "political authority of the great family landlords in both Chin dynasties was built directly on the foundation of the *chan-t'. ien* and *k'o-t' ien* landholding systems."[142] Kao Min seems to agree, noting that although commoners were obliged to purchase their land on the open market, so much of the estates of the great literati families came from official grants of state land that "a system of state landownership was a precondition" for their very emergence.[143] Such great families, therefore, did not have to "despoil themselves" at all in upholding the law, but on the contrary might have benefited materially from promoting it. Undoubtedly, many great families improved on their positions still more by exceeding the legal limits of the system.

At the other extreme, the poor, who might have been expected to welcome state-imposed land redistribution, or at least regulation of the presumably predatory landlords, might not actually have perceived even a genuinely equal distribution of farmland as being in their own best interests. A half century before the birth of Christ, one writer was already complaining that, "as for the poor people, even if you give them land, they still sell it cheaply in order to go into trade."[144] Presumably some commoners, at least, thought they could do better as merchants than as petty farmers. Derk Bodde concurs that, although the Northern Wei equal fields system was "no doubt intended, at least in good part, to improve the livelihood of the peasant, at the same time—to the extent that it actually operated—[it] severely curtailed his freedom of economic choice by confining him to whatever plot of land happened to be allotted to him."[145] Since, in any case, the true motivation of the government in promoting land redistribution might have been as much to stabilize its own revenue, derived from a per-capita land tax, as to benefit the common farmer altruistically, it would not be surprising if some poor farmers had found the system not to be to their advantage.[146]

When the central government was weak, as it was through so much of the Southern dynasties, literati had little to lose from support for the imperial land regulation systems. In the same way that the literati had captured the Nine Ranks system (described below) to support their claims to office, they could also use Southern dynasties land regulation laws to augment their economic position. What at first appears to be a curious paradox, then—the simultaneous existence of great landed estates and imperial land regulation laws—is resolved by the simple fact that not only did the land regulation laws permit and even create some landed estates, but members of the literati class benefited from both the regulations and the abuses of them.

Some evidence also suggests that for many literati, particularly after their hold on the Nine Ranks system had become firmly consolidated, official salary was a more important consideration than landownership. As Yen Chih-t'ui complained at the end of the sixth century: "The gentlemen of the courts of Chiang-nan, following the [Eastern] Chin restoration, came south across the [Yangtze] River and ended up as visitors. Down to the present, for eight or nine generations, they have never cultivated fields, but always depended on their salaries to eat."[147] A surprising insignificance for landed estates is suggested by the following Sui dynasty description: "Tan-yang was the location of the old capital, and its populace was originally flourishing. Petty people were mostly merchants, and gentlemen lived off of their official salaries."[148]

Private landownership was therefore far less essential to the identity and even the economic well-being of the Southern dynasty literati than was office holding. A significant part of the land that the great medieval literati did hold was obtained through their privileged relationship with the state. Despite what Chairman Mao said, politics might not have been "the concentrated expression of economics." Rather, economic benefit might have followed as an extension of political power.

Commercialization

Complaints of great family monopolization of the land are plentiful in the early medieval period, but so are complaints that land was not being cultivated at all. When all China was briefly united under the Western Chin dynasty in the late third century, a younger brother of Emperor Wu worried that "today there is an abundance of land, but those who do not farm are legion."[149]

The southerner Lu Chi understood one reason for this widespread reluctance to engage in farming: commerce seemed to be both easier and more lucrative. "Now, merchants are at ease, yet their profits are substantial. Farmers toil, yet their reward is slight," he wrote.[150] The difficulties of farming and the lure of easy money through trade combined to drive many agriculturalists from the land. As Wen Ch'iao (288–329) wrote in the early-fourth-century south, "Today those fellows who do not farm have ten thousand calculations for their actions."[151] Although the stereotypical Confucian fears underlying these complaints were unjustified, such statements may be evidence that significant numbers of individuals were attracted to commerce during this period.

Small-scale business seems to have flourished during the Southern dynasties. Rafe de Crespigny writes that during the third century, "the waters of the Yangzi [Yangtze] and its tributaries saw an explosion of commercial development."[152] Government officials and aristocrats enjoyed special trading privileges (such as tax exemptions) that made commerce irresistible for many of them as well.[153] As early as 259 the emperor of the southern kingdom of Wu was complaining of civil and military officials in the provinces and commanderies who were trading by boat up and down the Yangtze River to the alleged detriment of agriculture.[154] A splendid example of this kind of aristocratic capitalism in Southern dynasties China is provided by the sixth son of Emperor Wen of Liang (r. 550–551), who "had several tens of lodges in the capital from which he floated loans with contracts. Whenever the time on the contract expired for a field, home, lodge, or store, he would drive out the owner and seize [we might almost say 'repossess'] his home."[155]

Confucian moralists were appalled and lost no occasion to attack this "capitalization" of the economy. At the beginning of the fourth century Lu Pao, an earnest recluse about whom little else is known, wrote a bitter satirical essay in which he claimed that moral decay was so great that "for the people of today there is only money."[156] Since the end of the Han dynasty the principal concern of such Confucian ideologues had been that the "fundamental occupation," agriculture, would suffer because of neglect.

Wen Ch'iao, for example feared that "for each fellow who does not farm there must be someone who goes hungry."[157] Such writers could not understand the potential of trade to generate new wealth and even to stimulate agriculture without causing corresponding shortages elsewhere.

The following late-third-century complaint by Fu Hsüan's son Hsien (239–294) illustrates, in an amusing fashion, the limitations of Confucian economic vision:

> The wastefulness of [current] extravagance is worse than a natural disaster. The ancients were fortunate to have thatched cottages, but today's common people struggle to make their homes luxurious. Ancient ministers of state did not have delicacies to eat, but today's common traders all reject millet and meat [as not good enough]. Ancient imperial consorts alone had special adornments, but today's female slaves and concubines are clothed in fine silk. Ancient great officers alone did not go about on foot, but today's humble slaves ride chariots and drive fat [horses].[158]

Some might argue that such conditions were a "disaster" greatly to be desired.

The late third century, when Fu Hsien wrote the above complaint, was a time of exceptional stability and prosperity. It is likely that the dislocations accompanying the shift of the Eastern Chin court to Chiang-nan early in the fourth century created a temporary economic setback. In the south, however, a commercial dynamic gradually emerged that, over the course of several centuries, propelled Chiang-nan to the position it has enjoyed ever since as the most prosperous region in China.

During the Southern dynasties, as always, the imperial government was agriculturally oriented, but the Southern courts were not incapable of adjusting and turning this commercial development to their own advantage. Market taxes were levied on merchants, and, Wang Chung-lo reports, the transit taxes on the locks at the Ch'ien-t'ang and Pu-yang rivers alone collected as much as four million cash annually.[159] It was also during the Eastern Chin dynasty that the government first imposed a 4 percent sales tax on large items, which was continued through all of the Southern dynasties. "Because men competed in commerce and did not engage in agriculture, they were all compelled to pay this, with the wish that it would serve as a corrective. Although they [the government] used this excuse, its real benefit was in appropriations."[160]

The growing volume of Southern dynasty trade was not limited to domestic transactions; this same period also witnessed the development of a fairly extensive foreign trade. As early as the third century Chang Hua was writing that trade with Indochina across the southern sea was "uninterrupted."[161] In the fourth and fifth centuries the Southern dynasties, from their ports in Canton, explored even more distant maritime trade routes.[162] Archeological excavations reported in 1972 of Eastern Chin dynasty tombs at Hsiang-shan, Nanking, uncovered goods whose provenance lay as far afield as Persia and Syria.[163] It was at the start of the fifth century that the famous pilgrim Fa-hsien (abroad from 399 to 412) returned from his travels in India and Ceylon aboard a "great merchantman" that carried over two hundred persons—although this episode also reveals the continuing hazards of ocean travel, since the ship that Fa-hsien was riding foundered and sank in a storm.[164]

Burgeoning Southern dynasties foreign trade helped establish the conditions for the renowned cosmopolitanism of the following T'ang dynasty. More significant, it also set in motion the process that climaxed in the economic miracle of the Sung, during the tenth through thirteenth centuries. Mark Elvin has written a classic description of what he calls the "medieval economic revolution," but most of the important innovations that led to this age of Sung economic prosperity and technological supremacy were already in place well before the Sung dynasty began in 960.[165] It was during the Southern dynasties that the splendid capillary network of waterways in Chiang-nan began to be developed, facilitating the commercial exchange that underlay Sung prosperity. Multicropping of rice was already familiar in the Southern dynasties, and such inventions or discoveries as paper, water mills, the abacus, written contracts, porcelain (or, at least, protoporcelain), and the combustibility of coal all had been made before the end of the period of division. Even printing and gunpowder, although their impact on society was minimal until the Sung, were invented in the T'ang. A recent popular survey of one hundred important Chinese technological inventions and discoveries lists only eight that were made after the year 1000.[166] The Sung economic miracle should be understood, then, not as a sudden new revolution, but rather as the culmination of trends begun as early as the fourth century.

This analysis suggests a new image for Southern dynasties China as a time of surprising creativity and energy. If these were dark ages, they were also times of remarkable change and development, and the medieval Chinese economy was certainly a good deal more complex than can be explained simply by the persistent image of a subsistence feudal manorial system.

Commerce flourished during the Southern dynasties. However, like military command and landed wealth, this trade was at best tangential to the self-conscious identity and personal interests of the dominant literati class. The true foundation of literati authority, instead, remained bureaucratic office holding, based on the old Han imperial model. Mori Mikisaburō notes that the medieval Chinese elite grew up within the framework of the imperial system and remained dependent to a very great extent on office holding for both prestige and income.[167] Even under the Eastern Chin, at what may have been the height of real literati power, the normal process of governing continued to be through imperial decree, based on the corporate advice of the great families.[168]

John Fairbank was right. China never really did develop a dominant social class that was entirely outside of the framework of the state, even during the Northern and Southern dynasties. At the height of their power, the medieval *shih-ta-fu* did achieve a considerable degree of effective independence from autocratic imperial interference, thanks to their near monopoly of access to high office; but the Confucian state remained the basis for their legitimacy. *Shih-ta-fu* supremacy required an economic base, but it was their privileged position in the state that secured the *shih-ta-fu* access to land and salary. The Confucian state also provided the sanction of legitimacy, which made constant recourse to violence unnecessary and obviated the need for a knightly or samurai-style feudal military class. The irony of the literati triumph was that, although it made possible a high degree of independence from imperial autocracy, it would have been impossible without that same imperial system.

In Southern dynasties society, official position within the state was the key to literati ascendance; this position, in turn, was based on a system of self-selection through cooptation. Approved literati demeanor and credentials—and subtle skill at winning favor among established members of the class—determined admission to the ranks of the elite and a corresponding share of the state's power and wealth. This system of cooptation, founded in the ruins of the Han and rejected finally by the restored autocracy of the Sui, was known as the Nine Ranks system.

4

THE INSTITUTIONAL MACHINERY OF LITERATI ASCENDANCE

In the sixth century, toward the end of the Northern and Southern dynasties, Yen Chih-t'ui complained of scholars who "cultivate their persons for themselves, to seek advancement." Yen claimed that these ambitious contemporaries contrasted unfavorably with the selfless scholars of old, who cultivated themselves only in order to benefit all humankind.[1] Although it is doubtful that such altruistic individuals ever really existed anywhere except in Yen's own imagination, Yen's concern that ambitious individuals were seeking political or social advancement through personal self-cultivation is both revealing and striking. It suggests a social order in which ideal ethical behavior was expected to be rewarded with promotion.

During the Southern dynasties, admission to the ranks of the social and political elite became very much a matter of heredity. Family status determined the government positions that a man could legitimately aspire to and his place in the social hierarchy. The rigidity of the social structure eventually approached the dimensions of a caste system; but before that happened, during the period when this medieval literati class was beginning to coalesce in the third and fourth centuries, membership could not yet have been determined automatically by blood.[2] Instead, the composition of the incipient literati class was determined by conscious and unconscious choices in the definition of what it was that qualified a man for government office. These choices were expressed through the vehicle of the civil service selection system.

The literati ascent took place relatively rapidly. Using modern social science techniques, Mao Han-kuang has traced the expansion of literati families *(shih-tsu)*, defined principally as those families who attained rank five or higher in two out of three generations, from 29 percent of the governing stratum in the late second century (A.D. 196–219) to 80.8 percent in the late fourth century (371–396).[3] This period of two hundred years witnessed the formation and maturation of *shih-ta-fu* society. During this period certain of the notable old Han dynasty families were transformed from local military, social, and economic leaders into a self-perpetuating national political and cultural elite.[4]

In addition to the decline of effective autocratic imperial control after the fall of the Han, the factors that contributed to the rise of the literati included, specifically, the gradual spread of Confucian ideals through education over the course of the Han dynasty, the affair known as that of the "Pure Stream" *(ch' ing-liu)* at the end of the Han, and the establishment of the Nine Ranks selection system in the third century. Indeed, as Patricia Ebrey observes, the underlying assumption of much modern Chinese and Japanese scholarship has been that "the establishment in 220 and abolition in 583 of the nine-rank system was the primary determinant of the rise and fall of the aristocratic families."[5]

The diffusion of Confucian education led to the spread of what Ebrey calls "the ideal of the gentleman" throughout Han society.[6] This development can be traced back to the much publicized adoption of Confucianism as state orthodoxy by Emperor Wu (r. 140 B.C.–86 B.C.) of Han a century before the birth of Christ. The Confucian view, as Donald Munro has demonstrated, was that self-cultivation both disciplined a man for the demands of political leadership and made him a role model for others that deserved to be encouraged. The cultivated gentleman was therefore thought of as being "entitled to a privileged place in the social order."[7]

It was explicitly hoped that Confucian selection criteria would have an effect in modifying the behavior of aspirants to office. As Ko Hung (283–343) later observed during the fourth century, if academic examinations are instituted as the measure for determining access to government office, "then there will inevitably be many who carry their book bags a thousand *li* to seek the acquaintance of teachers."[8] When knowledge of the Confucian classics is made the route to political power, ambitious men will devote themselves to Confucian scholarship.

In the view of Ku Yen-wu (1613–1682), the bureaucratic selection system was intended to provide incentives for the amelioration of behavior: "In local selection you must first examine his entire life. If there is one flaw in the *ch' ing-i*, he will never be promoted. [In this way] gentlemen will have a fear of the law, and petty men will preserve the style of being corrected out of shame."[9] The Confucian gentleman is to be rewarded and encouraged, and all others are to be given incentives to emulate his achievements. Under such an ideologically driven formula for promotion, abstract ideals can take on real force in shaping the behavior of the most ambitious persons.

Thanks to the debunking efforts of H. G. Creel and others, it is now known that Emperor Wu of Han was moved to "adopt" Confucianism primarily for propaganda reasons, and legitimate doubt has arisen concerning the extent to which Confucian scholarship was promoted by the state in Emperor Wu's day.[10] However, a beginning was certainly made at this time, and Hirai Masashi has shown convincingly that Confucian scholars did succeed in making significant inroads into the ranks of officialdom by the time of Emperor Yüan (r. 48 B.C.–32 B.C.).[11] This success was then pushed to new heights by the selection system of the Later Han dynasty, regarding which Higashi Shinji has gone so far as to write that "above all else, achievement in Confucian scholarship was necessary."[12]

Higashi is aware of the many dimensions of late Han society and does not mean to imply that Confucian scholarship should be considered in isolation.[13] As Hsing I-t'ien observes, few of those who were recommended for office in late Han actually came from poor or uninfluential families; but, as Hsing also acknowledges, study of the Confucian texts had nonetheless become a nearly essential prerequisite for bureaucratic advancement by late Han times.[14]

The surprising degree of continuity between the Han bureaucratic selection system and the better-known civil service examination system of the late empire, detected in some recent Chinese scholarship, is interesting in this connection. Hsü Lien-ta and Lou Ching have argued persuasively that most of the essential elements of the renowned examination system, which is commonly assumed to have emerged only after the Sui and T'ang, were present already in reasonably complete form by early Han times.[15]

Specifically, candidates for office in the early empire were subjected to a formal examination. In the third century, for example: "The Chin [dynastic] command was that in the selection of 'Culti-vated Talent' it was necessary to pass all five questions to be saluted as a 'Gentleman.' If [a candidate] did not pass one of the questions, he could not be selected."[16] What distinguished the selection system of the Han from the more famous examination system of the late empire was the requirement that candidates for office be recommended or nominated by specific power holders before becoming eligible for examination. The examinations of late imperial China, in contrast, were open to nearly everyone who wanted to take them.

In the Later Han dynasty political patronage was still essential. There were, in the Han, three specific ways to be recommend-ed for government office. These were "local recommendation" *(hsüan-chü),* direct summons either by the emperor himself or by a ranking official, and inheritance—the "appointment of sons" *(jen-tzu).*[17] Among the three, inheritance did not lead directly to any significant office, and direct summons was of limited applica-tion, leaving "local recommendation" to become a kind of stan-dard channel into the imperial bureaucracy. As Emperor Ho (r. 89–106) proclaimed in A.D. 93: "The selection of outstanding talent is the root of government, [but] judgments concerning conduct and ability must come from the native villages."[18]

In this fashion recommendation for office in the central gov-ernment was supposed to hinge upon a candidate's reputation in his own home community—a reputation expressed in what even-tually came to be called *ch' ing-i,* or "pure criticism." Although the court reserved all decisions concerning actual bureaucratic ap-pointments to itself, in theory recommendations for those ap-pointments were based on local "public opinion" *(yü-lun).*[19]

An early-third-century court official, Fu Chia (c. 205–255), remembered the ideal:

> Of old, in the selection of talent by the former kings, it was neces-sary to begin with conduct in the hamlets and exposition of the Tao in the country schools. When conduct was perfected, they were called worthies. When the Tao was cultivated, they were called able. The village elders presented the worthy and able to the king, and the king respectfully received them.[20]

Because bureaucratic careers were expected to begin with this sys-tem of "local recommendation," it is not surprising that a pose, at least, of Confucian virtue and ability became a normal attribute of government officials by the late Han dynasty.

In practice, however, the system was subject to a number of abuses. Since "local public opinion" was forwarded to the central government by local officials rather than by the people themselves, these officials had considerable opportunity to adjust "local opinion" to suit their own interests. Ch'ü T'ung-tsu remarks that local officials often used the system simply to promote their own subordinates.[21] Jack Dull actually praises this particular abuse, moreover, for providing a kind of apprenticeship system for young bureaucrats.[22]

More ominous perhaps was the rise of powerful landed "great families" over the course of the Han dynasty. These powerful families spoke to local officials with voices louder than those of ordinary villagers, and by the end of the Han they had brought the system of official selection so thoroughly under their own control that Yang Lien-sheng concludes it became "difficult to distinguish the high officials from local great families."[23]

In general, there was a pronounced tendency in the late Han for those recommended for office to come increasingly from the ranks of families that had already established themselves in government.[24] However, the peculiar sequence of events attending the dissolution of the Han dynasty gave the evolution of the bureaucratic selection system an unusual twist. During the last half century of the Han, the court fell under the control of eunuchs, and "gentlemen were ashamed to be associated with them."[25] Great local magnates and pure Confucian scholars found themselves thrown together in a community of interest in opposition to this threat. In implied criticism of the corrupt eunuchs, a so-called pure stream of intellectuals began to rank the well-known figures of the day publicly according to Confucian standards of worthiness, calling them the Three Lords, the Eight Eminences, the Eight Patrons, and so on.[26]

This Pure Stream movement represented perhaps the first conscious articulation of a new ideologically based claim that the literati, as a class, were, or should be, the legitimate repositories of public authority.[27] At the time, these criticisms from the Pure Stream merely succeeded in provoking government anger and suppression, but the ghostly memory of this Pure Stream eventually triumphed in the ensuing period of division and found itself reified in the new Nine Ranks selection system. The ideals symbo-

lized by this Pure Stream movement had become, in Patricia
Ebrey's words, "the ideological basis for reforms of the recruitment system."[28] Satō Tatsurō, in fact, regards the man who first
suggested the Nine Ranks system to the court early in the Three
Kingdoms Wei dynasty to be the pivotal figure in the transformation of the late Han Pure Stream protesters into the power-wield-
ing literati-officials of the age of divisions.[29]

The last half century of the Han has been called the "womb"
from which the medieval Chinese literati class was born.[30] The enduring imprint the late Han Pure Stream made on medieval
memory is illustrated by the fourth-century Mao Shan Taoist revelations, which filled their heavenly bureaucratic hierarchy with
(among others) deified members of the Pure Stream returned as
sainted examples of the new Confucian literati ideal.[31] According
to Yü Ying-shih, it was in these clashes with the supposedly corrupt court of the late Han that the literati class first gained its corporate sense of identity.[32]

From the late Han Pure Stream, medieval ideology extracted
the ideal of "purity" *(ch' ing)*. Japanese scholars (who might be
expected to be particularly fascinated by this phenomenon in
view of Japan's own traditional fixation with "purity") such as
Ueda Sanae and Watanabe Shinichirō have demonstrated how
the medieval elite became obsessed with the word "purity" and
elevated it to the status of "their most important ideal in life."[33]
The late Han desire to remain unsullied by contact with a corrupt, eunuch-dominated court then translated into aloof indifference to government in general in the period after Han's fall, cu-
minating in the third and fourth century impulse to pursue lofty
(and pure) Neo-Taoist and Buddhist metaphysical studies.

Although the Han dynasty selection system could not be maintained amid the chaos surrounding the collapse of the dynasty,
the warlord Ts'ao Ts'ao was advised that examination of reputations at the village level was still the only way to obtain capable
officials for his own administration.[34] This impulse to restore at
least a modified version of the increasingly idealized Han selection system resulted in the creation of the new Nine Ranks and
Arbiters system *(chiu-p' in chung-cheng)* by Ts'ao Ts'ao's heirs in the
Wei Kingdom, after 220. Significantly, similar circumstances led
to the establishment of a nearly identical system in the rival Wu
Kingdom to the south.[35]

Under the Nine Ranks system, officials called "arbiters" *(chung-*

cheng) were appointed by the Wei court for each commandery in the kingdom, and senior arbiters were appointed for each province after 249. These men were then held responsible for evaluating all candidates for office within their jurisdiction and ranking them on a scale from one to nine, and for reviewing and augmenting their judgments every three years. The appropriate ministries of the central government were then notified of these rankings and made appointments to office on the basis of this rating system.[36]

What distinguished this Nine Ranks system from its Han dynasty predecessors, aside from the formal rank scale itself, was the fact that the man responsible for local selection was now a single official directly appointed for that purpose by the central government. In the Han, local officials had merely been expected to forward the recommendations made by "public opinion" to the court. This innovation might have been intended to enhance central supervision over the local recommendation process, and it can be considered part of an overall Wei program to restore imperial power.[37] Yet the Wei attempt at imperial restoration ultimately proved abortive, and the Wei throne was usurped by the Ssu-ma family in 265, an event usually regarded by historians as marking the temporary abandonment of strong Ch'in-Han–style imperial aspirations by the court. At that point the Nine Ranks selection system became a wedge between court and countryside, threatening not only true popular influence over the selection of officials (which might always have been a myth), but also the real degree of central imperial control over the system. Neither court nor countryside now controlled the official selection process; rather, it was controlled by members of the official class themselves.

In the Wei Kingdom the Nine Ranks system might have genuinely been concerned with enhancing the bureaucratic efficiency of the centralized imperial administration. Ts'ao Ts'ao had enjoined his government that in the civil service "only talent be promoted."[38] However, Yano Chikara's research, described in the Introduction, reveals that the nature of the evaluations given by arbiters to prospective civil service candidates changed over the course of the third century, and individuals increasingly came to be praised for such apparently unbureaucratic accomplishments as painting and calligraphy, music, and philosophical conversation. The arbiters still claimed to recognize talent and ability, but the practical administrative concerns of the centralized monarchy were increasingly overlooked.[39]

Viewed from a position close to the throne, the danger posed by this Nine Ranks and Arbiters system was all too apparent. As Liu I (c. 210–285) wrote: "Today we set up arbiters to determine the Nine Ranks. The high and low accord with their wishes; honor and disgrace are in their hands. They seize the majesty of the ruler of men [i.e., the emperor] and snatch the power of the heavenly court."[40]

From the end of the Wei Kingdom in the mid–third century, therefore, the arbiters can be said to have represented neither the interests of the monarchy nor those of the common people of China, but rather those of the incipient literati class itself. Certain literati held the office of arbiter and used it to recommend fellow literati. Since the supporters of the coup that overthrew Wei dynasty power and established the Western Chin dynasty in the mid–third century were mostly drawn from the ranks of the great families, these established families were able to make use of this Nine Ranks system virtually to monopolize government offices of the fifth rank and higher.[41]

As the system became closed to outsiders, the evaluations of arbiters, which were supposed to reflect Confucian talent and virtue, and constitute a measure of suitability for government employment, gradually became the escutcheons of a new aristocratic class—one that was born to office. From this time on, in Shen Yüeh's words, "metropolitan arbiters were vulgar men, and, in assessing the needs of the times and making evaluations, they looked around and followed the path of expedience. This is what Liu I meant when he said: 'There are no eminent families with low evaluations or humble families with high evaluations.' "[42] Because the Wei court had appointed members of prominent families as arbiters, Liu Fang concluded in the mid–eighth century that the Chin and later dynasties "began to esteem family itself, and then their division between noble and base, and separation of gentleman and commoner, could not be changed."[43] The evaluations of the arbiters became effectively hereditary.

The Nine Ranks system cast a hierarchical net over the entire land, establishing clear vertical relations between all the literati, but the bottom ranks of the Nine Ranks system extended only as far as the edge of the pool of prospective candidates for office.[44] Only gentlemen, or *shih*, were ranked by this system; commoners, or *shu-jen,* were excluded. The greatest split in the new medieval hierarchy, consequently, was the one between gentlemen and commoners: between those who participated in the Nine Ranks system and those who did not. As Chao I wrote in the eighteenth century, they "took the distinction between *shih* and *shu* to be the division between noble and base, and through long practice it became a fixed regulation."[45] The *shih* (or *shih-ta-fu,* meaning something like "gentleman-official") thus came to constitute the new medieval literati class.

Since the literati emerged out of and were defined by selection systems that were originally intended simply to staff the imperial bureaucracy, the incipient aristocratic class was initially indistinguishable from the class of government officials or those who were eligible for such office but refused. Great family control over the selection process insured that membership in this exclusive group became more and more a hereditary prerogative, however, and the result was a curious hybrid bureaucratic-aristocracy. In Liu Fang's eighth-century analysis, the Han dynasty had centuries earlier rejected the classical Chou feudal aristocracy by employing only men of demonstrated ability in its administration, thus beginning the practice of honoring office rather than birth. But during the age of division, as a reversion to aristocratic ways took place, this aristocratic mentality fused together with the Han imperial ideal (and Confucianism's blurry memory of Chou-style feudalism derived from the classics), and both office and birth came to be honored simultaneously. "Therefore, in office there were generations from the same families, and in the genealogies there were generations of officials."[46]

The late Han dynasty bureaucratic selection system and the *ch' ing-i,* or "pure criticism," that emerged out of it were supposed to measure nothing less than Confucian "virtue." These Confucian ideals were given renewed impetus by the Nine Ranks system. In 265, for example, the emperor "commanded all of the Commandery arbiters to use six conditions for raising up the obstructed, the first being honest reverence and self abnegation, the second filial respect exhausting the rites, the third kindness to brothers, the fourth personal purity and diligent modesty, the fifth faith that righteousness will overcome, and the sixth scholarship for its own sake."[47]

One of the pillars of the Confucian ethical system is the system of rites, or *li.* This system had been the ideal code of China's ancient bronze age aristocracy, which Confucius himself longed to restore. According to the Confucian classics, adherence to the code was one distinction between aristocrats and commoners: "The rules of ceremony [*li*] do not go down to the common people. The penal statutes do not go up to great officers," observes the *Li-chi*.[48] Since the early medieval literati identified themselves with this idealized ancient Chou nobility, familiar to them from their reading of the classics, they made an absolute fetish of these rites.

Kamiya Noriko has demonstrated that the early medieval literati held themselves seriously accountable for violations of the *li*.[49] At the same time, however, literati familiarity with the *li* and music also exempted them from any need to be subjected to the full weight of the law.[50] Wolfram Eberhard goes so far as to say that rigid application of the *li* became one of factors that "changed the gentry [*sic*] into a closed society, differing from the lower classes in their behavior, their language, their gestures, their morals."[51]

The spread of Confucian ideals rekindled the memory of ancient Chou patterns of aristocratic behavior. In the early Western Chin dynasty (mid–third century), for example, Yü Ch'un proposed relaxing restrictions concerning proper mourning observances, noting:

> The reason the ancients emphasized lineage was that the various lords succeeded to their titles, and the *shih-ta-fu* succeeded to their emoluments. They clarified their lineages in order to guard against [succession] struggles between them. Now there are no [feudal] states or hereditary emoluments, and there is nothing to guard against.[52]

Yü's suggestion provoked a burst of objections from Confucian scholars, however, and it was ultimately not adopted because it violated the ideal enshrined in the classics.

On the basis of their supposed Confucian virtue and conformity to the *li*, the early medieval literati class came to be ever more exclusive. A contemporary comment about the famous calligrapher Wang Hsien-chih (344–388)—he was "by nature extremely correct and lofty; he did not communicate with [people] who were not his kind"—describes typical literati behavior.[53] The gap between such lofty gentlemen and commoners gradually widened and grew more tangible as medieval society matured. As early as the late third century, a sumptuary law had been drafted to specify what apparel was appropriate for commoners and what was reserved for gentlemen, although this law was evidently viewed at first with some derision.[54] By the middle of the fifth century, the natural inclination of literati families to intermarry only with other literati families had become a legal requirement.[55] By this time status as *shih* or *shu* had become firmly fixed in one's household registration and was a matter of legal documentation.[56]

Ironically, and perhaps significantly, however, it was also at this time that the practice of forging household registrations to enter the literati class began: "Vulgar fellows who possessed the means all followed each other in struggling to bribe away humble entries and write in new registrations. . . . For only about ten thousand cash they who yesterday were lowly today are among the company of officials," a T'ang dynasty compendium records.[57]

Since the "merit" literati believed set them apart from commoners consisted of adherence to the Confucian *li* or to Buddho-Taoist metaphysical wisdom, rather than efficient administration, even while in government office many literati felt little obligation to apply themselves actively to their official duties. As Kan Pao complained in the fourth century, "Those who are in office regard contemplating the void to be lofty and laugh at diligence and effort."[58] If the literati formed a hybrid bureaucratic-aristocracy, they were a remarkably parasitic one.

Pien K'un (281–328) was more conscientious in office than most of his contemporaries, and his explanation was caustic: "All the gentlemen extend themselves with the Tao and its virtue, admiring each other for their style. If K'un doesn't manage the petty details, who will"?[59] Beginning in the third century, the higher ranks of the imperial civil service, on the whole, contributed little to the real task of governing the empire. But officials did continue to draw their salaries and extend their perquisites, rendering the bureaucracy an increasing burden on the subject population.

Some evidence exists that the medieval bureaucracy had swollen to grossly bloated proportions. In late imperial China Hung Mai observed a stone inscription from Nan-hsiang Commandery dated to the Western Chin dynasty. On the reverse side of this tablet were inscribed the names of 351 subordinate officials who served in the commandery at that time, yet the entire population of the eight counties in this commandery during the period 265–275, Hung Mai noted, was only twenty thousand households (an average of one official for every fifty-seven households).[60] With that kind of ratio between those who paid taxes and those whose salaries came out of taxes, Hung Mai concluded, "how could the people's strength not be wearied?"[61] By the end of the period of division, in 583, one northerner dryly remarked that government officials were so numerous in proportion to the population that it was like employing nine shepherds to watch ten sheep.[62]

The early medieval literati did not justify their status in terms of administrative efficiency, however, but by the spiritual example they set through self-cultivation. To many distinguished literati, therefore, bureaucratic service to an emperor or a functional role in the administration came to seem less important than personal fulfillment. Confucian belief in self-cultivation as the key to universal harmony conspired with a complex of new ideas drawn from Buddhism and Taoism to turn many great Southern dynasties literati away from a life of active service to the state toward types of activities they regarded as considerably more noble.

5

LITERATI CULTURE

The third-century withdrawal of so much of the Chinese elite from active public service to a life of individual self-absorption is surprising.[1] Classical Chinese philosophy had been notably this-worldly in orientation, and the Chinese elite has traditionally been dedicated, above all else, to a life of service to the state. This uncharacteristic third-century retreat requires some explanation, therefore. How did such an attitude of lofty detachment ever come to typify early medieval literati behavior?

A Genealogy for the Fourth-Century Mind

The classic explanation for retreat into transcendent philosophy, religion, and even libertinism in the third century is that it resulted from despair at the collapse of the Han imperial world order and an acute fear of political engagement in an increasingly turbulent age of war and coups d'état. This conventional explanation has some merit. Third-century Chinese had legitimate excuses for feelings of despair.

Official Chinese population statistics show a dramatic decline from a Han imperial height of 56,486,856 in A.D. 157 to a mere 16,163,863 a century later, in A.D. 280.[2] These figures may be deceptive: Hans Bielenstein has raised serious doubts as to the accuracy of the third-century census data, and both he and Earl Pritchard have speculated that post-Han population decline might actually have been minimal.[3] Even so, there is no reason to doubt that mortality rates were indeed very high during this period, and conditions only grew worse as first civil war and then external invasion wracked north China in the early fourth century. This was a time when, according to the histories,

> In six provinces there was a great [plague of] locusts, and all vegetation and even the hair of cattle and horses were devoured. In addition there was a great epidemic. When combined with the famine and the people who were killed by insurgents [during the wars], drifting corpses filled the rivers and bleached bones covered the land.[4]

Not only were wars and lesser conflicts endemic from the final years of the second century and foreign invasions from the beginning of the fourth century, but it has also been suggested that China underwent a bacteriological invasion at this time that resulted in disastrous outbreaks of plagues and epidemics.[5] Sakuma Yoshinari has tabulated data to suggest that natural disasters such as droughts and floods occurred with much greater frequency in the third and fourth centuries than previously, although these data are perhaps better explained by a declining state capacity to adequately maintain the infrastructure than by a change in climatic conditions.[6]

There is some evidence that people did not live as long in early medieval China, for whatever reason, as they had during the Han. Of fifty-three notable Chinese gentlemen born in the first century of the Later Han, between the years A.D. 1 and A.D. 100 (inclusive), for whom dates of birth and death were recorded, the average age at death was 70.87. For a similar group of 139 figures born during the first century of Chin dynastic rule, between the years 250 and 350, the average age at death was 54.9, or a decade and a half younger.[7] These figures do not represent statistically reliable "life expectancies" for either of those two periods, but they may have some sort of comparative value and suggest at least that gentlemen at the highest levels of society survived to a venerable old age less often in the two Chin dynasties than they did during the Han.

Even fifty-four is a respectable age to reach in a premodern society, however, and early medieval China is hardly unique in world history for its frequency of wars and natural disasters. For members of the incipient new medieval Chinese literati class, moreover, life offered numerous privileges and pleasures despite its being relatively short. The tone pervading much of what is recorded of third-century thought is one of liberation rather than despair, and even superficial acquaintance with the content of third-century thought shows that it had origins dating back to the most flourishing periods of the Han. Despair at the fall of the Han is not, therefore, sufficient explanation for the introspective turn taken by the Chinese elite in the third century.

The road that led from traditional Confucian political activism in the Han to Buddho-Taoist reclusiveness in the third and fourth centuries was long and complicated, and although it cannot be denied that the fall of the Han empire played a pivotal role in the retreat, explanations need to be sought for it at a variety of levels. The new medieval worldview provided consolation in a time of uncertainty and escape from dangerous political commitments, but it also provided amusement for a comfortable new literati class that no longer had to justify itself through service to the state. It further established an ideological framework legitimizing the new social order. But the worldview of the early medieval literati cannot be explained so easily. There is no simple equation that permits us to interpret thought directly as a projection of material conditions. We must not overlook the obvious: the early medieval worldview was an intellectual development. It was generated, to be sure, by people whose lives had been patterned and conditioned by specific historical circumstances—but it was generated in their minds, and play with ideas as such must be included among those specific historical circumstances. To understand the worldview of the early medieval literati we need to examine the history of ideas in late Han and post-Han China. Only in the light of these ideas will literati behavior, an early medieval history, become fully explicable.

The characteristic mode of philosophical discourse in the third and fourth centuries was known as *hsüan-hsüeh*. This term translates into English as something like "abstruse learning," but it is conventionally labeled "Neo-Taoism." Sometime after 438 a *hsüan-hsüeh* academy was officially established at the Southern dynasties capital together with other academies dedicated to the study of the Confucian classics, history, and literature.[8] This event can be taken as a kind of seal of imperial recognition and a benchmark for the final arrival of *hsüan-hsüeh* as an established discipline. Ironically, it also coincides with the period by which "Neo-Taoism" had already been largely superseded by Buddhism in the mainstream of Chinese thought.

Over the course of the Han dynasty, schools had grown up around famous masters, each of whom specialized in the meticulous study of a single Confucian classic and taught his interpretations of that classic to family and followers. Students would often spend an entire lifetime devoted to the intensive study of one book. This style was known as "chapter and verse" *(chang-chü)* scholarship. Its tedious scholasticism had already provoked a negative reaction as early as the time of Ma Jung (79–166), who attempted to interpret the Confucian canon broadly in its entirety and added a Taoist-tinged inclination toward introspection.[9] Students at the Imperial Academy then began ignoring the interpretations of established "schools" and freely voicing their own opinions not just about one text, but about the entire range of existing learning. Pedants criticized this practice as "insubstantial" *(fu-hua)*, but it marks the birth of the free-floating conversational style of medieval philosophy.[10]

Some experts assert that the seeds of later *hsüan-hsüeh* thought were planted even earlier, by the great Han philosopher Wang Ch'ung (27–97) in a book he completed around A.D. 82 called the *Lun-heng*.[11] Although a direct transmission of the text of the *Lun-heng* to the famous third-century Neo-Taoists Wang Pi and Juan Chi has been demonstrated, the supposed resemblance between Wang Ch'ung and *hsüan-hsüeh* thought is not very obvious.[12] What connects Wang Ch'ung to the later Neo-Taoists is their common rational, materialistic outlook. Wang Ch'ung was a rational skeptic, and the main theme of his long book was an attack on teleology: the belief that the various phenomena of the world must have some higher purpose. "The principle of Heaven is spontaneity, good and bad luck happen by chance," he wrote.[13] This theme presents a sharp contradiction to the prevailing "Han Confucian" outlook espoused by Tung Chung-shu (c. 179–104 B.C.), who claimed that "Heaven's purpose is humane, and its way is justice."[14]

Wang Ch'ung was not the first to deny an anthropomorphic moralistic heaven, however. A generation earlier Huan T'an (43 B.C.–A.D. 28) also advocated this same kind of rational agnosticism.[15] When someone remarked to him, for example, that since "Heaven produced medicines that kill people, there must be medicines that make people come alive," Huan demolished this specious symmetry by observing that poisons were not created by Heaven for the purpose of killing people. Poisons are simply things that are not suitable for people to eat.[16] As Timoteus Pokora observes, it was Huan's practice, in this fashion, to contrast "an idea with some well established fact from the world of nature to find whether the idea were [sic] right or wrong."[17]

This modern-sounding rationalism drained the universal order of any sort of providence and eventually brought its practitioners face to face with a heaven and an earth that were, as Lao-tzu had said long ago, "not humane." A better progenitor for third-century hsüan-hsüeh than either Wang Ch'ung or Huan T'an may be Yen Tsun, the somewhat mysterious first century B.C. Taoist who also argued, before either of these other men, that fortune came not from Heaven's dispensation, but from the natural order of the Tao. Yen also trumpeted the classic Neo-Taoist metaphysical position that all things began with nothing.[18] This bleak but unflinchingly rational understanding of the world of being as devoid of any higher purpose—the materialist denial of a benevolent heaven found in Yen Tsun, Huan T'an, and Wang Ch'ung in the middle of the Han—formed the intellectual foundation for what is often described as third-century Neo-Taoist "nihilism."

Indeed, although Fung Yu-lan praises Wang Ch'ung as "the greatest materialist philosopher of the two Han dynasties," he traces the origin of materialist thought in China much farther back, ultimately to the Taoist sage Lao-tzu. For Lao-tzu the Tao was a natural principle that followed regular, observable, laws and answered to no teleological higher purpose. The ineffable, mysterious quality of Lao-tzu's Tao weakened the force of his point, however, and ambiguously left a back door open to idealist tendencies—an ambiguity that later resurfaced in the third- and fourth-century Neo-Taoists.

It was only later at the Chi-hsia Academy in the Warring States kingdom of Ch'i (fl. 357–284 B.C.), Fung argues, that a group of scholars identified this Tao with a material substance called ch' i. Since the concept of ch' i was inspired by the image of breath or air, it had, like the old Western notion of "ether," the advantage of being a physical substance that was also formless and intangible, and that therefore elegantly satisfied all the requirements of a Taoist material universe. This ch' i then provided the foundation for a materialist vision of nature for Wang Ch'ung and subsequent philosophers.[19]

Although the materialist skepticism apparent in thinkers like Wang Ch'ung set them apart from much "Han Confucianism," these "skeptics" nonetheless shared many assumptions with the rest of their society, such as the concepts of yin and yang, the Five Elements, and the cosmic significance of the hexagrams in the *Book of Changes*. The rational material universe envisioned by Wang Ch'ung was composed of *ch' i*, responded to correspondences between heaven and earth, and followed the alternating cycle of yin and yang.[20] Wang saw no contradiction between his own skeptical logic and the numerical theories extrapolated from the diagrams in the *Book of Changes* by Yang Hsiung (53 B.C.–A.D. 18)—and, in the intellectual context of his day, there was no reason he should have.[21] Fung Yu-lan even emphasizes the role of such concepts as yin and yang, the Five Elements, and the hexagrams in the emergence of this materialist worldview in China.[22]

It is curious that most of these Han dynasty skeptics who are considered forerunners of *hsüan-hsüeh*—Wang Ch'ung, Huan T'an and Yang Hsiung—uncompromisingly denounced the so-called Taoist arts of immortality, when it is well known that the same medieval Chinese literati who perfected *hsüan-hsüeh* were also often avid practitioners of the immortality cult.[23] The best-known exponent of the medieval immortality cult, Ko Hung, for example, although not usually considered to be a prime example of *hsüan-hsüeh* thought, is classified by Jay Sailey as a rational humanist very much in the tradition of Ma Jung and Wang Ch'ung.[24]

The inconsistency was on the part of Ko Hung and the medieval immortality cult, however. The original Taoist classics had denied not only the possibility of individual immortality, but even its desirability. Chuang-tzu wrote that "the height of wisdom is to live out one's allotted years and not die prematurely."[25] The immortality cult that flourished in medieval China was a departure from this main line of Taoist philosophy, and even the most ardent practitioners of the immortality cult could not avoid a certain uneasiness about their faith. The late Han classic of religious Taoism *T'ai-p' ing ching*, for example, warned of "physicians and spirit-healers [who] only want to get people's money," and in the third century, when the rulers of the Wei kingdom assembled specialists in the occult arts at their court, the emperor's brother somewhat self-consciously explained that "we all consider this to be laughable and do not believe it."[26]

An explanation for the pseudo-Taoism of the immortality cult and its divergence from the main line of rational materialism is

provided by Ssu-ma Ch'ien's monumental history the *Shih-chi.*
There it is recorded that the immortality cult originated in the
Warring States period among men who propagated but "could
not understand" sophisticated yin and yang metaphysics.[27]
Whether this claim is historically accurate or not, it is metaphorically satisfying. The cult of immortality shares many of the materialist assumptions that inspired Wang Ch'ung's rational skepticism: the universe is composed of a solitary, nondecaying,
element labeled *ch' i,* which undergoes continuous transformation and whose patterns of change can be understood and manipulated through investigation. Adherents of the immortality cult
failed to appreciate the ultimate philosophical implication of
their own ideas, however, which was that individual human identity is temporary. Eventually all things must revert to the original
matter they called *ch' i.* Wang Ch'ung and the Neo-Taoists shared
a common background of rational materialist ideas, but the faithful of the immortality cult naively reintroduced an element of
hopeful idealism.

If *hsüan-hsüeh*'s ancestry can be traced back to the middle of the
Han dynasty, something dramatic must still have happened at the
end of the Han in order to spawn *hsüan-hsüeh* itself. When the
Han court slipped under the sinister influence of eunuchs in the
middle of the second century A.D., gentlemen often responded
by withdrawing from active participation in the government, and
from their lofty remove they then made sweeping criticisms of
important political personalities, known as *ch' ing-i,* or "pure criticisms." This movement was forcefully suppressed, and in the
interests of self-preservation many intellectuals then allegedly
shifted their debate away from political criticism to abstract—and
often abstruse—metaphysics.[28] "Pure criticism" then took on a
new philosophical orientation, and was transformed into "pure
talk," or *ch' ing-t'an.*[29]

The final collapse of the Han in 220 completed the process by
liberating thought from the constraints of Han orthodoxy (although the new Wei court did promote a variety of favored doc-
trines). The arrival of large numbers of ethnic non-Chinese to the
Central Plain by the third century probably also contributed to a
general receptivity to new ideas. One recent estimate suggests
that already, by the third century, as many as 54 percent or more
of the population might have been non-Chinese.[30] It was then,
during the Cheng-shih period (240–249) of the Three Kingdoms

Wei dynasty, that the classic phase of Neo-Taoist *hsüan-hsüeh* took shape in the minds of Wang Pi and Ho Yen (c. 190–249).

In tracing the origins of *hsüan-hsüeh* thought, it is useful to remember that the reason English speakers often call it Neo-Taoism is that it derived so much of its content from the classic Taoist texts *Lao tzu* and *Chuang tzu*. As the balance of intellectual interest turned from politics toward metaphysics at the end of the Han, philosophers had little choice but to reopen these Taoist classics. There were few other metaphysical works in the Chinese canon to turn to. In China only the *Book of Changes* and the Taoist classics were sufficiently metaphysical to provide ammunition for *hsüan-hsüeh* thought. As a consequence, these became the standard texts of the new movement.

If *hsüan-hsüeh* was argued from written texts, however, it was generally if not exclusively expounded orally. *Ch' ing-t'an,* or "pure conversation," was the predominant medium through which *hsüan-hsüeh* expressed itself. Initially, at least, *ch' ing-t'an* was simply a name for talk among friends about suitably lofty, or "pure," philosophic subjects. It has been suggested by modern scholars that in the third century pure conversationalists divided themselves into two groups on the basis of their preferred topics: those who preferred to talk about "names and coherences" (or "names and principles," *ming-li*) and those who spoke mysteriously about the "self-so" ("nature," *tzu-jan*). The Names and Coherences group are thought to have been Confucians who insisted on rigid adherence to the conventional proprieties and a life of public service, whereas advocates of the Self-so were "Taoists" who favored withdrawal and libertinism.[31]

This analysis might have originated with Liu Ta-chieh's seminal *Essay on Wei-Chin Thought (Wei-Chin ssu-hsiang lun)*. It is essentially sound but requires a number of caveats so as not to be misleading. First of all, it was very common, especially after the mid–third century when the political and intellectual schisms that had rent the Wei dynasty were terminated by the Ssu-ma usurpation and the establishment of the new Chin dynasty, for individual thinkers to follow both groups simultaneously without apparent contradiction.[32] In the fourth century, for example, Sun T'ung's younger son "excelled at Names and Coherences and annotated the *Lao tzu.*"[33]

Even when, somewhat earlier, Names and Coherences and the Self-so might have been separate schools, they were never really contradictory. A footnote to the *San-kuo chih*, for example, describes a conversation between an expert at Names and Coherences and a devotee of "the abstruse and distant" (the Self-so) around the year 227. "Although their purposes were the same, there were some points that were mutually unintelligible at that instant." The impasse was resolved to everyone's satisfaction, however, by the arrival of an intermediary who understood both arguments.[34] Although no more historically reliable than any other anecdote, this story does illustrate the idea that the two schools were hardly irreconcilable.

The school of the Self-so is associated with hedonistic behavior, and it is true that flagrant disregard of conventional propriety became fashionable for a time in the third century. Wang Ch'eng (269–312), for example, "was heedless and unrestrained, and the age spoke of him as 'transcendent.' "[35] However, few of the more famous third-century followers of the school of the Self-so really rejected the Confucian value system. Instead, as contemporary opinion clearly emphasized, they showed their contempt for rigid adherence to the outward forms of propriety *(li)* only to exhibit greater genuine sincerity in the traditional virtues, especially filial piety, than the so-called Confucians themselves. Juan Chi's extreme grief at his mother's death is a case in point, as is that of the famous "libertine" Chang Han (early fourth century), whose "nature was utterly filial. When he was in mourning for his mother, his distress exceeded [that dictated by] propriety."[36] The Confucian classics themselves had long insisted that sincerity of intention was more important than outward conformity with ritual, and great third-century libertines such as Juan Chi merely observed and exaggerated this distinction, with the effect of magnifying rather than renouncing their Confucian virtue.[37]

The Neo-Taoist metaphysical interests of third- and fourth-century Chinese gentlemen caused few if any of them to reject Confucianism. They simply superimposed their new interests as an additional and higher layer over the traditional Confucian substrate. The Confucian classics remained the foundation of all education, and Confucian virtues stood unchallenged. But *hsüan-hsüeh* thinkers had higher, cosmic principles in mind that caused them to reevaluate the importance of political activity, traditionally the focus of Confucian attention, and relegate it to a subsidiary position.[38] As Chih Tun (314–366) wrote in the fourth century, "The Tao of being a person is said to be humanity and justice [the basic Confucian virtues], but humanity and justice have roots, which are called the Tao and its virtue [the classic Taoist values]."[39] The Tao and its virtue could then be cultivated for Neo-Taoist or even Buddhist ends without the slightest challenge to Confucian orthodoxy. In this way the traditional Confucian agenda for social and political action was simply superseded by *hsüan-hsüeh* and Buddhism.

The hypothetical division of Pure Conversationalists into Confucians and Taoists presents a further difficulty. That is, the supposedly "Confucian" school of Names and Coherences actually played an important theoretical role in the elaboration of "Neo-Taoism." Whatever the term *ming-li hsüeh* ("the study of names and coherences") or its equivalents meant in antiquity, by the third century it had come to consist primarily of an examination of the relationship between names and reality, with particular reference to the evaluation of human ability for public service.[40] It implied that there might be a discrepancy between the names we give things and their true nature; and, in fact, the notion that "words do not fully express ideas" *(yen pu chin i)* was an old and venerable concept in China in both the Confucian and Taoist traditions.[41] It followed that if names do not always accurately denote realities, inquiry should discard meaningless names and pursue reality itself.[42] To push the point further, not just words but the entire realm of material being fails to satisfy the relentless search for ultimate truth. As Hsün Ts'an (c. 212–240) wrote in the Three Kingdoms era, "The subtleties of principle are not brought out by the semblances of things."[43] At this point it becomes apparent that truth must be sought in the immaterial world of the Neo-Taoist "original void."

In part, the Neo-Taoist rejection of "this world" was motivated by a desire to escape the dangers of political involvement in the tumultuous third century. A painful awareness of the transience of all worldly success was characteristic of contemporary thought. Shu Hsi (261–300) wrote, for example:

> In the morning you wander exalted palaces, and in the evening you plunge into the awesome abyss. During the day you laugh, and at night you sigh. At dawn you bloom, and at dusk you fall. Loyalty is not enough to protect yourself, and prayer cannot prepare for the next world. Therefore gentlemen shun ascending court and strive to enter the forest.[44]

The attitude was not unique to the stressful post-Han era, however. Yang Hsiung had expressed a similar feeling centuries before, asking: "Why be covetous of wealth and honor? It only ends by destroying yourself and endangering your family."[45] The realization that worldly success depends on chance and the recognition of others, while personal self-cultivation is all that is really under the individual's own control, is a classic philosophical posture, common to Lu Chi (261–303) in third-century China and *Candide* in the early modern West.[46]

The introspection of medieval Chinese thinkers, however, was much more than simple resignation from the dangers or uncertainties of the external world. It was viewed as a positive step in the direction of higher truth as well. When Shu Hsi, in the essay quoted above, was asked if active public service at the court was not the true way of the world and the only method for stimulating effective imperial rule, Shu Hsi replied that "nonaction [*wu-wei*] can be used to release the world's confusion, and tranquility can be used to rescue the anxiety of the state." In Shu's prescription, instead of active service at court, the gentleman should "prune the wilderness of the sagely classics, summarize the one truth of the many sayings, complete his pure conduct in the mountain garden, and turn his back on the strings [of official caps] to retire in perpetuity."[47]

The mysterious priority of nonaction made introspection a key to the universe and the only path suitable for a great gentleman. As the Buddhist Tsung Ping wrote in the fifth century, "Though one practice elegant nobility and gather swarms of disciples up to a million, one [must] first by himself alone, body and soul, sit and await the infinite."[48] Enlightenment came alone to the individual, and it was in the scholar's study, in lonely contemplation of the Tao, where medieval Chinese heroes dwelt. Thus Chih Tun could write with pride in the fourth century, "Since I enjoy the solitude of a country house and longed to dig up medicines, I stayed there [on the mountain] alone. Waving my hands I sent away all thoughts of the road to fame, and, quietly folding my hands within an empty house, I awoke to the purity beyond my body."[49]

The significance of intellectual trends in late Han and early post-Han China is that they led Chinese intellectuals inexorably away from the traditional commitment to public service toward retreat and introspection. "Lock out depravity by trusting to the quiet chamber, solitary, vacant, and true," wrote Chih Tun.[50]

These developments coincided with the growth of a new literati class that was, if still quite dependent upon government office for financial security and social validation, largely untroubled by actual administrative concerns. This body of thought helped shape the growth of the literati class even as it also provided a rationale for sometimes eccentric literati behavior.

To those for whom the heights of *hsüan-hsüeh* metaphysics were unscalable, which probably included the vast majority of the population, the mysterious dignity and obscure subtlety of literati activities could be all the more impressive. The prestige of literati behavior was further reinforced by the rise of new religions at this time, which added supernatural force to the literati reputation of *hsüan-hsüeh*.

The so-called Taoist religion was born in the middle of the second century at the hands of Chang Tao-ling (fl. c. 142) and others like him. Chang had gone into reclusion on a mountain in what is present-day Szechuan to "study the Tao of immortality."[51] Some accounts have it that he was visited there by the deified spirit of Lao-tzu, who provided him with secret texts and regalia, and endowed him with command over the spirit world.[52] Whatever the truth of the matter, the Taoist religion he helped create envisioned a heavenly hierarchy that closely paralleled the imperial bureaucracy on earth but was superior to it—especially as the secular Han empire began heading toward disintegration.[53]

Although many literati subscribed to or at least flirted with the new Taoist faith, salvationist religion had greater appeal to the less well educated and especially to the disenfranchised who were excluded from enjoying any benefits from the new aristocratic social order. Tsuzuki Akiko has argued that the Taoist religion, which reached scriptural maturity in the fourth-century south, was largely the product of poor southern families who imagined a religious order based on Confucian ethical ideals as an escape from the brutality of a real world that bore little resemblance to the ideal.[54] And yet, this popular faith reinforced the ideological leverage of lofty literati within the "cultural nexus," giving them at least potential ascendance over what Tanigawa Michio and others of the Kyoto school have called the moral "community."[55]

The Paradox of Neo-Taoism

In the wake of the Han dynasty, China experienced a remarkable burst of enthusiasm for weighty ontological speculation about the ultimate nature of existence. The central concern of this *hsüan-hsüeh* philosophy was to probe those mysterious regions that lie beyond the universe of ordinary existence but presumably precede all such existence and engender it. These Chinese philosophers posed the classic riddle: What existed before the universe began? What lies beyond the borders of heaven and earth? Their answer to this conundrum was, Nothing.

The distinctive Chinese approach to the momentous metaphysical problem of existence might have been conditioned, in part, by the Chinese use of a verb *(yu)* to express the idea of existence that functions quite differently from Indo-European verbs of being. As A. C. Graham has demonstrated in a particularly effective essay, the Chinese *yu* is a transitive verb that requires an object—"there is" something, or someone "has" something—unlike the intransitive English verb, which allows us to say that something simply "is." "Thus in Chinese one approaches existence from something outside, usually undefined, which has, in which there is, the thing in question."[56] By grammatical necessity, all things in Chinese exist in relation to an external subject.

When the totality of existence itself is under consideration, logically, the only conceivable external subject it could be related to is the infinite field of nothingness *(wu)* that lies beyond all things. Pushing the possibilities to the limit, must not even nothingness be contained in something else? Unraveling the logical implications of such ideas leads naturally to the kind of "Chinese boxes" approach to ontology seen already in the last century before Christ in Yen Tsun, who playfully spoke of a Tao that was "the nonexistence of the nonexistence of nonexistence's nonexistence" *(wu wu wu chih wu)*.[57]

In the Western philosophical tradition deriving from Parmenides, the abstract ideal of being itself has often been elevated to the level of a reality that is superior to the flawed objects of this material world—purer and truer than any mere physical thing. In Chinese, however, *yu* describes only concrete, material things—only they are said to "exist." When used as a noun in the technical Taoist sense, then, *yu* expresses the abstract idea of concrete existence. In the interests of precision, therefore, it might be translated as "(material) existence." To avoid confusing *yu* with the quite different Western concept of being, however, a lengthening roster of scholars, including Roger Ames, A. C. Graham, and D. C. Lau, prefer to render *yu* as "something."[58]

The opposite of something is nothing, or *wu*. In the Indo-European tradition, it is possible to invoke a supreme being—immaterial, but present—to explain the mystery of physical existence. When St. Augustine (354–430) observed that God could not have created heaven and earth from anywhere within heaven and earth, he was not distressed by this dilemma, since for him God was a transcendent being who stood beyond time and space, and brought them both into existence.[59] As Roger Ames puts it, in the Western tradition, "God is more real than and stands independent of his created world."[60] For the Chinese *hsüan-hsüeh* philosophers, however, there was no being apart from physical being and no escape from the riddle of existence other than to observe that before there was something there must have been nothing. And so this "nothing," labeled *wu,* acquired much of the priority of the Christian God within the *hsüan-hsüeh* metaphysical system. "All being originated from nonbeing," comments Wang Pi (226–249) in the Rump and Chan English translation.[61]

This formula is really no more than a tautology, however. As the negation of something, nothing is a logically necessary category. But you cannot actually make something out of nothing, either in China or in the West. It is easy enough to say, as Lao-tzu does in D. C. Lau's translation, "The myriad creatures in the world are born from Something, and Something from Nothing"; but, unlike the immaterial purity of the creator in the Western tradition, in China *wu* does not exist at all, by definition.[62]

The Neo-Taoist philosophical obsession with *wu* (and its superficial similarity to Western concepts of being) has led some readers to overlook the explicit premise of the *yu/wu* formula: the world of something is all that really exists. Sometimes it is supposed that Neo-Taoists such as Wang Pi must have understood *wu* to be an actual "substance"—some sort of quintessence "which is ontologically distinct from and prior to 'being.' " In this sense *wu* would have formed a kind of material substrate to our world of things. But *wu* means, literally, "nothing." A sophisticated review of the Neo-Taoist commentaries makes clear that Wang Pi used the term *wu* simply as a kind of heuristic device to suggest the grandeur of a Tao that exceeds the capacity of human language. Wang Pi knew better than to posit the existence of any substance beyond existence itself.[63]

In playful Taoist fashion Wang Pi danced metaphorically around the margins of comprehension, and any clumsy literal interpretation will always miss the point. This analysis of Wang

Pi's Neo-Taoism suggests that, despite the conventional designation of *hsüan-hsüeh* thought as "idealist" *(wei-hsin p'ai)*, it was actually predicated upon the profoundly opposite materialist assumption that this physical universe that we inhabit is the entire sum of all things, beyond which nothing lies. Despite all appearances to the contrary, Neo-Taoism was a thoroughly materialist doctrine. One reason why Neo-Taoists were so attracted to the immortality cult is that physical immortality was the only kind of immortality that was conceivable to them. As a fourth-century Buddhist critic observed, "Taoist doctrine supposes the self to be reality; therefore they take medicines to nourish life."[64]

The paradox is that Neo-Taoism nonetheless exalted the non-existent "nothing," the original void, above all else. This puzzle was already clearly laid out by Chuang-tzu centuries before the time of Christ: "Was there anything before heaven and earth that gave birth to them? What makes things things is no-thing. The creation of things does not permit any prior things. If there were something . . . if there were something, it would be the void.[65]

Chuang-tzu's position was not unique. It is echoed almost precisely in the *Lieh tzu*, parts of which may derive from the same classical age that produced the *Chuang tzu*, but which did not take its present shape until the early medieval period. It may therefore be regarded as a faithful reflection of fourth-century Neo-Taoist thinking.[66] In an entertaining dialogue form, Lieh-tzu writes: "T'ang of Yin asked Chi of Hsia, 'In the beginning of time, was there matter?' Chi of Hsia replied, 'If there were no matter at the beginning of time, where would the matter that exists today have come from?' "[67] Matter, it seems, must have always been present since the universe began. Before the beginning of time, there was nothing.

The early Taoist materialism of Chuang-tzu remained a fixture of the Neo-Taoist movement of the third and fourth centuries. It is evident in Juan Chi's (210–263) "Essay Penetrating *Chuang tzu*" *(Ta Chuang lun)*, where he writes: "Heaven and earth are born of nature, and all things are born of heaven and earth. Nothing exists outside of nature; therefore heaven and earth are named therein. Things do exist within heaven and earth; therefore all things were born therein."[68] When P'ei Wei (267–300) wrote his famous essay "In Praise of Actuality" *(Ch'ung-yu lun)*—in which he pointed out that it was not possible for anything to be produced out of a perfect void *(chih-wu-che wu-i neng sheng)*—therefore, it may be true that he was pointedly rebuking some of the logical and practical absurdities that flourished within the *hsüan-hsüeh* movement, but he was at the same time reiterating an old, established Taoist truth.[69] The clear-eyed among the Neo-Taoist movement, at least, must have had no doubt that the material world of things was absolute and inescapable, even though they might have been more fascinated by the subtle logical abstraction they called nothing. Neo-Taoist metaphysics emerges, then, as a quixotic quest to break free from the fetters of a physical existence that, in the end, the Neo-Taoists themselves did not really believe could be escaped. Only the void stands beyond material reality, and the void, of course, does not exist.

This absolute finality of our material world has tremendous implications for human life. It means that although the human spirit may be what gives animation to the inert physical body, the spirit itself is also imprisoned in the world of physical forms and cannot escape it. "Therefore the gentleman knows that form depends on the spirit to stand, but the spirit requires the form to exist," wrote Hsi K'ang (223–262).[70] Not only was the spirit trapped within the material world of forms, it was material itself— simply an especially refined product of the basic element in the Chinese material universe, *ch'i*.[71]

> Although the spirit is a subtle thing, it certainly is still something that is transformed by yin and yang. With transformation it is born, and with another transformation it is dead. As it is brought together it begins, and as it disperses again it ends. . . . The very fine and the very coarse [are composed of] the same *ch'i* and, first and last, abide together.[72]

Yang Ch'üan (third century) used the metaphor of fire to emphasize the purely material nature of human life:

> People contain *ch'i*, and so live. When their essence is exhausted, they die. It is like being drained dry or being extinguished. It may be compared to fire. When the fuel is exhausted and the fire is extinguished, there is no light. Therefore, in the remains of a fire that has been extinguished, there is no residual flame. After a man dies there is no residual spirit.[73]

It is dangerous to generalize about Chinese eschatological thought—ordinary Chinese have always believed in the presence of ghosts and spirits, and it is doubtful if many ever worked out all of the logical ramifications of their beliefs—but by the Han the Chinese intellectual mainstream had apparently crystallized around a belief that the spirit, whether or not it could exist apart from the body, was itself merely an especially rarefied version of the same *ch' i* that composed the body.[74] Chinese tradition has had a powerful inclination to visualize even the "spirit world" in concrete physical terms. Although it was commonly believed in Han times that each individual had not one but two souls, both souls tended to be conceived of in materialist terms as permutations of *ch' i*, one relatively coarse and one relatively fine.[75]

This native Chinese materialism was challenged by the arrival of Indian Buddhism in the first few centuries of the Christian era, and it can be said to have culminated in a conscious nativist reaction against Buddhist mysticism in Fan Chen's (c. 450–515) famous "Essay on the Extinction of the Spirit" *(Shen-mieh lun)*, written during the late fifth century. In this essay Fan argues that body and spirit are actually different facets of the same thing. Body is a word for its material substance, and spirit is a word for its function, "like the sharpness of a knife." There can be no talk of sharpness surviving the destruction of the knife.[76]

Within this world of things everything is composed of *ch' i*. "A stone is a lump of *ch' i*," wrote Yang Ch'üan.[77] A human being was also a lump of *ch' i*, as was the human spirit and also heaven itself, which encompassed humankind's entire realm of action, according to Lieh-tzu.[78] It was reasonable to suppose that if death occurred when the *ch' i*, which had temporarily combined to compose one's body and spirit, disintegrated into its original components once again, death could be postponed by attempts to hold together this volatile combination of *ch' i*. By the late Han, so-called Taoist adepts therefore elaborated such practices as "shutting off *ch' i* and swallowing it, calling it embryonic breathing, and swallowing [the fluid] coughed up from the well beneath the tongue, calling it embryonic feeding," to prolong their lives.[79]

This immortality cult became vastly popular among the medieval Chinese elite. One text from the medieval period lists no fewer than thirty-six different methods for nourishing one's nature and attaining immortality, ranging from "breathing and visualizing the cinnabar field" to "using sacrifices to bring spirits" to eremitism.[80] Yet many of the more thoughtful gentlemen realized that such techniques, at best, were postponing the inevitable. An early skeptic was Huan T'an, who wrote:

The "nourishing of nature" practiced by people today may be able to make lost teeth return, white hair turn black, and flesh and face radiant. It is like those who would force the wax back onto a candle. The utmost extreme of longevity is still only death . . . and those who wish to change their nature and seek a different Tao are deluded.[81]

Even the classic philosophical Taoists, Chuang-tzu and Lieh-tzu, concurred that the popular "Taoist" pursuit of immortality was misguided.[82]

Ch' i was inescapable because it was infinite and timeless, although constantly changing in its visible forms.[83] It followed that if death or dissolution was the fate of all particular combinations of *ch' i,* such as a single individual, a kind of material immortality was nonetheless assured through the unity of all things in primordial *ch' i.* This half optimistic, half fatalistic point is made by Chang Chan (c. 370) in a footnote to his fourth-century redaction of the *Lieh tzu:*

> The sage knows that life is not permanent existence, and death is not eternal extinction. The many forms are the result of transformations of a single *ch'i.* The many forms go through many transformations, but that which does not change remains. Reverting to the unchanging, it is called the Spring of Action [*chi-che*]. The Spring of Action is the beginning of all existence and the ancestor of motion.[84]

In a sense, then, because of the endless permutations of *ch' i,* it is really death that is the delusion, not immortality, even though no personal human identity can survive the transformation process.[85] No individual thing can escape eventual dissolution, but the collective *ch' i* is eternal, and the most sagacious response to this analysis of existence is simply to accept it. As the Buddhist Chih Tun wrote in the fourth century, "The great mind abandons itself to the passing of the body and untiringly follows the transformations."[86]

Medieval Chinese were fascinated by the possibilities for physical mutation presented by the transformation of *ch' i.* Kan Pao, for example, wrote an essay "On the Natural Transformations of Yin and Yang," describing how one material object could dissolve into another through the process of mutation.[87] *Lieh tzu* contains a long passage enumerating various, presumably fantastic, examples of such phenomena.[88] In the third century Chang Hua (232–300) included the following in his encyclopedic treatise known as the *Po-wu chih:* "If you bury a dragonfly's head on the fifth day of May beneath a west-facing door and leave it there for three days without eating, it will turn into a true black pearl."[89]

In theory at least, anything could become almost anything else. It was a natural impulse, then, to inquire what the natural patterns of transformation were and to wonder if human beings might not somehow be able to control or channel these transformations. The tantalizing possibility surely existed that human beings could master the natural process of chemical change and "alchemically" produce whatever they desired. Ko Hung, for example, noted that it was possible chemically to reproduce the effect of "clouds, rain, frost, and snow" and that such phenomena were "no different from the real thing."[90]

The technique known as "moving *ch' i*" *(hsing-ch' i)*, a method of mentally manipulating the body's internal *ch' i* (and the distant ancestor of modern *ch' i-kung* exercises), is mentioned in inscriptions as early as the late fifth century B.C.; and by the later Han dynasty, methods of mental concentration for the purpose of manipulating *ch' i*, referred to by such terms as "guarding the one" *(shou-i)* and "concentrated thought" *(ts'un-ssu)*, were widely practiced.[91] In the Han and after, these techniques were principally intended to cure diseases. A Han period text attributed to the mythical Chinese Methuselah P'eng Tsu claims, for example, that "whoever moves his *ch' i* with the desire of doing away with the hundred diseases concentrates on wherever they are located."[92] In the fourth century Ko Hung wrote of an earlier adept who "moved *ch' i* to cure other people's diseases" and taught how to shield oneself from illness by "imagining the *ch' i* from your five internal organs emerging from your two eyes to surround your body like a mist."[93]

Although rooted in a mechanical understanding of the physical nature of the universe, the attitude exemplified by *hsing-ch' i* techniques is essentially mystical idealism. It postulated an organic unity to the cosmos that breathed with life and purpose. This transcendent cosmic spirit was identified with the mind, and the early Han philosopher Tung Chung-shu concluded, drawing upon much older sources, that "all *ch' i* follows the mind."[94] While not exactly what we usually think of as Confucianism, this was certainly "Han Confucianism," and it was echoed by the noted third-century Confucian philosopher Fu Hsüan (217–278), who agreed that "the mind is the master of all things."[95]

If Han Confucianism espoused such a mystical view of the capabilities of the mind, it should come as no surprise that religion happily embraced the same concepts. The late Han religious Taoist classic *T'ai-p' ing ching* states, for example, "What human beings can imagine they can always bring about."[96] In another passage the same source explains: "The mind and thought are the pivotal mechanism for heaven and earth and must not be carelessly moved."[97] As is well known, Mahayana Buddhism, at least after the translation of the *Mahāparinirvāṇa-sūtra* in the early fifth century, also advocated the mystical supremacy of a cosmic mind.[98] Thus Tsung Ping (375–443), in explaining Buddhism to the Chinese, quoted "the Buddhist sutras" as saying that "everything and all laws follow ideas to produce forms" and "the mind is the origin of the law—the mind created the halls of heaven, the mind created hell."[99]

Hsüan-hsüeh philosophy took a more materialist, skeptical, path, however. While sharing the same physical understanding of the universe as consisting of a solid field of *ch' i,* the Neo-Taoists realized that the Tao of the universe ultimately could not be diverted from its own path, and the technology of "moving *ch' i,*" even if effective, could do no more than temporarily ward off death. As Huan T'an had said centuries earlier, "The utmost extreme of longevity is still only death."

Many *hsüan-hsüeh* philosophers dabbled with the cult of immortality and the alchemical transmutation of elements, but they generally took a somewhat more gloomy view of humanity's insignificance in the universe and our limitations in an entirely material world. Paradoxically, however, the very rigor of their materialism, which forced them to deny the mystic view of a transcendent and purposeful spirit filling the universe, allowed *hsüan-hsüeh* thinkers to lift their sights above this physical world of "something" to the superior realm of nothing that lies beyond.

The *hsüan,* or mystery, that *hsüan-hsüeh* thinkers contemplated was described by Ko Hung as that which is "above forms" *(hsing erh shang)*—the same words Sung dynasty Neo-Confucians later used to describe the ultramundane principle of coherence they called *li,* equated by Ko Hung with the Tao itself.[100] For Ko Hung this Tao was the intangible impulse that shaped the material world, and logically took priority over and was ultimately more real than matter itself. "Coherences [or ultimate principles] are what induce [material] circumstances, which are like the responses of a shadow or an echo—they are representations and not real," wrote Ko Hung in a very Platonic vein.[101] And, as the prototypical *hsüan-hsüeh* thinker Wang Pi defined it, this "Tao is an expression for nothing [*wu*]."[102] Embracing all things within it, the Tao comes full circle and returns to the infinite void.

Nothingness, or nonexistence, was the origin of everything and the ideal underlying *hsüan-hsüeh* thought. Such reasoning has an elegant symmetry: all things begin as nothing and eventually return there. Simply put, this was the mystery of *hsüan-hsüeh*. As Chang Chan summarized the message of the *Lieh tzu*, this book "clarifies the varieties of existence, taking perfect void to be ancestral [*tsung*] and ultimate extinction to be the experience of all things."[103]

The void is infinite and defies ordinary human comprehension, but humankind cannot resist the temptation to analyze and try to understand it. Perhaps the ever-mysterious Tao exhibits regular patterns that can be observed and reported. "Anciently, when the sages made the Yi [the *Book of Changes*], it was with the design that (its figures) should be in conformity with the principles underlying the natures (of men and things), and the ordinances (for them) appointed (by Heaven)."[104] The hexagrams in the *Book of Changes*, therefore, allegedly provide a code for the interpretation of complex universal patterns of change. These hexagrams were the inspiration for what is thought to be the earliest *hsüan-hsüeh* text, Yang Hsiung's *T'ai-hsüan ching*, or *Classic of Great Mystery*, composed at the end of the Former Han dynasty.[105] Yang used symbolic numerology to represent the patterns of the Tao schematically and to predict their repetition using yarrow stalk divination.[106] These schematic diagrams of the Tao remained a central concern for such classic third-century Neo-Taoists as Wang Pi.[107]

Since everything was contiguous through the unified field of *ch' i*, all things were interrelated, and the patterns of the Tao must therefore reveal themselves equally everywhere. This understanding suggested what Edward Schafer has called the "theory of correspondences," which maintained that events on earth had equivalent "counterparts" in heaven.[108] Watching the heavens and noting the interplay of regular motions and anomalies there was presumably easier than detecting similar patterns in the human world, and such astronomical observation could theoretically be used to take the pulse of the Tao.

The heavens accurately reflected the patterns of life on earth because of the attractive force of similarities, which, like modern gravity, formed currents through the universal field of *ch' i* and produced discernible patterns. Thus a Chin dynasty writer explained the connection between the lunar cycle and the ebb and flow of the tides as a consequence of the fact that "the moon is the essence of water."[109] In this way all natural laws could be deduced from the reciprocal influences of *ch' i*, and each item of creation therefore had potential significance for explaining the mysterious pattern of transformation.

The process applied not just to gross physical objects, but to higher-level abstractions as well. As the *T'ai-p' ing ching* put it toward the end of the Han: "The matters of the world each follow their own kind. Therefore, if the thoughts of emperors and kings are tranquil, their governments will also be at peace because of the attraction of [like] kinds."[110] In this manner the mystical, idealist side of Han philosophy reasserted itself to suggest that if the patterns of the Tao could only be understood, humankind could intervene to redirect these transformations toward some desired end.

Reality is intransigent, however, and rarely conforms obediently to any theory. In practice the possible combinations of interaction between physical entities are bewilderingly complicated, and it is difficult or impossible empirically to discern any pattern in nature through the mere observation of things. Realizing this, some *hsüan-hsüeh* thinkers finally came to despair that human intelligence, mired as it is in the world of *ch' i*, could ever penetrate the mysteries of the Tao.

From an infinite and randomly disposed array of data, no conclusions can ever be reached inductively. Chang Chan wrote in the fourth century:

> In all things you can make deductions based on patterns of coherences [*li*], but you cannot prove them using things. Therefore, believing what one knows consciously and not realizing that there are ultimate boundaries to what can be known is superficial knowledge. He who trusts what his ears and eyes hear and say without realizing that there are limits to vision and hearing is an ordinary man. As for the intelligent man, he fuses with mysteries cut off by the conscious mind, awakens to the subtle coherences beyond knowledge, understands what is excluded by vision and hearing, and obtains strange forms beyond matter.[111]

The inability of human beings to see the whole picture from their limited vantage point on earth became a basic tenet of *hsüan-hsüeh*. Chuang-tzu's dictum that "what a man knows is not the equal of what he does not know" was echoed repeatedly by the Neo-Taoists and in the fourth century by the Buddhist monk Chih Tun.[112] This ineffability of the natural order, after all, was why so many Chinese thinkers, following Yang Hsiung's *T'ai-hsüan ching*, had chosen the word "mystery" *(hsüan)* to describe the Tao.

Hsüan-hsüeh thinkers found evidence for their belief in the mysteriousness of the Tao in singularities they detected everywhere about them in nature. In the third century Chang Hua soberly described a man who had been born withered and who was neither consumed by fire nor cooled by water. Chang Hua assures his readers that this is a true incident, citing the personal observation of the local magistrate.[113] In the fourth century the famous calligrapher Wang Hsi-chih described a stone produced through the condensation of brine, which remained dry when placed in water but became wet when removed, and which vibrated spontaneously without external causes. Such a stone clearly violated the laws of physics as medieval Chinese understood them and constituted a dramatic refutation of their validity. Wang concluded, "How can we seek after the physical coherences of this world using thought?"[114]

If such singularities were true, then no "laws of physics" could hold, and anything was possible—this, in essence, is what the *hsüan-hsüeh* thinkers believed.

> Though there be perfect illumination, not all things that have form can be seen; though endowed with supreme hearing, not all things that have sound can be heard. . . . Though one possess the wisdom of Yi in [Great] Yü's [time], or Ch'i Hsieh [the author of a book of unusual tales], what we have learned is still not as much as what we do not know. The myriad things, and so on—what is there that does not exist?[115]

In a thoroughly infinite universe all conceivable possibilities, logically, must exist somewhere, and all patterns must ultimately dissolve into chaos.

By means of this rigorous chain of reasoning, skepticism was undermined, and medieval Chinese were prepared to accept all manner of miraculous behavior. Such reasoning helps explain the high level of interest in the "supernatural" in post-Han China that has often been remarked upon. Charlatans and mountebanks of assorted kinds preyed upon this credulity—for example, the central Asian monk Buddhacinga (Fo-t'u-teng, at Loyang in the north after 310), who claimed to be over a hundred years old, to be able to summon spirits, and to be able to see events hundreds of miles away in the palm of his hand—and it underlay the cult of immortality that was notably popular among the greatest intellectual figures of the day.[116] Yet, for the southern literati at least, this approach was based upon a rigorous logic of sorts—a skepticism even of the grounds for skepticism—and consisted not so much of vain "superstition" as of simply maintaining an open sense of the possibilities of the universe.

Empirical analysis of an infinite universe cannot escape eventually confronting singularities—exceptions to the normal rules derived from more limited sets of experience; but, when you soar intuitively above the realm of the particular to the infinite itself, ultimate truth can be found in the Tao.[117] *Hsüan-hsüeh* thinkers thus reasoned away the material world as a random and meaningless string of singularities and extolled instead the life of pure intellection in communion with the mysterious principle of ultimate nothingness. This Neo-Taoist position bears a remarkable resemblance to Mahayana Buddhism.

Chih Tun and the Buddhist Inversion

Neo-Taoists extolled "original nothingness" *(pen-wu)* as the womb from which our familiar world of things emerged and the ultimate reality; yet, in practice, this Neo-Taoist ontology was trapped by the paradox that, by definition, "original nothingness" simply does not exist. Nothing may enjoy logical priority over something, but it is an abstraction offering little concrete satisfaction. Any philosophy based on the idea of the original void is vulnerable to the charge of being "nihilism."

Europeans instinctively avoided this trap by assuming the superiority of existence. St. Anselm's (1033–1109) famous "proof" of the existence of God even hinged on this assumption—since God is perfect, and existence is superior to nonexistence, God must exist. As A. C. Graham has noted, however, in Neo-Taoist thinking the priorities were reversed: anything that exists is by definition incomplete and therefore imperfect.[118] Only nothing can be infinitely flawless. The Chinese *hsüan-hsüeh* logic was more carefully reasoned than St. Anselm's Ontological Argument, but it was also less emotionally satisfying.

Some Neo-Taoists, such as Kuo Hsiang (d. 312), twisted their way out of the paradox by interpreting the Taoist advocacy of *wu-wei* (nonaction) to mean "taking no unnatural action," rather than literally not acting at all.[119] This sort of adjustment is necessary to accommodate the awkward fact that literal nonaction is not possible for one living in this world. Such an interpretation, furthermore, represents no real distortion of mainstream classical Taoist philosophy, which had always emphasized following the natural spontaneity of the Tao rather than complete inactivity.

"Original nothingness" cannot be sidestepped so easily, however. It must be understood literally for it to mean anything. Thus, when queried as to whether the void and human activity were not incompatible and whether absolute void is not destroyed even by the act of doing nothing, the fourth-century Buddhist layman Ch'ih Ch'ao (336–377) conceded (or perhaps he was just gloating at the Neo-Taoist predicament), "Nothingness really is nothing, and if you inquire after nothingness, you will be frustrated."[120]

Only if we call it the Tao and invest it with positive qualities as a kind of cosmic code for the universe can "original nothingness" engage us in our lives in this world. Neo-Taoists were consequently forced to contort themselves into advocating merging with the Tao and identifying with nothingness by simply relaxing and accepting the world of things. In his "Essay on Nourishing Life" *(Yang-sheng lun),* Hsi K'ang, for example, advises taking the immortality cult medicines, drinking wine, listening to music, and ceasing to strive. "Forget enjoyment and take pleasure in satisfaction; neglect life, and your body will be preserved."[121] Although the Tao was equated with a void that preceded and transcended the physical world of matter, the Neo-Taoists were trapped within the physical world. It is no exaggeration to say, therefore, that Neo-Taoist philosophy must have been inherently somewhat frustrating.

There is a grim satisfaction to be had in Neo-Taoist "nihilism": a stern stoic consolation from which those of powerful intellect may draw guidance for life in a treacherous world. Less vigorous intellects will find little comfort in this doctrine, however; for them the religious promise of salvation in the next world is a more attractive possibility. This promise, essentially, is what Buddhism contributed to medieval Chinese thought. Buddhism restored the kind of supernatural providence that the remorseless logic of Neo-Taoist materialism had stripped away.[122]

Buddhists stood the *hsüan-hsüeh* equation on its head. For Neo-Taoists original nothingness reigned supreme in theory, but in practice did not even exist. Buddhism fundamentally challenged this proposition and asserted instead that it is actually the material world that is illusory, while the void ("emptiness," *śūnyatā*, Chinese *k'ung*) is in fact real and the only reality that there is or even can be. In this sense Buddhism offered a much more positive, emotionally satisfying ontological system, especially after the early fifth century when the Mahayana vision of a reified cosmic Buddha-nature seemingly began to endow even emptiness with humane spiritual attributes. With Buddhism, medieval Chinese thought moved from the existential nihilism of native Chinese *hsüan-hsüeh* to a triumphant religion of salvation.

The change was fundamental, yet it was also a subtle one. Buddhism presented itself in China essentially as a refinement of Neo-Taoism. The Buddhist concept of ultimate emptiness, *śūnyatā*, for example, in many ways resembled the corresponding Taoist concept of *pen-wu*, and the similarity was underscored by the use of Taoist terminology in translating the imported Indian texts. Chinese and Indian thought had arrived independently at many of the same conclusions, and the real distinctions between the two systems of thought were blurred in the process of transmission.

When the Chinese thinkers encountered the novel Indian concept of *samsara*, the cycle of reincarnation, they quite naturally interpreted it in the light of the native Chinese belief in the spirits of the dead. The Chinese assumed that some personal identity must pass from incarnation to incarnation in order for there to be rebirth, and it was logical to equate this personal identity with the spirit. Ironically, in so doing these Chinese Buddhists unwittingly violated a critical tenet of Indian Buddhism, that there is no eternal "soul."[123]

Indian Buddhists originally denied that human beings had any absolute spiritual identity. This belief is known as the doctrine of *anātman*. Samsara, to these Indians, was but an unbroken chain of physical cause and effect *(karman)*, in which the passing away of

individual beings—who possessed no individual reality anyway—
was of little concern. For them there was no independent spiritual identity in this life and no soul to be reborn in the next. In
this respect Indian Buddhism actually resembles Chinese Neo-
Taoist materialism, with its belief in endless physical transformation. But early Chinese Buddhists found this conception to be a
nearly insurmountable intellectual hurdle. Reincarnation, to
them, implied that something, like a soul, had to be reborn.

Evidence for ancient Chinese belief in spirits of various kinds
appears in the earliest written records, but, by the Han dynasty if
not sooner, Chinese intellectuals who seriously thought about
such questions tended to regard both spirit and body as material
objects, of varying degrees of refinement, within the realm of
"something" (yu). A fifth-century essayist observed that in pre-
Buddhist China "it was commonly supposed that the body and
the spirit were extinguished together" at death.[124] But when this
Chinese materialist concept of the spirit was superimposed over
the Indian Buddhist idea of samsara, a concept more akin to the
Western idea of a soul—an absolute spiritual identity that transcends physical existence—was born.[125] From this idea of the
soul, it was but a short step for Chinese Buddhists to identify the
spirit of individuals with the supreme spirit of the Buddha and to
merge the Buddho-Taoist concept of ultimate void with the positive characteristics of a cosmic soul.

This trend in Mahayana Buddhism was not yet clear in the
fourth century, but already Buddhism had undermined the primacy of physical existence. The shapes and forms of the world of
material existence are but kaleidoscopic permutations resulting
from the endless play of cause and effect upon the body of ch' i.
Physical matter, whether it is "real" or not, has no permanence,
no purpose, and no meaning, and the world of things is therefore
"empty" (k'ung). The futility of existence in this world can be transcended, however, simply by giving it up and surrendering to the
original nothingness of the void (for Buddhists, also k'ung).

Even before the void was reified as the cosmic Buddha-nature
in later Mahayana thought, Buddhism reversed the polarity of
Neo-Taoism by asserting that only the void was real and that the
apparent reality of physical matter was an illusion. This assertion
came as a revelation to many Chinese, by whom it could easily be
understood as a correction of the fundamental flaw in hsüan-
hsüeh thought and an improvement upon existing Chinese philos-

ophy. As Tsung Ping argued in the fifth century, "Those Buddhist sutras include the moral excellence of the [Confucian] Five Classics, with the addition of a vast [metaphysical] reality, and contain the void of Lao-tzu and Chuang-tzu, but they add the ultimate [truth] that all things are empty."[126]

Although Buddhism had been known in China since about the time of Christ, it first won wide acceptance during the fourth century. A T'ang dynasty scholar estimates that the number of monks and nuns in China multiplied almost six and a half times during the course of the century.[127] Although some may argue that Tao-an (312–385) and Hui-yüan (334–416) made greater original contributions to the developing Chinese Buddhist tradition, no monk did more to help the spread of the Buddhist message in south China at this time than did Chih Tun, who was unquestionably the Buddhist most esteemed by his own contemporaries.[128]

Not only was he of outstanding importance to the developing Buddhist church, but Chih Tun also was a prominent figure in the secular world of his day and a significant player in the world of fourth-century social history. He appears no fewer than forty-eight times in a collection of anecdotes concerning famous literati from the period, the *Shih-shuo hsin-yü.* This is two times more than Wang Hsi-chih, one of China's most highly regarded calligraphers, and only a little less than half as many times as the great statesman Hsieh An, the most outstanding individual of the entire century.[129] It is no exaggeration to say that Chih Tun was one of the more important personalities of the Eastern Chin dynasty.

Judged by literary talent or philosophical brilliance, however, Chih Tun would not merit much attention today even from specialists. He is not one of the great creative forces in Chinese intellectual history, but he makes a fine spokesman for the fourth-century southern Chinese *weltanschauung.* Precisely because Chih is not a genius who stands above his time and place, he is paradigmatic: representative, if not typical, of his age.

As a Buddhist monk, Chih Tun was not considered to have been enough of a "historical" figure to merit treatment in the standard sources of biographical data for premodern China, the so-called dynastic histories. These works still reflect the traditional Confucian bias toward purely political history. When Chih's name does appear, therefore, it is usually in the role of companion to some important political figure, such as Hsieh An or Wang Hsi-chih.[130] To reconstruct his life it is necessary to turn to other sources, such as the stories in the *Shih-shuo hsin-yü* or the clerical counterpart to the dynastic histories, the *Biographies of Eminent Monks (Kao seng chuan)* compiled by Hui-chiao (497–554) around A.D. 530.[131]

Chih was born in 314 in north China to a "family that had served Buddha for generations."[132] While he was still an infant, his family must have gone south with the general migration at the end of the Western Chin dynasty, sometime before 317. Later, he settled in reclusion on Mt. Yü-hang, just a few miles southeast of modern Hangchow, where he was initiated into the mysteries of the *Prajñāpāramitā-sūtras*. At age twenty-five he left his family to become a monk, and by the year 342 at the latest, he had made his way to the capital at Chien-k'ang, where he won ready acceptance into fashionable society.

Then, in 343, Chih left the crowded capital to retire to a small ridge on Ang Mountain, in Shan County (modern Sheng), Chekiang. This location was favored for its lovely scenery and was frequented around this date by many notable clergymen.[133] At some later point he moved to nearby Shih-ch'eng Mountain, where he established a monastery and where he appears to have resided for some time and done a large part of his writing. After the coronation of Emperor Ai in 362, Chih was summoned back to court. This time he lingered in the capital for three years, living at the Tung-an monastery and lecturing on the *Aṣṭasāhasrikā-prajñāpā-ramitā-sūtra*. Finally tendering his excuses to the emperor, Chih retired to the Eastern Mountains, where he died, possibly at his home on Mt. Shih-ch'eng in Shan, in 366 at age fifty-three.[134]

Only a small body of writings attributed to Chih Tun have survived. In the sixth century there were apparently thirteen *chüan* (scrolls) in Chih's collected works, but today only two *chüan* and a supplement remain, some of the most significant parts of which have had to be reconstructed from fragments quoted in other sources.[135]

Chih Tun subscribed to the Prajñā school of Mahayana Buddhism, and his most important surviving complete work is his "Preface to a Comparative Copy of the Essentials of the Larger and Smaller Versions [of the *Prajñāpāramitā-sūtra*]" (*Ta-hsiao p' in tui-pi yao-ch'ao hsü*), in which he compared the two principal translations from the *Prajñāpāramitā-sūtras* that had been made in the second and third centuries, one of which was notably larger than the other. This work has been painstakingly translated into English and studied by Leon Hurvitz, but unfortunately it is of little philosophical interest.[136] Like much of Chih's writing, it is full of rhetorical flourishes, and its principal message seems to be simply that both versions of the sutra are equally valuable in their own ways for seeking enlightenment. This message is in keeping with Chih's reputation for being interested in only the basic meanings and principles of the sutras, even at the expense of "sometimes forgetting chapters and verses," but it is somewhat at odds with the purpose of his scholastic exercise in textual comparison.[137]

The current of thought leading to *hsüan-hsüeh* in the third century had begun, in part, with a reaction against the absurd extremes of scholasticism attained by classical studies in the Han, and this rejection of arid "chapter and verse" pedantry remained in vogue in the south during the era of division.[138] Chih's eclectic approach to a comparison of the larger and smaller translations from the *Prajñāpāramitā-sūtras* is, consequently, representative of his era. At the same time it is also a reflection of the sincere concern of Chinese Buddhists in this early period to recover the true and often elusive meaning of the Indian scriptures.

Chih's preface remains an important artifact in the history of early Chinese Buddhism, but more significant expositions of his own Buddhist thought are to be found in his "Essay on Matter Itself" *(Chi se lun)* and in his thoughts on the Pure Land of the Western Paradise. His reputation as a lofty gentleman in his own day, moreover, rested largely on his Buddhist-tinged commentary to the "Free and Easy Wandering" *(Hsiao-yao yu)* chapter of *Chuang tzu,* which is often considered to be his most characteristic single work.[139]

The "Free and Easy Wandering" chapter, with its delightful parable of the great P'eng bird and the little quail, has long been a favorite of *Chuang tzu* devotees. In suitably enigmatic Taoist fashion, the true meaning of the story is ambiguous. Whatever the original Chuang-tzu intended, the standard Chinese interpretation of this text was penned shortly before Chih Tun's birth by Hsiang Hsiu (c. 221–300) and Kuo Hsiang. Their commentary explained that although a vast disparity of scale existed between the high-flying P'eng bird and the tree-hopping quail, since each was following its own natural disposition, each was equally wandering free and easy in its own terms.[140]

It is often claimed today that the Hsiang and Kuo commentary reflects the rigid class-consciousness of China's emergent medieval literati class, in its assumption that one's lot in life is apportioned by fate and that one can do no more than complacently accept it. It is also possible, however, to read this commentary as the radical equalizing philosophy of a rising literati class engaged in challenging the established autocratic authority of kings and emperors. The basic thrust of the commentary, after all, is that no one really is better than anyone else.[141]

In any case, Chih Tun was not satisfied with the Hsiang and Kuo interpretation. He objected that if following one's nature were all there was to free and easy wandering, then even great villains could wander free and easy simply by satisfying their naturally evil inclinations.[142] This Taoist moral relativism was repugnant to Chih's Buddhist sensitivities. Sometime around 342, therefore, while he was first living in the capital, Chih composed his own commentary to the "Free and Easy Wandering" chapter and thereby won for himself a measure of renown in Neo-Taoist literati culture.

Now, that which wanders free and easy is clearly the mind of the Perfected Man. Master Chuang spoke of the great Tao and expressed his meaning with the P'eng bird and the quail. Because the P'eng bird's path through life is far reaching, it neglects [spiritual] satisfaction beyond the body [*P'eng i ying-sheng chih lu k'uang, ku shih shih yü t'i-wai*]. Because the quail is nearby, it laughs at what is distant and is pleased with itself in its heart. The Perfected Man [however] ascends heaven directly and joyfully wanders endlessly in freedom. He treats things as things and is not treated as a thing by other things. Consequently, he is distant and unself-conscious. He acquires mysterious influence—he does not act and is not hasty, yet he is quick. Consequently, he is aimless, and there is nothing to which he is not agreeable. This is how he wanders free and easy. With regard to having desires, he treats them as something that is satisfied. To be satisfied by that which is satisfied is to cheerfully bear a resemblance to heaven. It is truly like the hungry, once full, and the thirsty, once satiated, not being able to forget to make the winter and autumn sacrifices with parched grain or to stop their cups when they come to the dregs! If you are not perfectly satisfied, how can you wander free and easy?[143]

Where the P'eng bird and the quail were both wandering free and easy in the Hsiang and Kuo interpretation because each was following its own natural disposition, in Chih Tun's interpretation

neither could wander free and easy because both remained
chained to the circuit of this world.[144] In this respect Chih's is an
entirely Buddhist interpretation, regarding free and easy wandering—or, more precisely, nirvana—to be attainable only by the
Perfected Man who has broken all attachments and dependen-
cies to the material world and has realized his Buddha-nature.[145]
Such a Perfected Man then drifts freely through the world of
material existence, encountering the physical world directly in it
own terms but never himself becoming an object in the world of
things.

In the second half of his essay, Chih Tun makes clear that realizing the Buddha-nature to wander free and easy is accomplished
through the elimination of desires, a classic Buddhist prescription deriving from the original Four Noble Truths. Chih suggests
that this can be accomplished simply by obstinately treating all
desires as if they are already satisfied. When one is satisfied in all
of his desires, how could he not be wandering free and easy?

It was a common practice at this time to explain Buddhist precepts with reference to well-known Taoist or even Confucian texts
and ideas. Ch'en Yin-k'o suggests that Chih's clarification of the
"Free and Easy Wandering" chapter of *Chuang tzu* in the light of
the *Prajñāpāramitā-sūtras* might have originated earlier in north
China and been brought to the south by Chih Tun's family in the
exodus at the end of Western Chin.[146] Despite Chih's use of Taoist
language and despite this suspicion that his analogy between free
and easy wandering and the Buddhist Perfected Man was not
original with him, his was a genuinely Buddhist interpretation. It
has been suggested that Chih Tun might have come closer to
understanding the true meaning of the Prajñā sutras than any
other Chinese monk in the period before Kumārajīva brought
the definitive Indian interpretation to China after 401.[147]

Chih Tun's thought about the Western Paradise is noteworthy
chiefly because it is such an early expression of ideas that would
later become identified with the Pure Land sect. Chih composed
"An Encomium to a Portrait of Amitābha, with Preface" *(A-mi-t'o-
fo hsiang tsan, ping hsü)*, which is still preserved in his collected
works. In it, he cites the scriptures as assuring the faithful that

If there is someone who serves the true Buddhist precepts and in-
tones the Amitābha sutra, he is sworn to be [re-]born in that
[Pure] Land, without surcease. When those of sincere heart come

to the end of their lives, their spirits pass through transformation toward it. When they see the Buddha's spirit [there], they are enlightened and immediately attain the Tao.[148]

Chih also appeals in this piece to the habitual *hsüan-hsüeh* pose of uncertainty about what exists outside of the range of one's own personal experience to claim that the cosmic world of the Western Paradise occupies a realm beyond all ordinary human cognition and is not to be understood in earthly terms.

Chih Tun's surviving writings reveal him to have been a man of wide-ranging interests, both Buddhist and otherwise, and his fame among contemporaries was largely due to his new Buddhist perspectives on the *Chuang tzu;* but the core of Chih Tun's Buddhist thought, around which his own school of Prajñā interpretation coalesced, is contained in his "Essay on Matter Itself."[149] There were, reportedly, "six schools and seven sects" of Prajñā interpretation in the fourth century.[150] Chih Tun was the chief architect of one of these schools, known as the school of Matter Itself, and the principal text for the exposition of his views was presumably his essay that bears the same title.

In view of the critical importance of this essay to understanding Chih Tun's Buddhist philosophy, it is much to be regretted that almost nothing of the work has survived to the present day. A mere fragment has been preserved in the form of a footnote to the *Shih-shuo hsin-yü.*[151] Clues to Chih Tun's interpretation can also be found in scattered comments that appear in the exegetical works of other monks, beginning as early as a generation after Chih's death.

All of the fourth-century schools revolved around competing understandings of the crucial Prajñā concept of *śūnyatā*, or emptiness.[152] This question greatly vexed thoughtful Chinese, and Wang Ch'ia (323–358), a son of the powerful minister Wang Tao, wrote to Chih Tun asking for instruction about it. It was clear from the *Prajñāpāramitā-sūtras*, Wang wrote, that matter was empty, but it was far from obvious from the scriptures what exactly "empty" meant. Wang inquired, "Is it that we get it [physical existence] by extension from analogy with what is beyond [the world of] appearances?"[153] Wang evidently was groping for an understanding of *śūnyatā* that vaguely resembles the Platonic "ideals" familiar from Greek thought: beyond the material world there is an absolute reality, of which the phenomena of our world are mere shadows or imperfect projections. Wang's understanding is respectable philosophy, but from a Buddhist perspective it is wrong. One can only wish that Chih Tun's reply to this letter had been preserved.

The six or seven fourth-century Chinese schools of Prajñā Buddhism can be condensed into three major competing interpretations. According to Whalen Lai, they all evolved from a first school, known as the school of "Original Nonexistence." The name of this school, in turn, was borrowed from the Neo-Taoist concept of *pen-wu.* By its denial of the ultimate reality of matter, this school could be accused of the nihilistic fallacy of trying to reduce things to nothingness. The error of this school was soon matched by the countererror of the school of "Mental Nonexistence" *(hsin-wu).* Following the Indian Buddhist concept of *anāt-man,* this school affirmed the reality of existence and claimed that it is human consciousness or personal identity that is empty. The school ran counter to the overwhelming Chinese Buddhist belief in the reincarnation of a spiritual identity and was incompatible with the mainstream of Chinese Buddhism, but it did provide a healthy antidote to the errors of the school of Original Nonexistence. In Whalen Lai's analysis Chih Tun finally offered a "dialectical synthesis," or compromise, between the positions of these two earlier schools, which formed the last major fourth-century interpretation of *śūnyatā.* Chih argued that (material) things are real, but transitory and conditioned by cause and effect, and therefore empty. Both emptiness and physical objects are real, and "we discover emptiness in the midst of these very real forms themselves while going along with or abiding in them."[154]

The surviving fragment of Chih Tun's essay reads as follows:

> Now, matter[155] does not have an intrinsic nature of its own as matter. Since matter does not intrinsically exist, it is empty, despite its being material. Therefore it is said [in the *Prajñāpāramitā-sūtras*]: "Matter itself is empty, but matter, again, is different from [true] emptiness."[156]

The first part is clear enough. Phenomena in this world of things have no ultimate reality because they are merely the transient products of cause and effect. Because they are lacking both permanence and inherent meaning, their manifestation in the realm of matter is ultimately "empty." This much is unmistakable from the language of the text and is also a common Buddhist idea. The unique twist that was then given to this concept by Chih's School of Matter Itself, however, is less clear. With his borrowed quotation from the sutra, Chih seems to be saying that while matter is ultimately empty and meaningless in a negative sense, this emptiness is not to be confused with the positive spiritual value of transcendent "emptiness" to be found in nirvana. Chih thus postulates two levels of "emptiness": the hollow emptiness of our world of material existence and the true void of Buddhist enlightenment.

This position, if indeed this is what Chih Tun meant, was soon superseded by the new directions taken by Chinese Buddhist exegesis in the early fifth century. The T'ang dynasty monk Yüan-k'ang (fl. 627–650) later criticized Chih Tun for his theory, writing, "This Dharma Master Lin [Chih Tao-lin, i.e., Chih Tun] only understands that matter is not so of itself, being the product of causation [*karman*], but he does not understand that matter is [also true] emptiness and still retains [the doctrine] of the falsity of things."[157] Yüan-k'ang's criticism should be understood in the light of the Mādhyamika Buddhism that was introduced to China at the very beginning of the fifth century by Kumārajīva (350–413) and developed by his brilliant disciple Seng-chao (384–414).

Seng-chao insisted that samsara and nirvana are not a duality, but instead are different perceptions of a single truth.[158] That is, instead of two levels of emptiness—the false emptiness of this world and the true emptiness of some ultimate void—there is only the one truth of *śūnyatā*. The sage need only realize his transcendent spiritual emptiness within the meaningless physical existence of this world to attain enlightenment. Previous, fourth-century, Chinese Buddhists had followed the Neo-Taoist tradition, based on the *Lao tzu,* of assuming that nothing has precedence over something. But Seng-chao, himself following Chuang-tzu's ideas of the relativity of all things (especially developed in the *ch' i-wu lun* chapter, "On the Equalization of Things," in *Chuang tzu*), showed that, as opposites, something and nothing generate each other and are bound together by causation. Nothingness *(wu)* itself is still locked within the wheel of samsara, and it is only by transcending the traditional Chinese opposition between *yu* and *wu* that one can reach the unity of *śūnyatā*.[159] In his essay "On Untrue Emptiness" *(Pu chen k'ung lun),* Seng-chao accordingly denies this duality and affirms that by the apprehension of the natural emptiness of things, the sage may "ride the thousand transformations without changing and walk through ten thousand delusions with constant understanding."[160]

According to this interpretation, Chih Tun was right to say that matter itself was empty of independent meaning, but he was mistaken when he failed to see the supreme principle of ultimate emptiness itself. Chih's inability to penetrate this mystery compelled him to invent an unnecessary and false duality where unity in fact prevails.

Another early fifth-century innovation, unknown in Chih Tun's day, was the discovery in the *Nirvāṇa-sūtra* of the concept of the Buddha-nature within all beings, from which comes the idea that one's "true self" is eternal and one with the Tathāgata.[161] This important Mahayana theory presented yet another path to enlightenment: instead of an intellectual search for the emptiness of *śūnyatā*, one need only realize one's spiritual identity with the transcendent being to join with the cosmic soul of Buddha. Here again, Chih's thought differs from the fifth-century developments, but his notion of transcendent Buddhist truth to some extent prefigures this idea.

Chih borrowed the old Chinese word "coherence" (sometimes translated "principle," *li*) to describe his concept of higher truth. According to him, "coherence" is an immutable conceptual proposition existing somewhere beyond the material world of ceaseless transformation.[162] The chief difference between Chih's concept of ultimate coherence and the later Mahayana concept of the cosmic soul is that Chih refused to anthropomorphize his principle into a deity. In this respect, Chih's thought may even be philosophically superior to the later Mahayana religion. Within his philosophical system Chih must have identified his principle of coherence with the ultimate truth of *śūnyatā*.

Although Chih made a distinction between the emptiness of this world of matter and the transcendent principle of ultimate emptiness, the road to enlightenment still led through this material world and consisted of a process of detachment. An indication of how Chih thought this could be accomplished appears in his commentary on the "Free and Easy Wandering" chapter of the *Chuang tzu*. Chih writes that the Perfect Man "treats things as things and is not treated as a thing by other things"—a passage that is as well turned in Chinese as it is clumsy in English.[163] The idea seems to be that it is possible to live in this world while remaining serenely above it, oblivious to the "empty" joys and sorrows of life. In yet another text Chih expresses the same idea, writing that the Prajñā scriptures "treat things as if they are non-existent in the midst of things, and therefore are able to maintain equilibrium among things."[164] In a world of empty sense impressions, the "Perfect Man complies with things and nothing more."[165] Like the enlightened layman Vimalakīrti, he "drifts through forms and names," responding with equanimity to every transformation.[166]

Thus far Chih Tun's idea of the Perfect Man seems to resemble the Neo-Taoist sage, who also is unaffected by worldly events and responds naturally to the Tao, drifting through life "like an unmoored boat."[167] Hsi K'ang, for example, had written an essay "On Letting Go of the Self" (Shih-ssu lun) in which he noted: "When honors do not stick in the mind, you are able to transcend the school of names and employ the self-so; when emotions are not bound by your desires, you are able to judge the noble and base and penetrate the conditions of things. . . . Therefore Kuan-tzu said: 'The gentleman performs his Tao and forgets that he is an individual.' "[168] But, as materialists, the Neo-Taoists were still chained to their physical identities. They advocated drifting through life as the best formula for a long and not unhappy life, but the Buddhist Chih Tun advocated detachment, because he was completely indifferent to life and sought unity with his higher principles.

Perhaps the clearest explanation of Chih Tun's views is to be found in the "Essentials of Practicing the Dharma" (Feng-fa yao) composed by his lay disciple Ch'ih Ch'ao.[169] As an eminent monk, Chih Tun was given to lofty flights of abstruse language, and his ideas are often obscured by his rhetoric. This was part of his mystique. As a layman and an amateur, Ch'ih Ch'ao could afford to be less pretentious, and perhaps a more easily comprehensible exposition of Chih Tun's philosophy can be found through him.

According to Ch'ih Ch'ao, śūnyatā, true emptiness, is a mental state rather than a physical one. Something and nothing depend on the mind, not in the sense that the mind actually creates or destroys material things, but in the sense that even as one exists surrounded by the objects and images of the physical world, by terminating one's perceptions of them through detachment, they cease to exist as far as one is concerned. In this way the supreme principle of śūnyatā can be realized. Ch'ih Ch'ao calls this practicing the ideal emptiness of *śūnyatā* amid the material emptiness of the world *(k'ung chung hsing k'ung)*.[170] This is, no doubt, what Chih Tun meant when he told the emperor shortly before departing the capital for his final retirement in 365 that he hoped to "cut off my desires and return to the ancestral, and wander in the ease of the empty origin."[171]

It is interesting that, in comparison to the brevity of the surviving fragment of Chih Tun's important "Essay on Matter Itself," an entire *chüan* of his current *Collected Works* is filled with poetry. The fourth century is known to have been the golden age of *hsüan-yen*, or metaphysical, poetry, and Chih's poems solidly exemplify this tendency. As such, they are unfortunately less readable today than the landscape poetry of the fifth century or the eternal masterpieces of the great T'ang poets.

It is a truism of literary criticism that poetry is a medium better suited for the lyric expression of feelings than it is for the logical working out of complicated philosophical ideas. Chih Tun's poetic efforts at philosophy really can do little more than attempt to stir deep emotional responses through allusions to already well-known ideas. Chih Tun's poetry should not be lightly dismissed—it does display real literary power and tackle magnificent themes—but its purpose appears to have been more to evoke sighs of admiration from like-minded companions than to expound Buddhist or Taoist philosophy seriously.

Studded as it is with strategic references to *Chuang tzu*, Chih Tun's poetry was calculated to impress the cognoscenti of his age, and it is consequently a very good index to the fourth-century worldview, regardless of whether or not it is great poetry. For example,

Poems that Sing My Soul, No. 2

Upright I sit by my own orphan shadow
And imperceptibly forget the toil of thought.
Haltingly I take up the spiritual bridle,
Savor the study of famous writings,
(5)   Touch upon *Lao tzu* and laugh over his "redoubled
            mysteries,"[172]
Open *Chuang tzu,* and toy with the Great Beginning.
Sing out, clear airs assemble.
Each thought encountered quietly pleases.
Looking down, I happily confront the text's obscurity,

(10)   Looking up, I lament the two masters' passing.[173]
       Mournfully, [the man] beneath the pillar [Lao-tzu
          recedes into the distance.
       Silently, Meng village [Chuang-tzu's birthplace] stands
          vacant.
       Empty—a thousand years of events
       Dissolve into nothingness.
(15)   Nothing—and yet what does it matter?
       Ten thousand differences return along one path.
       Taoist understanding values dim thought:
       It was "Imageless" who found the "mystic pearl"![174]
       Disappointed at the border of these muddy waters,
(20)   I almost forget their reflection in the pure stream.
       Approaching that mirror I revert to clear indifference,
       And without care or worry cherish union with the Tao.
       Of mind and coherence, it is coherence that is more
          fine.
       Of form and objects, it is objects that are coarse.
(25)   In solitude the affairs of humanity depart.
       Alone with spiritual insight I reside.[175]

Even in English translation, the majesty of Chih Tun's pose is unmistakable, but the poem does not really elaborate on any of its concepts, which are presented largely in the form of allusions, and it is unlikely that anyone not already converted to Buddho-Taoist philosophy would be persuaded to convert by this piece. The poetic medium may be unsuited for the logical development of abstract ideas, but that is not really what Chih Tun hopes to accomplish (and *hsüan-hsüeh* denies the efficacy of logic anyway): Chih simply expects his readers to admire his marvelous Taoist spirit. That, essentially, is the point. Chih Tun chose to express so much of his philosophy in poetic form because of poetry's prestige in the literati society of his day. Chih Tun's poetry was one of his ways of impressing people—which he was very good at—and winning patrons among the powerful laity.

Chih wrote a series of poems entitled "Poems That Sing My Soul." This title, which was a common one, suggests the belief that poetry is the best medium through which to express one's innermost feelings. However, poetry is also the most formal of all literary mediums, and for many poets the temptation is great to express not their true innermost emotions, but what they would like other people to think are their—suitably "poetic"—innermost feelings. Chih Tun's "Poems That Sing My Soul" reflect a carefully crafted persona that Chih presented to elite society, and they can safely be read as an index of what the fourth century admired in a gentleman.

In his third poem in this series, Chih writes:

> In a lonely stone chamber clear
> Is a gentleman who seeks transformation.
> His external body slips the worldly bonds,
> Embracing simplicity, he represses all thought of existence,
> And brandishing mystery, detaches himself from thought.[176]

Chih here provides a beautiful portrait of the ideal Buddho-Taoist hermit, inhabiting remote and forbidding mountain caverns, in communion with the Tao, and far removed from the vain pursuits of mundane terrestrial life. In the poem Chih explicitly vows to become like that hermit and casts himself in the approved role of Buddho-Taoist True Man.

6

"TRUE MAN": THE POWER OF A CULTURAL IDEAL

If Chih Tun was not an ordinary Buddhist monk, still less was he typical of the Eastern Chin literati as a whole. Yet Chih's religious devotion differed from that of many of his most distinguished secular contemporaries only by degree. It may even be said that Chih Tun is, indeed, representative of certain important tendencies in the early medieval elite carried to an extreme.

Chih's biography in Hui-chiao's *Lives of Eminent Monks* stresses his intimacy with several of the leading figures of his day, notable among whom were the future emperor Ssu-ma Yü, the renowned calligrapher Wang Hsi-chih, and the great fourth-century statesman Hsieh An.[1] The ease with which Chih Tun circulated in fourth-century high society was due to his skill in the accepted social graces. Miyakawa Hisayuki observes, for example, that Chih's adroitness as a calligrapher in both the grass and clerical scripts undoubtedly facilitated his acquaintance with Wang Hsi-chih.[2] Chih won the respect of other literati with his outstanding ability in *ch'ing-t'an*, as did his Buddhist colleague Hsü Hsün (c. 358).[3] When the two of them collaborated in a public discussion of the *Vimalakīrti-nirdeśa-sūtra*, the literati audience was reportedly awed by their performance.[4] They exhibited the established literati accomplishments with a new Buddhist twist. The histories record that Chih Tun "was famous at the time for *ch'ing-t'an*. There were none of the fashionable nobles who did not honor him, supposing his achievement in forging subtleties sufficient for him to have participated in [the great *hsüan-hsüeh* debates of] the Cheng-shih era."[5]

Chih Tun won admission to literati circles because of his cultural brilliance, and historians of Buddhism have correctly emphasized Chih's important role in converting the Chinese literati to Buddhism by making that unfamiliar Indian religion socially acceptable.[6] His Buddhist message contributed greatly, then, to the religiously charged ideological atmosphere of medieval China. In many ways the Buddhist monk Chih Tun exemplifies a new cultural balance that was achieved by Eastern Chin literati during the fourth century.

Chih's good friend and admirer Hsieh An subscribed to a very similar vision of the ideal life. Hsieh rose to the political summit of fourth-century south China, to the posts of grand protector *(t'ai-pao)* and, posthumously, grand tutor *(t'ai-fu);* but, the historian records, to the end of his life, Hsieh An's "ambitions for the Eastern Mountains [that is, reclusive inclinations] never changed and always revealed themselves in his speech and appearance."[7] Indeed, his conspicuous disdain for office was the very lure that brought upon him ever more insistent offers of appointment. Although one contemporary critic did slyly suggest that Hsieh should be allowed to have his wish and spend the rest of his life in retirement, by spurning government service for the first forty-odd years of his life Hsieh only managed to burnish his political credentials.

Hsieh's indifference to politics, moreover, was allegedly the secret of his success when he finally did take a position in the government. Hsieh was able to face down warlords and save China from barbarian conquest at the battle of the Fei River because of his legendary poise and Buddho-Taoist equanimity—his ability to face even great physical danger with "unaltered expression" *(shen-se pu-pien)*.[8] Hsieh could govern well with nonaction. He could simultaneously be a Buddho-Taoist model of detachment, win widespread acclaim, and fulfill his Confucian responsibility to benefit the state. By doing nothing, the legend of Hsieh An suggests, nothing was left undone.

Human behavior is always constrained by established cultural expectations. Hsieh An and Chih Tun are both comprehensible only in the context of their times. As proud literati, they gloried in their cultural achievements, and they were rewarded with recognition by state and society. In return, by joining the political order, such literati as Hsieh An conferred legitimacy upon the state within the terms of the prevailing cultural paradigm. The precariousness of imperial rule at the start of the fourth century made it more necessary than ever for the court to intensify its reliance on what Richard Madsen has elsewhere termed "moral resources," and such moral resources were the special preserve of the Buddho-Taoist-Confucian literati.[9]

The key to literati power thus became, in Michael Rogers' words, their "aura of cultural superiority."[10] This intangible aura was sufficiently potent, moreover, that even a militarily powerful figure like Generalissimo Huan Wen felt a need to establish his own claim to it through displays of benevolent Confucian administration, learning, and conversational ability. Admission to the ranks of the anointed was jealously guarded by the literati themselves, however, and Huan Wen's cultural aspirations met with continued snubs from the literati community. One member rejected a marriage alliance with Huan on the grounds that Huan was a mere "military man."[11]

In China a special "intimacy between art and politics" has long existed. It is still possible to write of the fine art of calligraphy as a "system of power" even in the modern People's Republic.[12] It should not be surprising, therefore, that in early medieval China Buddhism, abstruse *hsüan-hsüeh* philosophy, and *ch'ing-t'an* altered expectations for political behavior in profound and sometimes astonishing ways. When the northern capital fell to invading armies in 311, for example, the leading official at the doomed Western Chin court was a notorious nihilist who claimed to be completely uninterested in politics. His aloof indifference to practical considerations has long been blamed for the magnitude of the disaster.[13] Later in the century, Ssu-ma Yü was so absorbed with philosophy that Wang Hsi-chih had to implore him (unsuccessfully) to divert his attention from *ch'ing-t'an* long enough to prevent an ill-considered invasion of the north. "I wish your majesty would temporarily set aside your thoughts of the distant void to rescue us from the impending emergency," Wang wrote.[14]

These are extreme cases, but they are not isolated aberrations. Such seemingly odd behavior becomes almost normal, in fact, within the context of the prevailing ideological system. By the third century, conspicuous withdrawal from an active interest in politics in favor of a contemplative life of retreat and self-cultivation had become an ennobling act.[15] Because it was highly esteemed, a gesture (at least) in the direction of lofty reclusion became almost obligatory even for those with political ambitions, to the extent that Wolfgang Bauer is able to write of "eremitism in power" during the Wei and Chin dynasties.[16]

It became fashionable among Eastern Chin literati to affect "a style of transcending the world" *(mai shih chih feng)*.[17] Powerful and successful fourth-century Chinese gentlemen sought the seemingly incongruous companionship of religious hermits—like the "otherworldly relationship" Wang Hsi-chih had with one Taoist figure—and claimed to prefer seeking the Tao in a distant mountain cavern to presiding at court.[18] Such behavior earned them the coveted cultural halo of sanctity and appreciable status in society.

For some, ironically, conspicuous withdrawal then became a strategy for political self-promotion. Sincerity of motivation, thus, becomes a problem in the analysis of early medieval behavior. It is difficult, or impossible, to be sure who is cynically manipulating the ideological system and who is truly following his ideals. The literati class was composed of sophisticated persons, well aware of the classic Taoist admonition that "reversal is the movement of the Tao" and living in a sometimes deadly age of multileveled political maneuver. It is therefore impossible to pass judgment on the sincerity of individual literati members' motivation. The point is, however, largely irrelevant, since both cynical manipulation of the system and naive sincerity were likely to result in essentially the same behavior. There is, moreover, no reason to doubt that ambition often coincided with more elevated sentiments.

Traditional Chinese historiography has usually decried this medieval fashion for *hsüan-hsüeh* and *ch'ing-t'an*.[19] By diverting the elite from more "practical" concerns, some historians claim, *hsüan-hsüeh* created the conditions for the chronic political instability that plagued the era of division. The *Chin-shu* records, for example, that two third-century Neo-Taoists "commonly had great reputations in the world. Their mouths spoke of the fleeting void, and they did not obey the rules of decorum. They drew their salaries but neglected their duties, were doted upon, and in office did not attend to business."[20]

What is often overlooked, however, is that these seemingly impractical cultural pretensions had very real practical consequences for those who adopted them. By identifying themselves with the established cultural ideal, literati gained leverage in support of their own position. And, while, in individual instances, such a pose might be absurdly counterproductive, for the literati as a whole it helped create conditions for their own social stability amid continuous dynastic flux. David Johnson's astonishment is quite understandable when he observes that "it is truly remarkable that two-thirds of the Chin officials of Rank Five and above who have biographies in the *Chin shu* are of families still prominent four and five centuries later."[21] In an age notorious for its political instability, at a time when dynasties rose and fell with bewildering speed, literati society remained, at least collectively if not always for every individual member, oddly stable.

The peril in reading too deeply into early medieval Chinese history is that it often leaves one faced with an (apparent) choice between denial of the evidence or of what we assume to be the universal laws of history. Joshua Fogel is not mistaken in predicting that even many of those who do not profess to practice "historical materialism" will nonetheless find any claim that the medieval Chinese elite comported itself on a basis of "Confucian morality and Taoist selflessness" unacceptably "naive."[22] Except for rare individuals (at best), the medieval literati were not saints. But it is possible to be too cynical. Under certain circumstances— especially where favorable conditions have been consciously cultivated—a general process of moralization of behavior is not inconceivable.

Beyond the narrow limits of pure coercion, ultimately, the successful and sustained exercise of power depends on winning some degree of consent from those who are subject to it. Consent, in turn, is best won by some appearance of legitimacy. The early medieval literati class were specialists in legitimacy. In return, they acquired power. And, in part because so many of the presidents of the Board of Civil Office, entrusted with determining bureaucratic appointments, were themselves famous for their *ch'ing-t'an*, literati philosophical expertise joined traditional Confucian virtue as a measure of qualification for high office.[23] The ensuing cultural complex, while historically unique to early medieval China, is rationally explicable and in no way mysterious.

Thomas Metzger has spoken of what he calls the "transformative" moral ideal of Chinese high culture.[24] This is the claim that a man's moral posture, by itself, can change the world around him. "The principle which the superior man holds is that of personal cultivation," writes Mencius, "but the empire is thereby tranquilized."[25] The questions of whether it is possible to govern effectively in this Confucian manner, by moral example, and of the transcendent "truth" of that particular brand of morality are less relevant here than the crucial point that some medieval Chinese could have subscribed to this belief and altered their conduct accordingly.

Benjamin Schwartz has observed that an ambivalent tension between the demands of private personal self-cultivation and public service has always been central to Confucianism.[26] This contradiction between introspection and the active life of selfless public service is actually not a contradiction at all: in mainstream Confucianism the two are bound together by a formula that links successful government to the personal virtue of the ruler. "Only the sage can bring about an era of Great Peace."[27] Within Confucian society, personal cultivation is not an evasion of the responsibility for public service, but an essential prerequisite for it.

The definitive statement of the political importance of self-cultivation in traditional Confucianism is found in the famous chain syllogism of the *Ta-hsüeh*.[28] This formula had not been forgotten in medieval China. Fu Hsüan, who was probably the foremost Confucian political theorist between the Han and the late T'ang, paraphrased it in the third century.[29] Wang Tao, the all-powerful minister at the court of the early Eastern Chin, did the same around 317:

> People know that the reason literati are esteemed is because they preserve the Tao. Therefore they retire and cultivate their persons. They cultivate their persons so as to reach their families. They correct their families so as to reach the village. Study in the village is used to ascend to court. Reverting to the origin and returning to the beginning, everyone seeks it within himself.[30]

Introspection and even reclusion were therefore an acknowledged part of the Confucian political agenda. Taoism, for its part, although not necessarily advocating an active cognitive process of introspection, did condone withdrawal from active politics on the part of the ruler. "Let your mind wander in tranquility, combine your *ch'i* in indifference, go with things spontaneously, and do not tolerate the self—then the whole world will be well governed," urges Chuang-tzu.[31]

Roger Ames is surely right to conclude that self-cultivation was a shared theme linking classical Taoism with Confucianism.[32] Medieval literati had solid theoretical precedent, therefore, for their belief that through a process of self-cultivation, which might or might not require withdrawal from active participation in politics, the philosopher could come to an appreciation of the true Tao—which would then make him uniquely qualified to lead society. In this manner they easily came to view arcane philosophical activity, such as *hsüan-hsüeh* and *ch'ing-t'an,* as a demonstration of worthiness to rule.

It was not just that the self-cultivated literatus was assumed to better understand the workings of heaven, earth, and man: he was even supposed to have a physical influence over them. During the Han dynasty, Confucian theorists, such as Tung Chung-shu, had devised elaborate systems of correspondences, linking the behavior of individuals to that of the broader cosmos. It was theorized that, because heaven and earth are interconnected through a universal web formed of the substance known as *ch'i* and because of the resonance that exists between all mutually related categories, the rectification of a ruler's heart at the center would exert a kind of gravitational pull outward upon the entire world and bring even the seasons into their proper sequence.[33]

Although much of the "Han Confucian" worldview was discredited after the fall of the Han, this theory of an intricate network of correlations between the human and natural orders remained popular. Kan Pao, for example, attributed the droughts that afflicted the capital in 317–318 to disturbances caused by an unjust execution, and Wang Hung (379–432) accepted the blame for another drought that hit around the year 428, resigning from office with the comment that it was the responsibility of top officials to assist the ruler in "adjusting the yin and the yang."[34] This "Han Confucian" understanding was further strengthened by the development of religious Taoism during the age of division after the Han, which Livia Kohn has demonstrated drew a mystical "connection between cultivating oneself and governing the country."[35]

Buddhism, then, when it came of age after the fourth century, merely added the observation that politics—and everything else in this sorry world of being—is inconsequential anyway. All that matters is the transcendent goal of enlightenment, which is also to be reached by the common path of self-cultivation. This path, Buddhism promised, would deliver not only good government on earth, but eternal bliss as well:

Therefore, for the ruler of [a land of] ten thousand chariots or the lord of only a thousand, the day is growing late and he has no leisure even to eat. The people have been entrusted to him for only one transformation. How can he make luxuriant his spirit and become king of ten thousand transformations? Follow, now, Confucius of the Chou to nourish the people, and taste the law of Buddha to nourish your spirit. Then, in life you will be an enlightened monarch, and in death an enlightened spirit and eternal king.[36]

In his influential study of Chinese philosophy, Fung Yu-lan concludes that its ideal has consistently been what he calls "sageliness within and kingliness without."[37] Except perhaps in Buddhism, politics have never been far removed from the center of Chinese philosophy. But, as Charles Le Blanc has observed, if the ruler's personal virtue is what draws the universe into order, as the Han model of cosmic resonance asserted, then kingliness must be distinctly subordinate to sageliness. The classic function of the ancient sage-kings had been to serve as "mediators between the human and the divine world."[38] Since successful rule on earth depends on maintaining a harmonious cosmic balance, only the sage, or Buddho-Taoist True Man, can be the ideal terrestrial monarch. And, in the end, "the True Man can fulfill his calling without becoming a ruler. His oneness with Tao contains and transcends the political function."[39]

Aramaki Noritoshi has shown that the ancient Chinese ideal of the sage had broadened by the fourth century from the exclusive domain of royalty to include all properly self-cultivated literati.[40] Both religious Taoism and Buddhism seized upon this point to proclaim their superiority to earthly politics. In the second century A.D. the Taoist classic *T'ai-p'ing ching* announced that "the perfect gentlemen of the empire eschew office for immortality."[41] Buddhism delivered a similar message: even kings should renounce their thrones in the name of Buddhism's higher truth. An Shih-kao, for example, had been a prince in his central Asian homeland before he came to China in the mid–second century. When his father died, however, since "he was deeply aware of the emptiness of suffering and shunned rank, when he had finished conducting the mourning, he gave up his kingdom and together with his uncle left his family [as a monk] to cultivate the Tao."[42]

But even as the pursuit of Buddho-Taoist truth distanced the early medieval literati from the this-worldly political concerns of classical Chinese philosophy, it also qualified them, according to the accepted standards of the day, to be the directors of earthly affairs. As Tanigawa Michio writes, "The famous families regarded the administration of society as their own mission, on the basis of their discernment of the Tao of Heaven."[43] Understanding of the universal pattern of the Tao was the key to successful government, and under those circumstances an obsession with *hsüan-hsüeh* philosophy and a neglect of administrative details was not seen as necessarily irresponsible behavior on the part of a monarch like Ssu-ma Yü or a top official such as the "notorious nihilist" who lost the northern capital in 311. In fact, earlier in his career, as county prefect, this same nihilist "had spent every day in *ch'ing-t'an,* and yet county affairs were still [well] managed."[44] Within the medieval literati worldview the literati proclivity for abstruse metaphysical discussion was not viewed as a distraction from administrative duty, but the best qualification for public service.

The spiritual authority of emperors, it was now believed, was not the unique prerogative of monarchs, but could be shared as well by cultivated gentlemen in their mansions or places of retreat. Just as, in another land in a later era, Christian religion endorsed a new confidence in the individual capacities of Europeans, such that a poor sixteenth-century Italian miller could become convinced he possessed access to the truth equal to that of popes, kings, and princes "because he has within himself that spirit which God has imparted to all men,"[45] so too the religio-philosophical system of early medieval China supported a belief in the ability of individual literati to attain a higher truth—a truth that, furthermore, in China had profound political implications as well. As the commentary to the *Book of Changes* instructed them: "The gentleman sits in his house and sends out words. If they are good, then [people] will respond to them from over a thousand *li.* . . . Words and actions are what the gentleman uses to move Heaven and Earth. How could he not act with care?"[46]

The twin pillars of great family ascendance during the Southern dynasties were leadership in the local community and, especially, privileged access to court office—with the still superior psychological and material resources of the state at their disposal. The relative importance of each source of influence varied from family to family and sometimes from individual to individual. Many of the old southern families, who enjoyed relatively few privileges of access to high office, might have resigned themselves to an active involvement in their local communities; whereas, at least initially in the fourth century, many émigré literati would have found themselves detached from any actual local community and almost entirely reliant on office holding at the dynastic level. In both cases, however, status depended on position within a shared cultural continuum.

Deft maneuvers within the complex network of customary expectations and a display of at least apparently benevolent paternalistic leadership and material charity (as well as wealth itself and simple inertia) promoted local ascendance. The legacy of Confucian ideals and the Nine Ranks selection system established under the Wei dynasty laid down the cultural expectations for the national-level elite, while Buddho-Taoist philosophical and religious innovations in the third and fourth centuries extended the parameters and readjusted the emphasis of acceptable literati activity. The assumption of nearly hereditary literati access to office in the imperial government, by the time of the Eastern Chin, allowed the literati to disregard the immediate interests of the state and indulge their own cultural ideals to a sometimes fantastic extreme.

But the literati class, in office, were often grossly inefficient administrators. By doing nothing, some things were indeed left undone. Before the imperial glories of the vanished Han dynasty could be restored, therefore, it would be necessary to reinvoke the ancient Confucian imperative of dedicated, selfless service to the state. Such a reorientation of the Chinese elite back to dynastic service would be a difficult operation. In the end, however, the literati would finally be asked to sacrifice their considerable private privileges on the altar of raison d'état.

EPILOGUE:
IMPERIAL RESTORATION

They say the momentum of history was ever thus: the
empire, long divided, must unite; long united, must divide.

Lo Kuan-chung, *Three Kingdoms,*
translated by Moss Roberts

The memory of the Ch'in and Han imperial tradition was sustained throughout the period of division, both by monarchs who
aspired to recapture something of the lost imperial grandeur and
by a literati class whose very eminence depended on an ideological complex not easily detached from the imperial political tradition. The special favors showered upon certain temporarily impe-
cunious émigré literati by the Eastern Chin dynasty early in the
fourth century reflected both their usefulness to the court as cul-
tured guardians of the imperial ideal and the material reliance of
those same literati on the patronage of the court. For a time, in
the Southern dynasties, the literati and the state needed each
other.

The early medieval literati drew upon the weakened shell of
imperial government for their titles, salary, and ideological justification, while often behaving as considerably less than conscientious servants of that state. This literati behavior was parasitic, in
the sense of draining resources from the state to nourish their
own private interests, but in the end this parasitic posture left the
literati still dependent on the state and vulnerable to a restoration of centralized imperial power.

Although it would take centuries to eradicate fully the privileged position of the medieval great families in Chinese society,
imperial restoration came quickly; within a half century of the Sui
reunification in 589, the degree of literati independence that had
formerly marked the Chin dynasty had already come to seem
almost incomprehensible as well as inexcusable to the T'ang em-

peror T'ai-tsung (r. 627–649).[1] In his evaluation of Emperor Wu of Western Chin (r. 265–289)—the only monarch to unite the entire empire even briefly during the four centuries between 184 and 589—T'ang T'ai-tsung nonetheless criticized Emperor Wu because his "mind was frequently influenced by public opinion, and he did not decide matters according to his own plans."[2] By "public opinion," T'ang T'ai-tsung meant the opinions of Emperor Wu's literati companions. T'ang T'ai-tsung's ideal vision of imperial autocracy would have been impracticable in the third century, but by the early seventh century it had evidently once again become the expected norm. The "counternormal" Southern dynasties period of literati ascendance had ended.

Southern dynasties emperors had tried for years to achieve a restoration of imperial authority. The power of the court probably sank to its lowest ebb during the Eastern Chin dynasty, in the fourth century. When the dynasty collapsed into rebellion, beginning as early as 399, peace was forcibly restored by military men from the Northern Palace Army. After their leader, Liu Yü, established his own dynasty, the Sung, in 420, it is possible to detect a subsequent strong imperial resolve to exclude great literati families from positions of real influence (as distinct from important-sounding sinecures) in the government, both to escape the powerful influence of the literati and because great literati made such miserably ineffective civil servants. Mao Han-kuang estimates that the number of literati families wielding real military power declined from the nearly universal 70 to 94 percent in the fourth century to a mere 16.7 percent in the sixth.[3] Okazaki Fumio remarks that the "autocratic tendency" of the first Sung emperor created a "general crisis" for the literati class; and Dennis Grafflin, tracing the turning point even further back to the death of Hsieh An in 385, says that this event "marked the end of great family control of southern society."[4]

If active administrative posts in the imperial government were increasingly staffed by men of humble origin, however, great literati families continued to dominate Southern dynasty society for another two centuries. Such men could even afford to ignore the mundane details of actual civil service because their position was so secure. Southern dynasties attempts at imperial restoration were at best only partially successful, and in the end it was the heavily non-Chinese Northern empire, where literati *pouvoirs intermédiaires* had never been as intransigent, that triumphed where the Southern dynasty courts had failed in restoring imperial autocracy.

During three centuries of division, state and society in north and south China had pursued different courses. Armed strongmen remained prominent in the north, while poets, monks, and cultivated literati cut fine figures at the southern court and in their fashionable mountain retreats. Following the utter chaos of the fourth century, however, the situation in the north stabilized somewhat under the great Northern Wei dynasty (386–534). Thereafter, the remaining northern regimes began a process of institutional development that concentrated power into the hands of activist monarchs at the expense of local strongmen.[5]

The Northern Ch'i demonstrated considerable success at mobilizing manpower, conscripting a reported 1.8 million citizens to build a wall stretching some three hundred miles from the vicinity of modern Peking west to modern Ta-t'ung in 555.[6] In 587 Sui was able almost simultaneously to send over a hundred thousand able-bodied men north to work on a wall and to dig a canal in the south running to Kuang-ling, a city on the north bank of the Yangtze just downstream from and threatening the Southern dynasty capital.[7] It was the ability of the central state to mobilize manpower for war, however, that was to prove crucial.

In this regard the justly famous *fu-ping* conscription system of Western Wei, established sometime after 542, would have played a pivotal role.[8] When the centralized imperial system had first appeared in China many centuries earlier, during the Warring States period, a household registration system had proved to be an effective device in organizing the population for taxation and military service.[9] The mandatory two years of universal male military service that had characterized the early empire, however, collapsed amid the ruins of the Han dynasty, and for a time the empire ceased to have any effective central military organization.[10]

The *fu-ping* system of the Western Wei was an attempt to restore order to this organizational chaos by consolidating existing local forces under central control, under military commands known as the Six Pillars of the State. A percentage of wealthier men were conscripted for military service but compensated for their service with tax and labor-service exemptions and equipped with horses and other supplies by noncombatant households.[11] The resulting system bolstered military morale by confirming soldiers in a status superior to that of the ordinary peasants (and sharply different

from the servile status of soldiers in the Southern dynasties) and
at the same time neatly provided for the logistics of a large army.
It was, no doubt, in part owing to this *fu-ping* system of mobilization that in 588 the northern Sui regime was able to deploy an
army 518,000 strong against the last Southern dynasty, the Ch'en,
which reportedly could muster a force of scarcely 100,000 men to
oppose them.[12]

The last Southern dynasties, in the meantime, seem to have
been oblivious to this military force massing in the north. As one
northern minister wrote in 584 with fascinated contempt, the
decadent southern court dissipated its energy in versification:
"They connect chapters and amass books about nothing more
than the appearance of the moon and dew, and compile examples filling cases about only the forms of wind and clouds."[13]
Since royal favor and official promotion depended so much on
poetic ability and cultural refinement in the Southern dynasties,
gentlemen had become obsessed with literature to the detriment
of more serious government business, such as war.

The Southern dynasties, moreover, had always been politically
unstable. The Eastern Chin had lasted for 103 years, but its successor, the Sung, stood for only fifty-nine, Ch'i for a mere twenty-
three, Liang for fifty-five, and Ch'en for only thirty-two. In the
sixth century, the Liang dynasty provided a final blaze of cultural
splendor and economic prosperity for the Southern dynasties,
but Liang ended in a disastrous rebellion (that of Hou Ching,
beginning in 548) that devastated the old literati families. Yen
Chih-t'ui reported that "of those in the capital the destruction
was nearly complete."[14] The last Southern dynasty, the Ch'en,
established in 557, thus inherited a vastly weakened empire as
well as an increasingly formidable threat from the north.

The Southern dynasties came to an end at the hands of the
superior military power of the Sui.[15] Ironically, the Sui itself soon
succumbed to the excesses of its own second emperor, but the
T'ang dynasty that followed in 618 formed in all respects a continuation of the Sui pattern. Power was now more firmly concentrated in the central imperial administration than it had been at
any time since the fall of the Han, and T'ang T'ai-tsung was
accordingly able to enjoy the luxury of criticizing Emperor Wu of
the Western Chin for not having been autocratic enough.

A milestone in the restoration of imperial autocracy under the
Sui was the final abolition of the Nine Ranks system in 583. In its

place, beginning in 595, the Sui dynasty substituted an official selection system based on written examinations that, Miyazaki Ichisada notes, enabled T'ang T'ai-tsung to boast in the early seventh century that "the Heroes of the empire are all in my pocket!"[16] Gradually, over the course of the T'ang dynasty, this civil service examination system led to the replacement of the medieval great families by a professional scholar-official class more subservient to the needs of efficient central administration. To further undercut independent great family authority, the Sui also reimposed the old Han "rule of avoidance" forbidding officials to serve in their own home areas.[17]

The literati privilege of tax exemption—a major reason for the fiscal weakness of the Southern courts—had never been as widespread in the north, but in 585 the Sui ruler nonetheless ordered a careful new inspection of the much abused census (tax) registries to augment imperial revenue and labor sources.[18] The Sui also made a show of lowering tax rates, with the intention of making public "citizenship" more attractive than private dependence on some great family and enticing more farmers onto the state tax rolls.[19]

The old great families did not simply disappear after the restoration of unified imperial power at the end of the sixth century, however. David Johnson estimates that more than half of the chief ministers of early T'ang, during the years from 618 to 755, still belonged to what he calls the "medieval oligarchy."[20] But these T'ang great families enjoyed considerably less political independence than their Southern dynasties predecessors, and they were also already very different in kind from the literati who had taken shape in the third century and grown to maturity in the regimes in exile in the south.

The T'ang great families were a mixed Sino-Turkic elite, pronouncedly military in orientation and relatively little given to classical scholarship or poetic composition.[21] Despite its aristocratic character, this T'ang dynasty social elite bore little resemblance to the cultivated, civilian Buddho-Taoist literati of the Southern dynasties. By this time the old Southern dynasties literati were already approaching extinction. Their demise, at least metaphorically, is marked by the final disappearance from historical records of the once proud Hsieh family, with the death of Hsieh Chen in 585, exactly two hundred years after that of his esteemed Eastern Chin dynasty ancestor Hsieh An in 385.[22]

NOTES

1: Introduction

The I-shan text, which introduces this chapter, is the only one of the First Emperor's seven Eastern stone inscriptions not recorded in the *Shih-chi*. The original monument was lost in T'ang times, but a copy made in A.D. 993 still exists in the Pei-lin museum in Sian. A photograph of this copy is reproduced in Li Yü-cheng, ed., *Hsi-an pei-lin shu-fa i-shu* (Sian: Shan-hsi jen-min mei-shu ch'u-pan-she, 1992), p. 27. I am indebted to Professor Ho Ch'ing-ku for transcribing the archaic script into modern characters. The First Emperor's use of inscriptions to enhance his public image has been assessed by Ting I-hua in "Ch'in Shih-huang te cheng-kang hsüan-yen ho hsin-li chi-lu: Ch'in Shih-huang tung hsün k'o-shih wen-tz'u p'ing-i," *Ch'in-ling Ch'in-yung yen-chiu tung-t'ai* 1992.1: 3.

1. Fang Hsüan-ling, ed., *Chin-shu* (644; Peking: Chung-hua shu-chü, 1974), 6.149 (hereafter cited as *Chin-shu*). The name of the city was changed from Chien-yeh to Chien-k'ang in 313 to avoid a taboo name. See, for example, Fu Chao-chün, "Liu-ch'ao ch'eng-shih ching-chi te t'e-tian chi ch'i tsai hsin ching-chi-ch'ü fa-chan chung te tso-yung," *Hsüeh-shu yüeh-k'an* 1992.11: 68.

2. For Chiang-nan in antiquity, see Kanō Naosada, "Kan Bō to sono shūhen—Kōnan bunka no ichi kōsatsu," *Kodaigaku* 18.1 (1972): 33–34. The Han population increase is described in Lao Kan, *Wei-Chin Nan-Pei-ch'ao shih* (Taipei: Chung-kuo wen-hua ta-hsüeh, 1980), pp. 2–3; T'an Ch'i-hsiang, "Lun liang-Han Hsi-Chin hu-k'ou," *Yü-kung pan-yüeh-k'an* 1.7 (1934): 36.

3. It should not be supposed that north China was overwhelmed by conquering alien armies, however. Non-Chinese states, largely from the

marchlands of modern Manchuria, simply moved into the vacuum left in the Central Plain by the spontaneous disintegration of the Chinese dynasty. The invaders were thus "not predators . . . but scavengers." See the fascinating analysis in Thomas J. Barfield, *The Perilous Frontier: Nomadic Empires and China, 221 B.C. to A.D. 1757* (Cambridge, U.K.: Blackwell Publishers, 1989), pp. 91–92, 98, 100.

4. For some attempts to estimate the number of refugees, see Wang Chung-lo, *Wei-Chin Nan-Pei-ch'ao shih* (Shanghai: Shang-hai jen-min ch'u-pan-she, 1980), p. 345; Ni Chin-sheng, "Wu-hu luan-Hua ch'ien-yeh te Chung-kuo ching-chi," *Shih-huo pan-yüeh k'an* 1.7 (1935): 42; and "Wu-hu luan-Hua ming-jih te Chung-kuo ching-chi," *Shih-huo pan-yüeh k'an* 1.8 (1935): 19; and Yang Lien-sheng, "Notes on the Economic History of the Chin Dynasty," in id., *Studies in Chinese Institutional History* (Cambridge: Harvard University Press, 1961), p. 127.

5. Chou I-liang estimates that northern émigrés constituted less than 17 percent of the total population of the Southern dynasties ("Nan-ch'ao ching-nei chih ko chung jen chi cheng-fu tui-tai chih cheng-ts'e," in *Wei-Chin nan-pei-ch'ao shih lun-chi*, edited by Huang Lieh [Peking: Chung-hua shu-chü, 1963], p. 39). The role of old(er) southern families in the success of the Eastern Chin was indisputably crucial, but authorities agree that it was the émigré northerners who were dominant. See Chou's tables showing the preponderance of émigré northerners in high office during the Southern dynasties (pp. 55–56, 58). See also Han Kuo-p'an, *Wei-Chin Nan-Pei-ch'ao shih-kang* (Peking: Jen-min ch'u-pan-she, 1983), p. 176; Wu Hsien-ch'ing, "Nan-ch'ao ta-tsu te ting-sheng yü shuai-lo," *Shih-huo pan-yüeh k'an* 1.10 (1935): 4; and Kawakatsu Yoshio, "Tō Shin kizokusei no kakuritsu katei: Gunjiryoku to no kanren no moto ni," *Tōhō gakuhō* 52 (1980): 318–319.

6. Tsang Jung-hsü (late fifth century), "Chin-shu," in *Chiu-chia chiu Chin-shu chi-pen*, edited by T'ang Ch'iu (Kuang-ya shu-chü ts'ung-shu, n.d.), 1.8a; *Chin-shu* 19.584. See also Howard J. Wechsler, *Offerings of Jade and Silk: Ritual and Symbol in the Legitimation of the T'ang Dynasty* (New Haven: Yale University Press, 1985), p. 110.

7. Ho Fa-sheng (fifth century), "Chin chung-hsing shu," *Huang-shih i-shu k'ao*, edited by Huang Shih, Ts'ung-shu ching-hua edition (I-wen yin-shu-kuan, 1934), 29.56a–b; *Chin-shu* 68.1828–1830, 69.1842. Earlier, during the Western Chin, Emperor Wu had consulted the scholar Chang Hua for his knowledge of the details of the vanished Han palaces. See Anna Straughair, *Chang Hua: A Statesman-Poet of the Western Chin Dynasty* (Canberra: Australian National University, Faculty of Asian Studies Occasional Paper 15, 1973), p. 28.

8. See Yang Kuang-hui, "Kuan-p'in, feng-chüeh yü men-fa shih-tsu," *Hang-chou ta-hsüeh hsüeh-pao: Che-she-pan* 1990.4: 91. Shigezawa Toshirō

explains the new intensity of interest in studies of ceremonies and official deportment—defined now as a category of historical research—during the Southern dynasties as reflecting the importance of establishing behavioral norms for the new elite that were validated by tradition ("Bunken mokuroku o tōshite mita rikuchō no rekishi ishiki," *Tōyōshi kenkyū* 18.1 [1959]: 7–8).

9. Benedict Anderson, *Imagined Communities: Reflections on the Origin and Spread of Nationalism* (Revised ed.; London: Verso, 1991).

10. It is widely agreed that nationalism is a uniquely modern phenomenon. Anderson locates its inception in the late eighteenth century (ibid., p. 4). Leonard Tivey goes so far as to claim that "fully fledged" nationalism is not just modern but even "essentially contemporary" ("Introduction," in *The Nation-State: The Formation of Modern Politics*, edited by Leonard Tivey [New York: St. Martin's Press, 1981], p. 1.). Most peculiarly modern are the combination of mass political participation through democratic elections with a presumed link between state and (ethnic) nation, and the paradigmatic assumption that the world naturally divides into a series of such ethnic national entities. There can be little doubt that Chinese literati conceived of themselves as belonging to a Chinese cultural tradition that was already ancient by the fourth century. Yü Ying-shih observes that, although the concept of "state" *(kuo-chia)* had long been obscured by the vision of universal empire *(t'ien-hsia)* in premodern China, national consciousness (more cultural than racial in orientation) dates from Ch'in times if not earlier ("Min-tsu i-shih yü kuo-chia kuan-nien," *Ming-pao yüeh-k'an* 18.12 [1983]: 3–4; see also Michael Ng-Quinn, "National Identity in Premodern China: Formation and Role Enactment," in *China's Quest for National Identity*, edited by Lowell Dittmer and Samuel S. Kim [Ithaca: Cornell University Press, 1993], p. 57). At the beginning of the Southern dynasties, however, China faced an identity crisis of potentially serious proportions. Of the four common bases for modern national identity described by Rupert Emerson (*From Empire to Nation: The Rise to Self-Assertion of Asian and African Peoples* [Cambridge: Harvard University Press, 1960], p. 104)—territory, language, shared historical tradition, and identification with a preestablished state structure—by the start of the Eastern Chin dynasty the traditional Chinese territorial homeland had been lost, the émigré elite found itself submerged in a sea of unintelligible dialects, and the imperial state had been significantly weakened. It was not political loyalty to the dynastic state, with its hereditary monarchs, that sustained Chinese national consciousness through this difficult period so much as it was a supradynastic sense of cultural affinity reaching back to the Chou. This was not modern Western nationalism, but the historical self-awareness of traditional Confucianism (see Tu Wei-ming, "The Con-

fucian Tradition in Chinese History," *Heritage of China: Contemporary Perspectives on Chinese Civilization,* edited by Paul S. Ropp [Berkeley: University of California Press, 1990], p. 124).

11. Theodore C. Bestor, *Neighborhood Tokyo* (Stanford: Stanford University Press, 1989), pp. 2, 10, and passim.

12. A necessarily incomplete enumeration of the Man, Liao, and Li "minorities" by Chu Ta-wei indicates that they alone constituted more than half of the total population of the southern state in A.D. 464 ("Nan-ch'ao shao-shu-min-tsu kai-k'uang chi ch'i yü Han-tsu te jung-ho," *Chung-kuo shih yen-chiu* 1980.1: 59). On the re-creation of China in fourth-century Chiang-nan, see Dennis Grafflin, "Reinventing China: Pseudobureaucracy in the Early Southern Dynasties," in *State and Society in Early Medieval China,* edited by Albert E. Dien (Stanford: Stanford University Press, 1990).

13. In his pioneering modern study of the economic history of the Northern and Southern dynasties, T'ao Hsi-sheng confessed that he was surprised to discover just how distinctive the period from late Han to the mid-T'ang was. See T'ao Hsi-sheng and Wu Hsien-ch'ing, *Nan-Pei-ch'ao ching-chi shih* (1937; Taipei: Shih-huo ch'u-pan-she, 1979), preface, p. 1.

14. Charles Hucker, for example, speaks of "four centuries of disruption that have commonly been considered a 'dark age' in China . . . a dismal record of disunity, intrigue, strife, and alien encroachments, of which the Chinese have not been proud" (*China's Imperial Past: An Introduction to Chinese History and Culture* [Stanford: Stanford University Press, 1975], p. 133). See also T'ung Ch'ao, "Chung-kuo ta-lu te Wei-Chin Nan-Pei-ch'ao shih yen-chiu," *Studies in Chinese History* 2 (1992): 113. "The preoccupation with state power" on the part of modern Chinese nationalists—in reaction first to Western imperialism and then to Japanese invasion (see Michael H. Hunt, "Chinese National Identity and the Strong State: The Late Qing–Republican Crisis," in *China's Quest for National Identity,* edited by Lowell Dittmer and Samuel S. Kim [Ithaca: Cornell University Press, 1993], p. 76)—automatically damns the Northern and Southern dynasties in the eyes of many patriotic scholars. A certain northern cultural bias may also explain some of the neglect the Southern dynasties have traditionally suffered. See Wu Ch'eng-hsüeh, "Lun wen-hsüeh shang te nan-pei-p'ai yü nan-pei-tsung," *Chung-shan ta-hsüeh hsüeh-pao (she-hui k'o-hsüeh-pan)* 1991.4: 102–103.

15. Kuwahara Jitsuzō, "Shin shitsu no nan-to to nampō no kaihatsu," in *Tōyōshi setsuen* (Kyoto: Kōbundo insatsu-bu, 1927), pp. 113–115.

16. Mark Elvin, *The Pattern of the Chinese Past: A Social and Economic Interpretation* (Stanford: Stanford University Press, 1973). On economic development in Chiang-nan during the Southern dynasties, see Hsü Hui, "Lun Liu-ch'ao shih-ch'i ch'ang-chiang liu-yü ching-chi te cheng-t'i

k'ai-fa," *Chiang-hai hsüeh-k'an* 1992.4: 129; T'ung Ch'ao, "Chung-kuo ta-lu," p. 121.

17. Murakami Yoshimi, "Kizoku shakai no bunka," in *Kizoku shakai,* edited by Sotoyama Gunji (Osaka: Sōgensha, 1981), p. 69.

18. Mori Mikisaburō, *Rikuchō shidaifu no seishin* (Kyoto: Dōbōsha, 1986), pp. 193, 197. This section of Mori's book is a splendid introduction to the subject of absolutism and liberty in early medieval China.

19. Ibid., pp. 187–247; Yü Ying-shih, "Individualism and the Neo-Taoist Movement in Wei-Chin China," in *Individualism and Holism: Studies in Confucian and Taoist Values,* edited by Donald J. Munro (Ann Arbor: Center for Chinese Studies, University of Michigan, 1985), pp. 122, 125. "A tendency toward self-consciousness" is the first of four special characteristics of the period of division noted by Chu Ta-wei, in "Wei-Chin Nan-Pei-ch'ao wen-hua te chi-pen t'e-cheng," *Wen-shih-che* 1993.3: 39–41.

20. See Beatrice Spade, "The Education of Women in China during the Southern Dynasties," *Journal of Asian History* 13.1 (1979). See also Chu Ta-wei, "Chi-pen t'e-cheng," p. 40.

21. Yoshimori Kensuke discusses and confirms Yano's findings in " 'San-ku kei-ji' no kenkyū: Sei-Shin shoki no ribu senyō," in *Chūgoku kizokusei shakai no kenkyū,* edited by Kawakatsu Yoshio and Tonami Mamoru (Kyoto: Kyōto daigaku jinbun kagaku kenkyūsho, 1987), especially pp. 118–119. For the Wei policy, see Ch'en Shou (233–297), *San-kuo chih* (reprint; Peking: Chung-hua shu-chü, 1959), 1.32.

22. The term *fan-ch'ang* is used by Chin Kuan-t'ao and Liu Ch'ing-feng, in *Hsing-sheng yü wei-chi: Lun Chung-kuo feng-chien she-hui te ch'ao wen-ting chieh-kou* (1982; Taipei: T'ien-shan ch'u-pan-she, 1987), p. 225.

23. It would be conventional to add a third crisis involving the Spring and Autumn and Warring States disintegration of the classic Chou order, beginning in the eighth century B.C., as Li Yüan does in "Wo-kuo li-shih shang te san tz'u wen-hua wei-chi" (*Pei-fang lun-ts'ung* 1988.3).

24. See Kubozoe Yoshifumi, "Gi-Shin Nanbokuchō ni okeru chihōkan no honsekichi nin'yō ni tsuite," *Shigaku zasshi* 83.1 (1974), part 1, p. 2.

25. Tsang Jung-hsü, "Chin-shu," 13.1b. See also Lu I-t'ung, ed., *Yu-chün nien-p'u,* Mei-shu ts'ung-shu 4.9 (1855; Taipei: I-wen yin-shu-kuan, n.d.), p. 377.

26. *Chin-shu* 117.2980.

27. In *Heritage of China: Contemporary Perspectives on Chinese Civilization,* edited by Paul S. Ropp (Berkeley: University of California Press, 1990), pp. 67–72.

28. David G. Johnson, *The Medieval Chinese Oligarchy* (Boulder: Westview Press, 1977), pp. 1–2, 7, and passim. His choice of the term "oligarchy" is defended on p. 153, note 1.

29. Yang Kuang-hui, "Kuan-p'in," pp. 93–96. On hereditary titles, see also Dennis Grafflin, "Reinventing China," p. 150 and note 38.

30. Yü Ying-shih, "Individualism," pp. 123–124; Albert E. Dien, "Introduction," in *State and Society in Early Medieval China*, edited by Albert E. Dien (Stanford: Stanford University Press, 1990), pp. 21–24.

31. On the fief in medieval Europe, and its transformation into "the patrimony of the vassal," see Marc Bloch, *Feudal Society*, translated by L. A. Manyon (1940; Chicago: University of Chicago Press, 1961), pp. 163–175, 190–210. The proprietary principle in medieval Europe was so strong that even kings inclined toward a view of their realms as personal fiefs. See Herbert H. Rowen, *The King's State: Proprietary Dynasticism in Early Modern France* (New Brunswick: Rutgers University Press, 1980), pp. 1–26. In China, even the regimes of preimperial antiquity, which sometimes closely resembled European feudalism, always exhibited significant distinctions; and these quasi-feudal systems were thoroughly displaced by the new imperial order after 221 B.C. On this process, see Max Weber, *The Religion of China: Confucianism and Taoism*, translated by Hans H. Gerth (New York: The Free Press, 1951), pp. 33–62. Jack Dull characterizes ancient China as "patrimonial," and denies the applicability of the label "feudal" even for the preimperial Chou dynasty ("The Evolution of Government in China," pp. 56–62). Paul Wheatley is also at pains to distinguish the Shang regime from classic European feudalism. See *The Pivot of the Four Quarters: A Preliminary Enquiry into the Origins and Character of the Ancient Chinese City* (Chicago: Aldine Publishing Company, 1971), pp. 52, 56–61.

32. Patricia B. Ebrey, *The Aristocratic Families of Early Imperial China: A Case Study of the Po-Ling Ts'ui Family* (Cambridge: Cambridge University Press, 1978), p. 10. In 1914 Naitō Konan (1866–1934), in an analysis of the different "forms of aristocratic governance in China," distinguished Chou "feudalism" from the "great family politics" of the era of division. See Tanigawa Michio, "Problems Concerning the Japanese Periodization of Chinese History," translated by Joshua A. Fogel, *Journal of Asian History* 21.2 (1987): 153, note 2.

33. Chung Ch'i-chieh, "Nan-Pei-ch'ao shih-ch'i hsing-ch'eng pei-ch'iang nan-jo chü-mien chih tsai-hsi," *Pei-fang lun-ts'ung* 1992.3: 80. Emphasis mine.

34. Chien Po-tsan, "Ch'in-Han li-shih shang te jo-kan wen-t'i," *Li-shih hsüeh* 1 (1979): 26.

35. Wang Chung-lo, "Chung-kuo feng-chien she-hui te t'e-tien," *Li-shih yen-chiu* 1985.1: 6.

36. Chiang Ta-ch'un, "Li-shih li-lun," *Chung-kuo li-shih hsüeh ssu-shih nien, 1949–1989*, edited by Hsiao Li (Peking: Shu-mu wen-hsien ch'u-pan-she, 1989), pp. 27–28, 37–39. On Kuo Mo-jo, see Lin Chien-ming, "Ch'in-Han shih pu-fen," *Chung-kuo ku-tai shih tao-tu*, edited by Hsiao Li and Li Kuei-hai (Shanghai: Wen-hui ch'u-pan-she, 1991), pp. 102–103. Chang Chun-shu dates Kuo's innovation to 1928 instead of 1930 ("The

Periodization of Chinese History: A Survey of Major Schemes and Hypotheses," in *The Making of China: Main Themes in Premodern Chinese History*, edited by Chun-shu Chang [Englewood Cliffs: Prentice-Hall, 1975], p. 5).

37. Chiang Ta-ch'un, "Li-shih li-lun," pp. 34–37.

38. To illustrate the spread of this concept through the educational system: the single most pronounced change in a standard Chinese introductory middle-school history text between 1955 and 1981, apart from an increase in length, was the replacement of the traditional periodization by dynasties with the section titles "Slave Society" and "Feudal Society." Compare *Ch'u-chi chung-hsüeh k'o-pen: Chung-kuo li-shih*, vol. 1 (1955; Sian: Shan-hsi jen-min ch'u-pan-she, 1959), with Ch'en Kuang-chung and Tsang Jung, eds., *Ch'u-chi chung-hsüeh k'o-pen: Chung-kuo li-shih*, vol. 1 (1981; Peking: Jen-min chiao-yü ch'u-pan-she, 1985).

39. See Chang Chun-shu, "Periodization," pp. 6–7; T'ung Ch'ao, "Chung-kuo ta-lu," p. 115.

40. Ch'en Kuang-chung and Tsang Jung, *Ch'u-chi chung-hsüeh k'o-pen*, pp. 39–43, 54–55. Kuo Mo-jo has been a leading proponent of this view. See his *Nu-li-chih shih-tai* (1954; Peking: Jen-min ch'u-pan-she, 1973), pp. 1–75.

41. Su Shaozhi, "The Formation and Characteristics of China's Existing System," *Chinese Democracy and the Crisis of 1989: Chinese and American Reflections*, edited by Roger V. Des Forges, et al. (Albany: State University of New York Press, 1993), p. 19, note 10.

42. Erich Pilz, " 'Feudalismus' und Theoriebildung in der Volksrepublik China: Zur Debatte der 50er Jahre über die feudale Grundeigentumsform," *Oriens Extremus* 30 (1983–1986): 42–43. The description of late imperial conditions is from Lloyd E. Eastman, *Family, Fields, and Ancestors: Constancy and Change in China's Social and Economic History, 1550–1949* (New York: Oxford University Press, 1988), pp. 71–78.

43. Kao Min, *Ch'in-Han Wei-Chin Nan-Pei-ch'ao t'u-ti chih-tu yen-chiu* (Kaifeng: Chung-chou ku-chi ch'u-pan-she, 1986), pp. 1–2, 9, 70–167.

44. W. G. Aston, trans., *Nihongi: Chronicles of Japan from Earliest Times to A.D. 697* (1896; Rutland: Charles E. Tuttle Company, 1972), vol. 2, p. 217. The impact on Japan of the "Chinese doctrine" that "under the heavens there is no land which is not the king's land" is discussed in G. B. Sansom, *Japan: A Short Cultural History* (1931; Stanford: Stanford University Press, 1978), pp. 98–104. That this Chinese model was actually implemented in Japan in the Nara period is no longer seriously in doubt (see Bruce L. Batten, "Provincial Administration in Early Japan: From *Ritsuryō kokka* to *Ōchō kokka*," *Harvard Journal of Asiatic Studies*, 53.1 [1993]: 111–14), but the question of to what extent this external evidence from Japan corroborates the case for state land control in China has never been addressed.

45. Hou Wai-lü, "Chung-kuo feng-chien she-hui t'u-ti so-yu-chih hsing-shih te wen-t'i: Chung-kuo feng-chien she-hui fa-chan kuei-lü shang-tui chih-i," *Li-shih yen-chiu* 1954.1: 19–20, 22–23. Pilz, "'Feudalismus,'" pp. 50–61, reviews Hou's ideas. Ho Ch'ang-ch'ün wrote a monograph on the "Feudal System of State Landownership and the Equal Fields System between Han and T'ang" (*Han T'ang chien feng-chien te kuo-yu t'u-ti chih yü chün-t'ien chih* [Shanghai: Shang-hai jen-min ch'u-pan-she, 1958]). For a discussion of a post-Stalinist "Revival of the Theory of the Asiatic Mode of Production" in Europe and the Soviet Union, see Tanigawa Michio, *Medieval Chinese Society and the Local "Community,"* translated by Joshua Fogel (Berkeley: University of California Press, 1985), pp. 53–59.

46. See Tanigawa, "Problems." In Taiwan, Tu Cheng-sheng has recently suggested reconceptualizing the great transition from the classical age of Chou to the imperial age of Ch'in and after in terms of a move from feudal city states to a political structure based on registered households of equal citizens. See *Pien-hu ch'i-min: Ch'uan-t'ung cheng-chih she-hui chieh-kou chih hsing-ch'eng* (Taipei: Lien-ching ch'u-pan shih-yeh kung-ssu, 1990), p. iii. This analysis seems promising.

47. See Meng Mo and Sun Ta-jen, "Kuan-yü Chung-kuo feng-chien t'u-ti so-yu-chih te hsing-shih wen-t'i," *Li-shih yen-chiu* 1961.1: 30–31.

48. Kao Min, "Wei-Chin Nan-Pei-ch'ao shih pu-fen," *Chung-kuo ku-tai-shih tao-tu,* edited by Hsiao Li and Li Kuei-hai (Shanghai: Wen-hui ch'u-pan-she, 1991), p. 163.

49. On this point, see Etienne Balazs, "Chinese Feudalism," in *Chinese Civilization and Bureaucracy: Variations on a Theme,* translated by H. M. Wright (New Haven: Yale University Press, 1964), pp. 28–33.

50. The opening lines of Ko Chien-p'ing's essay on early medieval family ethics are illustrative: "The Wei, Chin, and Northern and Southern dynasties were a quite unusual historical period in Chinese *feudal* society. Great family [*men-fa*] rule constituted the most unique feature of this age" (emphasis mine). See "Tung-Chin Nan-ch'ao she-hui chung te chia-t'ing lun-ch'ang," *Chung-shan ta-hsüeh hsüeh-pao (che-hsüeh she-hui k'o-hsüeh pan)* 1990.3: 70.

51. *Ch'in-Han ching-chi ssu-hsiang shih,* by Shang-hai she-hui k'o-hsüeh yüan, ching-chi yen-chiu-so, ching-chi ssu-hsiang shih yen-chiu-shih (Peking: Chung-hua shu-chü, 1989), p. 481. Chang Po-ch'üan argues for the inevitability of Chinese unity in "'Chung-hua i-t'i' lun," *Chi-lin ta-hsüeh she-hui k'o-hsüeh hsüeh-pao* 1986.5.

52. Ch'en Kuang-chung and Tsang Jung, *Ch'u-chi chung-hsüeh k'o-pen,* p. 54.

53. Thomas Hobbes' famous description of conditions "during the time men live without a common Power to keep them all in awe." *Leviathan,* edited by Francis B. Randall (1651; New York: Washington Square Press, 1964), pp. 84–85.

54. "Kuo Ch'in lun," quoted in Ssu-ma Ch'ien (145–c. 90 B.C.), *Shih-chi* (reprint; Peking: Chung-hua shu-chü, 1959), 6.283.

55. Perry Link, *Evening Chats in Beijing: Probing China's Predicament* (New York: W. W. Norton and Company, 1992), p. 269.

56. Hung Mai, *Jung-chai sui-pi* (12th century; Taipei: Ta-li ch'u-pan-she, 1981), 8.103.

57. *Chin-shu* 56.1543.

58. T'an Yao, *(Chia-t'ai) Wu-hsing chih*, Wu-hsing ts'ung-shu (1201; Nan-lin Liu-shih chia-yeh-t'ang, 1914–1927), 16.22b.

59. See the case of Kan Pao in Li Heng, ed., *Shao-hsing fu-chih*, Chung-kuo fang-chih ts'ung-shu 221 (1792; Taipei: Ch'eng-wen ch'u-pan-she, 1975), 41.994; and the case of Li Ch'ung in Kao Ssu-sun, ed., *Shan lu* (early thirteenth century; Sheng County Yamen, 1828), 1.6b, 3.2b.

60. *Chin-shu* 56.1544.

61. Chang Chün-mai, *Chung-kuo chuan-chih chün-chu cheng-chih chih p'ing-i* (Taipei: Hung-wen-kuan ch'u-pan-she, 1986), p. 600. For a discussion of the tradition of attributing the loss of the north to the literati fashion for abstruse metaphysics, see chapter 6 of this book.

62. Chao I, *Nien-erh shih cha-chi* (18th century; Taipei: Hua-shih ch'u-pan-she, 1977), 12.254. For the rise of a rigorous new standard of Confucian loyalty in late imperial times, see Wang Gungwu, "Feng Tao: An Essay on Confucian Loyalty," in *Confucianism and Chinese Civilization*, edited by Arthur F. Wright (Stanford: Stanford University Press, 1959).

63. Wu Chu-chu, "Hao-men cheng-chih tsai nan-fang te i-chih: Wang Tao te 'K'uei-k'uei chih-cheng,'" *Fu-chien shih-fan ta-hsüeh hsüeh-pao: Che-she-pan* 1992.2: 111.

64. Huang Tsung-hsi, "Ming-i tai-fang lu," in *Ming-Ch'ing shih-liao hui-pien, ch'u-chi*, edited by Shen Yün-lung (reprint; Taipei: Wen-hua ch'u-pan-she, 1967), part 1, vol. 5, p. 5a. A translation of this passage can be found in Wm. Theodore de Bary et al., eds., *Sources of Chinese Tradition*, vol. 1 (New York: Columbia University Press, 1960), p. 534.

65. Rafe de Crespigny, *Generals of the South: The Foundation and Early History of the Three Kingdoms State of Wu* (Canberra: Australian National University, Faculty of Asian Studies Monographs No. 16, 1990.), pp. 512–523.

66. See, for example, Link, *Evening Chats*, p. 6

67. Mikiso Hane, *Peasants, Rebels, and Outcastes: The Underside of Modern Japan* (New York: Pantheon Books, 1982), pp. 21–22. Hane also notes 2,800 earlier peasant disturbances between 1590 and 1867 (p. 7).

68. Albert Feuerwerker, *Rebellion in Nineteenth-Century China* (Ann Arbor: University of Michigan, Center for Chinese Studies, 1975), p. 74.

69. Prasenjit Duara, *Culture, Power, and the State: Rural North China, 1900–1942* (Stanford: Stanford University Press, 1988), p. 251. See also

Edward Friedman, Paul G. Pickowicz, and Mark Selden, *Chinese Village, Socialist State* (New Haven: Yale University Press, 1991), pp. 11–12.

70. William G. Crowell, "Social Unrest and Rebellion in Jiangnan during the Six Dynasties," *Modern China* 9.3 (1983): 322, 343–345.

71. See, for example, Yoshimori Kensuke, "Shin-Sō kakumei to Kōnan shakai," *Shirin* 63.2 (1980): 46.

72. See Wang Chung-lo, *Wei-Chin Nan-Pei-ch'ao shih*, pp. 360–364, 433–438; Han Kuo-p'an, *Wei-Chin Nan-Pei-ch'ao shih-kang*, pp. 381–386.

73. Wang Chung-lo, "Feng-chien she-hui," pp. 8, 10.

74. For an essay on the futility of attempting to constrain an emperor from pursuing his own private agenda at the expense even of the dominant landlord class, see Yen Ts'un-hsin, "Feng-chien cheng-chih chih-tu te i ko ken-pen ch'üeh-hsien—tu *Shuo-yüan, chün-tao*," appendix to Hsieh T'ien-yu, *Chuan-chih chu-i t'ung-chih hsia te ch'en-min hsin-li* (Ch'ang-ch'un: Chi-lin wen-shih ch'u-pan-she, 1990), pp. 121–125.

75. T'ung Ch'ao, for example, estimates that two hundred scholarly articles on the Wei, Chin, and Northern and Southern dynasties period have been published every year in mainland China alone since the restoration of normal academic activities there following the Cultural Revolution in the late 1970s ("Chung-kuo ta-tu," p. 114).

76. Kao Min, "Pu-fen," pp. 167–168, 177–178. Tanigawa Michio provides a splendid survey of the development of Japanese contributions to the field in "Nihon ni okeru Gi-Shin Nanbokuchō shi kenkyū no kaiko," *Studies in Chinese History* 2 (1992). For the theme of the local community, see p. 225.

77. "'Kyōri' no ronri: Rikuchō kizoku shakai no *ideorogii*," *Tōyōshi kenkyū* 41.1 (1982).

78. See Duara, *Culture, Power, and the State*, pp. 5, 15–41.

79. See Kubozoe Yoshifumi, "1970–1989 nien Jih-pen te Wei-Chin Nan-Pei-ch'ao shih yen-chiu," *Chung-kuo shih yen-chiu tung-t'ai* 1991.12: 23. For the Japanese Marxist critique of Tanigawa, see the "Translator's Introduction" by Joshua Fogel in Tanigawa's *Local "Community,"* pp. xxv–xxviii; Tanigawa, "Kaiko," p. 226.

80. See Bhikhu C. Parekh, *Marx's Theory of Ideology* (London: Croom Helm, 1982), p. 214; Jorge Larrain, *The Concept of Ideology* (Athens: The University of Georgia Press, 1979), pp. 47–48.

81. Maurice Meisner, *Mao's China and After: A History of the People's Republic* (revised ed.; New York: The Free Press, 1986), p. 301. See also pp. 41–45.

82. Karlis Racevskis, *Michel Foucault and the Subversion of the Intellect* (Ithaca: Cornell University Press, 1983), p. 105.

83. Karl Marx and Frederick Engels, *The German Ideology*, parts 1 and 3, translated by R. Pascal (London: Lawrence and Wishart, 1940), preface, p. 1.

84. René Descartes, "Meditations," in *Discourse on Method and Other Writings*, translated by Arthur Wollaston (Baltimore: Penguin Books, 1960), pp. 144–169.

85. Arthur J. Vander, James H. Sherman, and Dorothy S. Luciano, *Human Physiology: The Mechanisms of Body Function* (New York: McGraw-Hill, 1970), p. 567; Herbert Butterfield, *The Origins of Modern Science, 1300–1800* (Revised ed.; New York: Free Press, 1957), p. 136.

86. See Samuel H. Beer, "Introduction," in Karl Marx and Friedrich Engels, *The Communist Manifesto* (New York: Appleton-Century-Crofts, 1955), pp. ix, xx–xxiv, 30.

87. See John R. Searle, *The Rediscovery of the Mind* (Cambridge: MIT Press, 1992), pp. 25–26, 46–48, 54, 85, 112–124. This remains true even if, as announced, Gerald M. Edelman has finally produced "a biologically plausible model of how consciousness could have emerged" (Oliver Sacks, "Making Up the Mind," *New York Review of Books* 40.7 [April 8, 1993]: 46).

88. Racevskis, *Michel Foucault*, p. 123. See the discussion in Lowell Dittmer and Samuel S. Kim, "In Search of a Theory of National Identity," in *China's Quest for National Identity* (Ithaca: Cornell University Press, 1993), p. 20.

89. Václav Havel warns us "to be suspicious of words," since the word "socialism" has been used for years in Czechoslovakia as an incantation to enchain his people ("Words on Words," *New York Review of Books*, 36.21–22 [Jan. 18, 1990], p. 8). Had the word been employed with less hypocrisy, this spell might (need?) never have been broken. It becomes necessary for a state to resort to violence and coercion only when authority founded on the popular recognition of legitimacy fails. See Hannah Arendt, "On Violence," in her *Crises of the Republic* (New York: Harcourt Brace Jovanovich, 1969), pp. 148, 153–155.

90. See Susan J. Hekman, *Hermeneutics and the Sociology of Knowledge* (Cambridge: Polity Press, 1986), p. 174.

91. Racevskis, *Michel Foucault*, pp. 110–112, describing Foucault's thought. Compare B. F. Skinner, *Beyond Freedom and Dignity* (New York: Alfred A. Knopf, 1980), pp. 169–171.

92. This paradox is outlined in Nakayashiki Hiroshi, *Chūgoku ideorogii ron* (Tokyo: Keisō shobō, 1983) p. 105.

93. Chung Chao-p'eng, quoted in Wang Hsiao-po and Chang Ch'un, "Ju fa ssu-hsiang yü Chung-kung te lu-hsien tou-cheng," appendix to *Hsien-Ch'in fa-chia ssu-hsiang shih-lun* (Taipei: Lien-ching ch'u-pan shih-yeh kung-ssu, 1991), p. 351.

94. *Chin chung-hsing shu*, quoted in Li Fang, ed., *T'ai-p'ing yü-lan* (983; Taipei: T'ai-wan shang-wu yin-shu-kuan, 1980), 216.1158. Compare Juan Fang's brief biography in *Chin-shu* 49.1367.

95. Shen Yüeh (441–513), *Sung-shu* (reprint; Peking: Chung-hua shu-chü, 1974), 91.2249–2250.

96. Watanabe Yoshihiro, "Kan-Gi kōtaiki no shakai," *Rekishigaku kenkyū* 626 (1991.11): 48.

97. W. Dilthey, *Selected Writings*, edited by H. P. Rickman (Cambridge: Cambridge University Press, 1976), pp. 175, 198.

98. Yü Ying-shih, "Individualism," p. 128.

99. Benjamin I. Schwartz, *The World of Thought in Ancient China* (Cambridge: Harvard University Press, 1985), p. 76.

100. *Chin-shu* 6.150.

101. English-language scholarship is more extensively reviewed in Scott Pearce, "A Survey of Recent Research on the History of Early Medieval China," *Studies in Chinese History* 2 (1992).

102. Etienne Balazs, *Chinese Civilization and Bureaucracy: Variations on a Theme*, translated by H. M. Wright (New Haven: Yale University Press, 1964).

103. De Crespigny, *Generals of the South*.

104. Aat Vervoorn, *Men of the Cliffs and Caves: The Development of the Chinese Eremitic Tradition to the End of the Han Dynasty* (Hong Kong: The Chinese University Press, 1990).

105. Donald Holzman, *Poetry and Politics: The Life and Works of Juan Chi, A.D. 210–263* (Cambridge: Cambridge University Press, 1976).

106. Richard Mather, *The Poet Shen Yüeh (441–513): The Reticent Marquis* (Princeton: Princeton University Press, 1988).

107. Martin J. Powers, *Art and Political Expression in Early China* (New Haven: Yale University Press, 1991).

108. Audrey Spiro, *Contemplating the Ancients: Aesthetic and Social Issues in Early Chinese Portraiture* (Berkeley: University of California Press, 1990).

109. Erik Zürcher, *The Buddhist Conquest of China: The Spread and Adaptation of Buddhism in Early Medieval China* (Leiden: E. J. Brill, 1959).

110. Such translations are too numerous to cite here. They appear in the Bibliography in the section titled "Modern Scholarship".

111. Carol Gluck, *Japan's Modern Myths: Ideology in the Late Meiji Period* (Princeton: Princeton University Press, 1985), p. 8.

2: Refugee State

1. Hu Mu, of the northern "Great Wei" kingdom, in A.D. 350. Quoted in Ssu-ma Kuang (1019–1086), *Tzu-chih t'ung-chien chin-chu*, Chung-hua ts'ung-shu (reprint; Taipei: T'ai-wan shang-wu yin-shu-kuan, 1966), vol. 5, 98.20.

2. See Wang I-t'ung, *Wu-ch'ao men-ti* (reprint; Hong Kong: Chung-wen ta-hsüeh ch'u-pan-she, 1978), vol. 1, p. 116. Fu Chao-chün discerns four major economic zones during the Southern dynasties: Ching-chou,

Yang-chou, the Szechuan region surrounding Chengtu, and the Ling-nan region focusing on Canton ("Liu-ch'ao," p. 68). Szechuan was beyond the pale of Eastern Chin jurisdiction for much of that dynasty (and going through a period of relative eclipse), however, and the rapid rise of Ling-nan in the far south is mostly a development of the later Southern dynasties (p. 70). For matters of political geography, see the excellent series of historical maps edited by T'an Ch'i-hsiang, *Chung-kuo li-shih ti-t'u chi,* especially volume 4, *Tung-Chin shih-liu-kuo, Nan-Pei-ch'ao shih-ch'i* (Shanghai: Ti-t'u ch'u-pan-she, 1982).

3. Seng Yu (435–518), *Ch'u san-tsang chi-chi,* Ch'i-sha tsang-ching (reprint; Shanghai: 1934–1936), vol. 450, p. 48b.

4. Lu I-t'ung, *Yu-chün nien-p'u,* p. 429.

5. Edward H. Schafer, *The Vermilion Bird: T'ang Images of the South* (Berkeley: University of California Press, 1967).

6. T'an Ch'i-hsiang, "Hu-k'ou," p. 35.

7. For a contemporary example of the term "Chung-kuo" used to designate the lower Yellow River valley, see *Chin-shu* 43.1237. For a more ancient usage, see Cho-yun Hsu and Katheryn M. Linduff, *Western Chou Civilization* (New Haven: Yale University Press, 1988), pp. 96–97.

8. Kan Pao (early fourth century), "Chin-chi tsung-lun," in Hsiao T'ung (501–531), *Wen-hsüan* (reprint; Tainan: T'ai-nan pei-i ch'u-pan-she, 1974), 49.688.

9. Ibid.

10. *Chin-shu* 26.791.

11. The system of local administrative units in exile is discussed in Sa Shih-chiung, "Wei-Chin Nan-Pei-ch'ao shih-tai te ti-fang chih-tu," *Tung-fang tsa-chih* 41.17 (1945): 31. The figures for Eastern Chin come from Li Chieh, *Wei-Chin Nan-Pei-ch'ao shih* (Taipei: Chiu-ssu ch'u-pan yu-hsien kung-ssu, 1978), p. 108.

12. Ōkawa Fujio, "Rikuchō zenki no Gokō gun no gōzoku—tokuni Bukō no Shin shi o megutte," in Risshō daigaku shigaku-kai, *Shūkyō sha-kai shi kenkyū* (Tokyo: Yūzankaku Publishing Co., 1977), p. 523.

13. *Chin-shu* 43.1237–1238. Helpful capsule biographies of these (and other) men are provided in Richard B. Mather, trans., *Shih-shuo Hsin-yü: A New Account of Tales of the World* (Minneapolis: University of Minnesota Press, 1976), pp. 584, 596.

14. Sun Sheng (c. 302–373), "Chin yang-ch'iu," in *Chin yang-ch'iu chi-pen,* edited by T'ang Ch'iu (Kuang-ya shu-chü ts'ung-shu, 1920), 2.18a.

15. Mao Kuo-chin, *Chin shih shan* (c. 1600), 11.25a–b.

16. The evolution of Japanese thought on this question is nicely surveyed in Kim Minsoo, "Tōshin seiken no seiritsu katei—Shiba-Ei (Gentei) no furyō o chūshin toshite," *Tōyōyshi kenkyū* 48.2 (1989): 69–70.

17. Tsang Jung-hsü, "Chin-shu," 1.8b.

18. Lu I-t'ung, *Yu-chün nien-p'u,* p. 374.

19. For the rebellion of 327–328, see Sun Sheng, "Chin yang-ch'iu," 3.7a–b. For Yü's succession to military command in the west, see Lu I-t'ung, *Yu-chün nien-p'u,* p. 375.

20. *Chin-shu* 65.1753.

21. Sun Sheng, "Chin yang-ch'iu," 3.12a.

22. Ibid., 3.13b–14b.

23. Ssu-ma Kuang, *Tzu-chih t'ung-chien chin-chu,* vol. 6, 100.49.

24. Sun Sheng, "Chin yang-ch'iu," 3.19a.

25. *Chin-shu* 9.220.

26. Ibid., 79.2074.

27. In a very influential article ("The Myth of the Battle of the Fei River [A.D. 383]," *T'oung Pao* 54.1–3 [1968]), Michael Rogers exposed some of the inconsistencies in the existing accounts of this legendary battle. Even if no battle actually took place at this site in 383 (which is the extreme revisionist position), however, there is no reason to doubt that there was an invasion and that it was repulsed by Eastern Chin armies.

28. See Tsang Jung-hsü, "Chin-shu," 13.1a.

29. *Chin-shu* 79.2076.

30. Chao I, *Nien-erh shih cha-chi* 8.158.

31. Shen Yüeh, *Sung-shu* 1.9.

32. Ibid., 2.46.

3: The Socioeconomic Order

1. John King Fairbank, *The United States and China* (4th edition, enlarged; Cambridge: Harvard University Press, 1983), p. 28.

2. Ou-yang Hsiu (1007–1072), *Hsin T'ang-shu* (reprint; Peking: Chung-hua shu-chü, 1975), 199.5679.

3. For a detailed periodization, see Mao Han-kuang, *Chung-kuo chung-ku she-hui shih-lun* (Taipei: Lien-ching ch'u-pan shih-yeh kung-ssu, 1988), pp. 35–41.

4. Mori Mikisaburō, "Rikuchō shidaifu no seishin," *Ōsaka daigaku bungakubu kiyō* 3 (1954): 26.

5. *Chin-shu* 14.414–415.

6. See the Introduction above. See also Derk Bodde, "Feudalism in China," in *Feudalism in History,* edited by Rushton Coulborn (Princeton: Princeton University Press, 1956), pp. 83–87.

7. Tu Yu (735–812), *T'ung-tien* (reprint; Peking: Chung-hua shu-chü, 1984), p. 61; *Chin-shu* 45.1272.

8. Yen K'o-chün (1762–1843), ed., *Ch'üan Shang-ku San-tai Ch'in Han San-kuo Liu-ch'ao wen* (reprint; Kyoto: Chūbun shuppansha, 1981), 48.1735 (hereafter cited by specific dynastic period—e.g. as the Complete Literature of the Chin Dynasty [*Ch'üan Chin wen*], the Complete Literature of the Three Kingdoms Era [*Ch'üan San-kuo wen*], etc.). Fu

Hsüan's writings have been translated by Jordan D. Paper as *The Fu-Tzu: A Post-Han Confucian Text* (Leiden: E. J. Brill, 1987).

9. *Chung-wen ta tz'u-tien* (revised edition; Taipei: Chung-kuo wen-hua hsüeh-yüan ch'u-pan-pu, 1980), vol. 3, p. 635, entry 56 (7583.56).

10. See Bodde, "Feudalism."

11. See the splendid essay on this debate in Min Tu-ki, *National Polity and Local Power: The Transformation of Late Imperial China,* edited by Philip A. Kuhn and Timothy Brook (Cambridge: Harvard University Press, 1989).

12. *Lü-shih ch'un-ch'iu chin-chu chin-i,* annotated by Lin P'in-shih (c. 239 B.C.; Taipei: T'ai-wan shang-wu yin-shu-kuan, 1989), 13.350.

13. Ts'ao Chiung, "Liu-tai lun," in Hsiao T'ung, *Wen-hsüan* 52.720–724. See also Lu Chi (A.D. 261–303) "Wu-teng lun," in *Wen-hsüan* 54.742–746.

14. T'ien Yü-ch'ing concludes that during the Eastern Chin the great literati families equaled or surpassed the emperor in real power, but that with Liu Yü's usurpation the balance of power tipped once more back toward the court. See *Tung-Chin men-fa cheng-chih* (Peking: Pei-ching ta-hsüeh ch'u-pan-she, 1989), pp. 330, 337, 343, 355.

15. See Ch'en Yung, "Liu Yü yü Chin-Sung chih chi te han-men shih-tsu," *Li-shih yen-chiu* 1984.6: 40. Jennifer Holmgren suggests that the Liu-Sung regime "exhibited a greater tendency towards 'aristocratic' practices in its selection of officials than any other regime" ("Northern Wei as a Conquest Dynasty: Current Perceptions; Past Scholarship," *Papers on Far Eastern History* 40 [1989]: 31).

16. *Nien-erh shih cha-chi* 12.254.

17. Li Yen-shou, ed., *Nan-shih* (c. 629; Peking: Chung-hua shu-chü, 1975), 36.943; 21.573–575. That this new-found aristocratic independence had its limits is revealed by the fact that Wang was eventually implicated in a rebellion and "allowed" to commit suicide in prison at age thirty-five.

18. The authority of the prince to legislate under Roman law was codified in *The Digest of Justinian* (translated by Charles Henry Monro [A.D. 533–534; London: Cambridge University Press, 1904], I. iv. 1, vol. 1, p. 23). Compare the second century B.C. Chinese view expressed in Pan Ku (A.D. 39–92), *Han-shu* (Pai-na pen, erh-shih-ssu shih [Taipei: T'ai-wan shang-wu yin-shu-kuan, 1988], 60.752), which asks: "Where did the three foot [laws] come from? What early lords considered right they made known as statutes. What later lords considered right they appended as ordinances." William Rowe is also undoubtedly correct to emphasize the almost total absence of "the rhetoric of 'rights' of *any* kind" in premodern China ("The Problem of 'Civil Society' in Late Imperial China," *Modern China* 19.2 [1993]: 149). Still, somehow, the medieval literati did achieve a perceptible degree of immunity to impe-

rial autocracy. See Chou Tao-chi, "Wo-kuo min-pen ssu-hsiang te fen-hsi yü t'an-t'ao," *Chung-kuo shih-hsüeh lun-wen hsüan-chi*, 5, edited by Wang Shou-nan (Taipei: Yu-shih wen-hua shih-yeh kung-ssu, 1984), p. 41.

19. See, for example, Kawakatsu Yoshio, "L'aristocratie et la société féodale au début des six dynasties," *Zinbun* 17 (1981): 157–159; T'ang Ch'ang-ju, *San chih liu shih-chi Chiang-nan ta t'u-ti so-yu-chih te fa-chan* (1957; Taipei: Pai-shu ch'u-pan-she, n. d.), pp. 21–23; de Crespigny, *Generals of the South*, p. 497.

20. Tsang Jung-hsü, "Chin-shu," 1.8a.

21. Mao Han-kuang, "Wu-ch'ao chün-ch'üan chuan-i chi ch'i tui cheng-chü chih ying-hsiang," *Ch'ing-hua hsüeh-pao*, new series 8.1–2 (1970): 262, 265; Okazaki Fumio, *Gi-Shin Nanboku-chō tsūshi* (Tokyo: Kōbundō shobō, 1943), p. 585.

22. Kawakatsu Yoshio, *Rikuchō kizokusei shakai no kenkyū* (Tokyo: Iwanami shoten, 1982), p. 250. See also Tanigawa Michio, "Kaiko," p. 224. Tanigawa was a close friend and sometime collaborator of Kawakatsu, and he provides a concise analysis of the evolution of Kawakatsu's thought from 1950 until his untimely death in 1984 in *Chūgoku chūsei no tankyū: Rekishi to ningen* (Tokyo: Nihon edeitā sukūru shuppanbu, 1987), pp. 255–278.

23. *Ch'üan Chin wen* 8.1507.

24. For a detailed study of *t'u-tuan*, see Yano Chikara, "Dotan to hakuseki—Nanchō no seiritsu," *Shigaku zasshi* 79.8 (1970). The translation "residence determination" is borrowed from William G. Crowell, "Northern Émigrés and the Problems of Census Registration under the Eastern Jin and Southern Dynasties," in *State and Society in Early Medieval China*, edited by Albert E. Dien (Stanford: Stanford University Press, 1990), p. 187. Crowell exhaustively catalogs these programs (pp. 189–204). See also Hu A-hsiang, "Shih-lun liang-Chin Nan-ch'ao shih-ch'i te t'u-tuan," *Nan-ching shih chih* 1992.5.

25. T'an Tao-luan, "Hsü Chin yang-ch'iu," in *Chin yang-ch'iu chi-pen*, edited by T'ang Ch'iu (fifth century; Kuang-ya shu-chü ts'ung-shu, 1920), 2.13a.

26. For the traditional ideal, see Ma Tuan-lin, *Wen-hsien t'ung-k'ao*, Wan-yu wen-k'u 2 (thirteenth century; Shanghai: Shang-wu yin-shu-kuan, 1936), 12.123. This work offers what is clearly an idealized discussion, but the adminstrative efficiency of the early Chinese imperial state should not be dismissed lightly. See the discussion of the Yün-meng documents below.

27. See Fu K'o-hui, "Wei-Chin Nan-ch'ao huang-chi chih yen-chiu," *Shan-tung ta-hsüeh hsüeh-pao: Che-she pan* 1989.1: 110.

28. *Chin-shu* 75.1986. See Crowell, "Northern Émigrés," pp. 180–183, and notes 26, 33.

29. Li Heng, *Shao-hsing fu-chih* 41.994.

30. Ho Fa-sheng, "Chin chung-hsing shu," 29.77b–78a.

31. Li Heng, *Shao-hsing fu-chih* 41.994.

32. T'an Tao-luan, "Hsü Chin yang-ch'iu," 2.13a.

33. Nakamura Keiji, "Kyūhin kanjin hō ni okeru kyōhin ni tsuite," *Jinbun kenkyū* 36.9 (1984): 67–68.

34. *Chin-shu* 100.2628.

35. Ibid., 67.1797.

36. See Ch'ih's biographical sketch in Mather, *Shih-shuo Hsin-yü*, p. 509.

37. See the discussion of biographical topoi in Denis Twitchett, "Problems of Chinese Biography," in *Confucian Personalities,* edited by Arthur F. Wright and Denis Twitchett (Stanford: Stanford University Press, 1962), p. 35.

38. *Chin-shu* 62.1694.

39. J. Holmgren, "The Making of an Élite: Local Politics and Social Relations in Northeastern China during the Fifth Century A.D.," *Papers on Far Eastern History* 30 (1984): 67–68 and passim.

40. Ebrey, *Aristocratic Families,* p. 116.

41. Tanigawa Michio's influential opinions concerning *kyōdōtai* have been translated into English by Joshua Fogel in *Medieval Chinese Society and the Local "Community."* A particularly forceful presentation of the *kyōdōtai* idea can be found in Naba Toshisada, "O-shu kō," *Tōa jinbun gakuhō* 2.4 (1943).

42. For Tanigawa's discussion of the "communitarian" bonds within refugee camps in early medieval China, see Tanigawa, *Local "Community,"* pp. 106–110.

43. In a major reconsideration of scholarly interpretation, however, Edward Friedman, Paul Pickowicz, and Mark Selden argue now that in the mid–twentieth century, "rural dwellers experienced themselves in terms of community and consanguinity as members of lineages, neighborhoods, and villages, not as members of exploited or exploiting classes" (*Chinese Village, Socialist State* [New Haven: Yale University Press, 1991], p. 81). Victor V. Magagna has also recently advanced the concept of "community" as preferable "to class as a basis for interpreting the logic of rural institutions" in European History (*Communities of Grain: Rural Rebellion in Comparative Perspective* [Ithaca: Cornell University Press, 1991], pp. 12–21, 49–58).

44. William Miles Fletcher, III, *The Search for a New Order: Intellectuals and Fascism in Prewar Japan* (Chapel Hill: University of North Carolina Press, 1982), pp. 112–113.

45. Tanigawa Michio, *Tankyū,* pp. 87–88.

46. See Friedman, Pickowicz, and Selden, *Chinese Village,* p. 81; Magagna, *Grain,* pp. 12–21, 49–58. See also Andrew G. Walder's study of modern conditions, *Communist Neo-Traditionalism: Work and Authority in Chi-*

nese Industry (Berkeley: University of California Press, 1986), pp. 4–7, 14–22, 244. Walder is at pains to show, however, that contemporary industrial clientage patterns are "generic features of modern communism" and not mere survivals of premodern Chinese forms (pp. 10, 12, 22–27).

47. Lucian W. Pye, *Asian Power and Politics: The Cultural Dimensions of Authority* (Cambridge: Harvard University Press, 1985), pp. 47–48, 51, 53. The "rational peasant" analysis advanced by Samuel Popkin rightly emphasizes the danger of romanticizing premodern patron-client ties and the real difficulty of sustaining any kind of cooperative effort in a peasant village even when it is genuinely directed toward a common good. But Richard Madsen adds that "collective action can and does occur among peasants when individualistic calculations of self-interest are embedded in compelling moral codes" (*Morality and Power in a Chinese Village* [Berkeley: University of California Press, 1984], pp. 4–8). Successful village leadership must orchestrate a variety of competing individual interests within the framework of some such accepted moral code.

48. Wang Ying-lin (1223–1296), ed., *K'un-hsüeh chi-wen,* annotated by Weng Yüan-ch'i, Kuo-hsüeh chi-pen ts'ung-shu (reprint; Shanghai: Shang-wu yin-shu-kuan, 1935), 13.1086. Under the influence of Legalist thought, to increase productivity and enhance political control, the Ch'in dynasty had required all adult males to form separate households. During the Han dynasty this provision wavered in the face of the Confucian ideal of the extended household, and in the third century it was discarded. See Chu Tsung-pin, "Lüeh-lun Chin-lü chih 'ju-chia-hua,'" *Chung-kuo shih yen-chiu* 1985.2: 115–116.

49. Fan Yeh (398–445), *Hou-Han shu* (reprint; Peking: Chung-hua shu-chü, 1965), 32.1119.

50. Ch'en Shou, *San-kuo chih* 23.663.

51. Shen Yüeh, *Sung-shu* 42.1312.

52. Tanigawa, *Tankyū,* pp. 106–107.

53. Joshua A. Fogel, "A New Direction in Japanese Sinology," *Harvard Journal of Asiatic Studies* 44.1 (1984): 245–246.

54. Mao Han-kuang, *Chung-ku she-hui,* pp. 73–75.

55. Chou Chi (1781–1839), ed., *Chin lüeh* (reprint; Wei-chün chai, 1876), 10.2:3a–b.

56. Tanigawa, *Tankyū,* p. 99.

57. Bestor, *Neighborhood Tokyo,* p. 255.

58. Kao Min, *T'u-ti chih-tu yen-chiu,* pp. 59–60. By Eastern Chin times Kao believes landlords had shed some of this lineage coloration (p. 224).

59. Michel Foucault, *The History of Sexuality,* vol. 1: *An Introduction,* translated by Robert Hurley (New York: Vintage Books, 1980), p. 86.

60. Duara, *Culture, Power, and the State*, p. 40.

61. Ma Tuan-lin, *Wen-hsien t'ung-k'ao* 12.123; Shang Ping-ho (b. 1871), *Li-tai she-hui chuang-k'uang shih* 15.4a.

62. *Chin-shu* 88.2282–2283.

63. For modern times Jack M. Potter has identified the following conditions as conducive to the growth of strong lineage organizations: the existence of frontier conditions, weak central government control, commercial development, and rich agricultural soil. "Land and Lineage in Traditional China," in *Family and Kinship in Chinese Society*, edited by Maurice Freedman (Stanford: Stanford University Press, 1970), pp. 130–138.

64. See T'ang Ch'ang-ju, *T'u-ti so-yu-chih*, p. 16.

65. Robert M. Somers, "Time, Space, and Structure in the Consolidation of the T'ang Dynasty (A.D. 617–700)," *Journal of Asian Studies* 45.5 (1986): 989.

66. See Ōba Osamu, *Ch'in-Han fa-chih shih yen-chiu*, translated from the Japanese by Lin Chien-ming et al. (Shanghai: Shang-hai jen-min ch'u-pan-she, 1991), p. 41; Lin Kan-ch'üan, "Lun Ch'in-Han feng-chien kuo-chia te nung-yeh cheng-ts'e: Kuan-yü cheng-chih ch'üan-li yü ching-chi fa-chan kuan-hsi te k'ao-ch'a," in *Ti shih-liu chieh kuo-chi li-shih k'o-hsüeh ta-hui: Chung-kuo hsüeh-che lun-wen-chi*, edited by Chang Lien-fang (Peking: Chung-hua shu-chü, 1985), p. 210; An Tso-chang, "Ts'ung Shui-hu-ti Ch'in mu chu-chien k'an Ch'in-tai te nung-yeh ching-chi," in *Ch'in-Han shih lun-ts'ung*, 1 (Sian: Shan-hsi jen-min ch'u-pan-she, 1981), pp. 30–31.

67. A. F. P. Hulsewé, *Remnants of Ch'in Law: An annotated translation of the Ch'in legal and administrative rules of the 3rd century B.C. discovered in Yün-meng Prefecture, Hu-pei Province, in 1975* (Leiden: E. J. Brill, 1985), p. 13.

68. G. William Skinner, "Introduction: Urban Development in Imperial China," in *The City in Late Imperial China*, edited by G. William Skinner (Stanford: Stanford University Press, 1977), p. 25.

69. See Shang Ping-ho, *Li-tai she-hui* 15.1a–b. In the Chou an official was supposedly charged with "recording the numbers of the many people" in registers. See Chang Ju-yü (c. 1200), ed., *Shan-t'ang (hsien-sheng ch'ün-shu) k'ao-so* (reprint; Yüan-sha shu-yüan edition, 1320), ch'ien-chi, 63.9a. It is difficult to know what to make of such undoubtedly idealized portraits of ancient China; the situation could never have been as neatly systematic as the classics pretend. For the evolution of the urban administrative unit known as the *li*, or neighborhood, up to the Warring States period, see Chao Shih-ch'ao, *Chou-tai kuo-yeh chih-tu yen-chiu* (Sian: Shan-hsi jen-min ch'u-pan-she, 1991), pp. 75–84, 326–329.

70. Miyazaki Ichisada, "Chūgoku ni okeru sonsei no seiritsu—kodai teikoku hōkai no ichimen," *Tōyōshi kenkyū* 18.4 (1960): 76–77.

71. See Miyakawa Hisayuki, *Rikuchō shi kenkyū: Seiji shakai hen* (Tokyo: Nihon gakujutsu shinkōkai, 1956), p. 439.

72. Ch'en Shou, *San-kuo chih* 11.363, note 6.

73. See Kao Ming-shih, "Yün-meng Ch'in-chien yü Ch'in Han shih yen-chiu: I Jih-pen te yen-chiu ch'eng-kuo wei chung-hsin," *Shih-huo yüeh-k'an*, new series 11.3 (1981): 38–39.

74. Miyazaki, "Sonsei," p. 86.

75. *Chin-shu* 36.1058.

76. Tang Changru describes the peasants as facing a choice between the government-sponsored "oppression of cruel taxes and corvée" or submission to a local strongman, in "Clients and Bound Retainers in the Six Dynasties Period," in *State and Society in Early Medieval China,* edited by Albert E. Dien (Stanford: Stanford University Press, 1990), p. 136.

77. *Chin-shu* 127.3170. Tang Changru explains that mention of the Ch'in and Chin dynasties "refers to the struggle ca. 370–99 between Former Qin and Eastern Jin" ("Clients and Bound Retainers," p. 123, note 32).

78. "Wu-teng lun," in Hsiao T'ung, *Wen-hsüan* 54.742–746.

79. Wu Shu-p'ing, "Yün-meng Ch'in-chien so fan-ying te Ch'in-tai she-hui chieh-chi chuang-k'uang," in *Yün-meng Ch'in-chien yen-chiu* (Peking: Chung-hua shu-chü, 1981), p. 102.

80. Lu I-t'ung, *Yu-chün nien-p'u,* p. 393.

81. Chang P'u (c. 1635), ed., *Chin Wang yu-chün chi* (photocopy of 1892 edition; Taipei: Hsüeh-sheng shu-chü, 1979), 1.5a–7a.

82. Shen Yüeh, *Sung-shu* 6.121.

83. *Chin-shu* 75.1985–1986.

84. Ibid., 100.2632.

85. Kao Min, "Shih-lun liang-Chin shih-ch'i she-hui chu-yao mao-tun te yen-pien kuo-ch'eng," *Shih-hsüeh shih-yen-chiu* 1989.2: 26.

86. Chu Shao-hou, *Wei-Chin Nan-Pei-ch'ao t'u-ti chih-tu yü chieh-chi kuan-hsi* (Chengchow, Honan: Chung-chou ku-chi ch'u-pan-she, 1988), introduction, p. 4. For a description of government exactions, see pp. 260–273. See also Wang Chung-lo, *Tse-hua shan-kuan ts'ung-kao* (1987; Taipei: T'ai-wan shang-wu yin-shu-kuan, 1990), p. 64.

87. For the text of "Peach Blossom Spring," see *Ch'üan Chin wen* 111.2098. For a translation, see Cyril Birch, ed., *Anthology of Chinese Literature: From Early Times to the Fourteenth Century* (New York: Grove Press, 1965), pp. 167–168. In this famous early short story villagers take refuge from the disasters of the Ch'in period (third century B.C.) in a grotto and lead an idyllic existence for centuries entirely oblivious to the rise and fall of dynasties outside.

88. Watanabe Yoshihiro, "Kan-Gi kōtaiki," p. 50. Dennis Grafflin describes what he calls a "collegial superelite," concentrated at the capital, as effectively excluding personalities of merely local prominence

from high national office by the late third century ("Reinventing China," pp. 155, 169).

89. *Chin-shu* 100.2629.

90. See Kawakatsu, "L'aristocratie," p. 107.

91. Chang Yüan-chih, *Wu-hsing shan-hsü ming* (late fourth century; Yün tzu-tsai k'an ts'ung-shu, 1891), p. 1a.

92. See Chu Yung-chia, "Lun Ts'ao Ts'ao te i-chih hao-ch'iang chi ch'i fa-chia ssu-hsiang," in *Ts'ao Ts'ao lun-chi,* edited by Kuo Mo-jo (Hong Kong: Sheng-huo tu-shu hsin-chih san-lien shu-tien, 1979), pp. 367–368, 372.

93. There is some reason to think that the military power of the Eastern Chin great families declined over the course of the dynasty. See Kawakatsu Yoshio, "Kakuritsu katei," p. 317; Ochi Shigeaki, "Nanchō no kizoku to gōzoku," *Shien* 69 (1956): 10; Yasuda Jirō, "'Shinan ō Shi Kun no hanran' ni tsuite—Nanchō monbatsu kizoku taisei to gōzoku dogō," *Tōyōshi kenkyū* 25.4 (1967): 57–58.

94. On the conversion of private armies into tenant farmers, see Wang Chung-lo, *Wei-Chin Nan-Pei-ch'ao shih,* p. 164.

95. Yang Ch'üan (third century), "Wu-li lun," in *Lung-hsi ching-she ts'ung-shu,* edited by Cheng Kuo-hsün (reprint; Shanghai: Shang-hai ku-chi shu-tien, 1962), p. 8a.

96. *Chin-shu* 91.2347.

97. *Men-sheng* is often translated simply as "retainers," but that expression obscures the critical distinction between the military followers of a European or Japanese feudal lord and the civilian followers of a Chinese literatus, who were at least represented as being his students. Ho Tzu-ch'üan, for example, understands the term to have meant the disciples of a Confucian scholar in late Han. See "Liang-Han hao-tsu fa-chan te san ko shih-ch'i," in *Ch'in-Han shih lun-ts'ung 3* (Sian: Shan-hsi jen-min ch'u-pan-she, 1986), pp. 112–113.

98. Mao Tse-tung, "On New Democracy," in his *Selected Works* (5 vols.; Peking: Foreign Language Press, 1975), vol. 2, p. 340.

99. For an orthodox modern interpretation, see Yang K'uan, *Chan-kuo shih* (2d edition; Shanghai: Shang-hai jen-min ch'u-pan-she, 1980), pp. 126–129, 392. For classical citations, see Tu Yu, *T'ung-tien* 9–10; Chang Ju-yü, *Shan-t'ang k'ao-so* 65.1a–b. For some interpretations of the new archeological evidence, see Kao Ming-shih, "Yün-meng," pp. 39–41; Lin Kan-ch'üan, "Nung-yeh cheng-ts'e," p. 211.

100. See Kao Min, *T'u-ti chih-tu yen-chiu,* p. 71.

101. Kao Shang-chih, "Ch'in-chien lü-wen chung te 'shou-t'ien,'" in *Ch'in-Han shih lun-ts'ung 3* (Sian: Shan-hsi jen-min ch'u-pan-she, 1986), pp. 25–26, 29–30, 32–34.

102. Liu Ch'un-fan, "Ch'in chuan-chih chu-i chung-yang chi-ch'üan-chih te ching-chi chi-ch'u," in *Ch'in-Han shih lun-ts'ung 3* (Sian: Shan-hsi

jen-min ch'u-pan-she, 1986), pp. 5–14. See also the lucid description in Yang K'uan, *Chan-kuo shih*, pp. 188–190 and notes.

103. Hsiung T'ieh-chi and Wang Jui-ming, "Ch'in-tai te feng-chien t'u-ti so-yu-chih," in *Yün-meng Ch'in-chien yen-chiu* (Peking: Chung-hua shu-chü, 1981), p. 77.

104. Hung Mai, *Jung-chai sui-pi*, hsü-pi, 7.295.

105. Chu Li, *Han-T'ang shih-chien*, Pi-chi wu-pien (fourteenth century; Taipei: Kuang-wen shu-chü, 1976), p. 232.

106. "Hsün shih-chung chi," quoted in Wang I-t'ung, *Wu-ch'ao men-ti*, vol. 1, p. 115. Nearly two centuries earlier Wang Mang had complained that the Former Han "reduced the land tax to one in thirty [3.3 percent] . . . but strongmen fraudulently took possession of the allotted fields, so that the nominal [one in] thirty was really a tax of five out of ten [50 percent]." Quoted in Pan Ku, *Han-shu* 24.255.

107. Liu Yü-huang, "Lun Han-Chin Nan-ch'ao te feng-chien chuang-yüan chih-tu," *Li-shih yen-chiu* 1962.3: 116; T'ang Ch'ang-ju, *T'u-ti so-yu-chih*, p. 1.

108. Mather, *Shih-shuo Hsin-yü*, chapter 30.

109. *Chin-shu* 43.1234.

110. Ibid., 69.1845.

111. Conversion figures are supplied by Yang Lien-sheng, "Notes," p. 132, note 66.

112. Shen Yüeh, *Sung-shu* 54.1533–1534.

113. U.S. Department of Commerce, Bureau of the Census, *1987 Census of Agriculture*, vol. 1, part 51, (Washington, D.C.: U.S. Government Printing Office, 1989), pp. 84–85, table 51.

114. Richard Hofstadter, *America at 1750: A Social Portrait* (New York: Vintage Books, 1973), p. 152. In 1815 Thomas Jefferson reported owning 5,640 acres in Albemarle County (Virginia) alone (see Garry Wills, "The Aesthete," *New York Review of Books* 40.14 [August 1993]: 9).

115. See Hu Ju-lei, *Chung-kuo feng-chien she-hui hsing-t'ai yen-chiu* (Peking: Sheng-huo, tu-shu, hsin-chih san-lien shu-tien, 1979), p. 35; Denis Crispin Twitchett, *Financial Administration under the T'ang Dynasty* (Cambridge: Cambridge University Press, 1963), pp. 18, 21.

116. Kuo Mo-jo, *Nu-li-chih shih-tai*, p. 5; Bodde, "Feudalism," p. 64. For an overview of preimperial landholding patterns, see Ts'ao Ke-ch'eng, "Chou-tai ts'un-she t'u-ti chih-tu te yen-pien," *Pei-fang lun-ts'ung* 1984.1. The effect of modern ideological biases on this historiographical debate in the early twentieth century is traced in sparkling fashion by Joseph R. Levenson in "Ill Wind in the Well-Field: The Erosion of the Confucian Ground of Controversy," in *The Confucian Persuasion*, edited by Arthur F. Wright (Stanford: Stanford University Press, 1960).

117. Ochi Shigeaki, "Concerning Various Aspects of Public Finance, Land Management and Corvée Allotment Outlined in the Chou-li," *Memoirs of the Research Department of the Toyo Bunko* 39 (1981): 34. For

Mencius' description of the Well Field system, see James Legge, trans., *The Four Books* (reprint; Taipei: Culture Book Co., 1979), pp. 617–620.

118. Tung Chung-shu's advice is quoted in Tu Yu, *T'ung-tien* 10. For a second century A.D. example, see Uchiyama Toshihiko, "Chū-chō Tō— Go-Kan matsu ichi chishikijin no shisō to kōdō," *Nippon Chūgoku gakkai hō* 36 (1984): 64. For an early-fifth-century example, see the case of Liu Yü, in Shen Yüeh, *Sung-shu* 2.29–30.

119. Ch'en Shou, *San-kuo chih* 15.467–468.

120. Studies of the Wei dynasty *t'un-t'ien* system include Kuang Shih-yüan, "Ts'ao-Wei t'un-t'ien k'ao," in *Wei-Chin Nan-Pei-ch'ao yen-chiu lun-chi* (Taipei: Wen-shih-che ch'u-pan-she, 1984); and Ochi Shigeaki, "Gi-Shin Nanchō no tonden," *Shigaku zasshi* 70.3 (1961).

121. The origin of the *t'un-t'ien* system is discussed in Chang Ch'un-shu, "Ku-tai t'un-t'ien chih-tu te yüan-shih yü Hsi-Han ho-hsi, hsi-yü pien-sai shang t'un-t'ien chih-tu chih fa-chan kuo-ch'eng," in *Ch'ü Wan-li hsien-sheng ch'i-chih jung-ch'ing lun-wen chi* (Taipei: Lien-ching ch'u-pan shih-yeh kung-ssu, 1978), especially pp. 563–565, 598.

122. T'ang Ch'ang-ju, "Hsi-Chin t'ien-chih shih-shih," in *Wei-Chin Nan-Pei-ch'ao shih lun-ts'ung* (1955; Sheng-huo, tu-shu, hsin-chih san-lien shu-tien, 1978), p. 37. Wu Shu-p'ing similarly regards the penal laborers used in great numbers in the third century B.C. by the Ch'in state for such projects as the construction of the First Emperor's tomb as essentially slaves of the state ("Yün-meng Ch'in-chien so fan-ying te Ch'in-tai she-hui chieh-chi chuang-k'uang," in *Yün-meng Ch'in-chien yen-chiu* [Peking: Chung-hua shu-chü, 1981], p. 110).

123. For a discussion of the *chan-t'ien* system, see Balazs, *Chinese Civilization,* pp. 104–106.

124. See Kao Min, "Kuan-yü hsi-Chin chan-t'ien, k'o-t'ien chih te chi-ko wen-t'i," *Li-shih yen-chiu* 1983.3: 54–58. Kao writes that this law brought legal recognition of private landownership to a new level (*T'u-ti chih-tu yen-chiu,* p. 151).

125. The principal source for the *chan-t'ien* land law is *Chin-shu* 26.790–791. For a review of current mainland Chinese interpretations of the law, see T'ung Ch'ao, "Chung-kuo ta-lu," p. 117.

126. Kao Min, *T'u-ti chih-tu yen-chiu,* pp. 194–195, 197. T'ang Ch'ang-ju argues persuasively that the *k'o-t'ien* provision was a measure intended to require people to cultivate at least 50 *mu* (*Wei-Chin Nan-Pei-ch'ao shih lun-ts'ung,* pp. 50–53).

127. Hsing T'ieh, "Liang Chin Nan-Pei-ch'ao shih-ch'i te hu-teng chih-tu," *Ho-pei shih-yüan hsüeh-pao: She-k'o-pan* 1991.4: 92–93.

128. Yoshida Fudōmaro, "Shindai ni okeru tochi shoyū keitai to nōgyō mondai," *Shigaku zasshi* 43.2 (1932): 215. For the expansion of "guest" keeping privileges in the fourth century, see Chiang Fu-ya, "Tung-Chin Nan-ch'ao te ta-t'u-ti so-yu-chih," *Chiang-hai hsüeh-k'an* 1992.2: 117.

129. Shen Yüeh, *Sung-shu* 54.1537.

130. As Ho Ch'ang-ch'ün writes, "You can see that the Southern dynasties and Northern dynasties uniformly, from the Sun-Wu [kingdom] on, had systems of public land for the distribution of fields on the basis of population" (*Feng-chien te kuo-yu t'u-ti chih*, p. 28).

131. *Wen-hsien t'ung-k'ao* 2.38.

132. Balazs, *Chinese Civilization*, p. 105.

133. T'ang Ch'ang-ju, for example, uses the comment of a court official, which he dates after the promulgation of the *chan-t'ien* law, to the effect that there were no fixed limits on the size of people's fields, as evidence that even the government acknowledged the ineffectiveness of the law (*Wei-Chin Nan-Pei-ch'ao shih lun-ts'ung*, p. 45).

134. Kwang-chih Chang, *Shang Civilization* (New Haven: Yale University Press, 1980).

135. Ikeda On, "T'ang Household Registers and Related Documents," in *Perspectives on the T'ang*, edited by Arthur F. Wright and Denis Twitchett (New Haven: Yale University Press, 1973), p. 123. Kao Min seems to concur in this assessment (*T'u-ti chih-tu yen-chiu*, p. 157).

136. Ikeda acknowledges that the system was "subject to wide variation and modification in actual practice" during the T'ang ("T'ang Household Registers," p. 49), and Balazs was still skeptical in 1954, suggesting that "the rights to allocation of land were often no more than a legal fiction" (*Chinese Civilization*, pp. 114–116). The very examples Balazs gives, however, indicate that the system was at least partially effective. Recent studies from the People's Republic of China support the hypothesis that the *chün-t'ien* system really was implemented, although there remains considerable disagreement as to the exact extent and manner of its implementation. See T'ung Ch'ao, "Chung-kuo ta-lu," pp. 118–119; Hou Hsü-tung, "Chin-nien li-yung Tun-huang T'u-lu-fan wen-shu yen-chiu Wei-Chin Nan-Pei-ch'ao shih kai-k'uang," *Chung-kuo shih yen-chiu tung-t'ai* 1992.5: 8.

137. Balazs, *Chinese Civilization*, p. 105.

138. Ibid., p. 116.

139. Kao Min, "Wei-Chin Nan-Pei-ch'ao fu-i huo-mien te tui-hsiang yü t'iao-chien," *Chiang-Han lun-t'an* 1990.6: 62–63.

140. *Chin-shu* 26.790–791.

141. Chin Kuan-t'ao and Liu Ch'ing-feng, *Hsing-sheng yü wei-chi*, p. 241. These figures are highly speculative but suggestive nonetheless.

142. Wu Tse, "Liu-ch'ao she-hui ching-chi cheng-chih te fa-chan kuei-lü ho t'e-tien," *Su-chou ta-hsüeh hsüeh-pao: Che-she-pan* 1990.3: 87–88.

143. Kao Min, *T'u-ti chih-tu yen-chiu*, pp. 176–177.

144. Pan Ku, *Han-shu* 72.895.

145. Bodde, "Feudalism," p. 91.

146. On the land tax, see Wu Tse, "Liu-ch'ao," p. 88.

147. Yen Chih-t'ui (c. 531–591), *Yen-shih chia-hsün* (reprint; Taipei:

T'ai-wan chung-hua shu-chü, 1974), 4.21b. For a translation, see Teng Ssu-yü, *Family Instructions for the Yen Clan: Yen-Shih Chia-Hsün* (Leiden: E.J.Brill, 1968), pp. 116–117.

148. *Sui-shu,* quoted in Okazaki Fumio, *Tsūshi,* p. 567.

149. *Chin-shu* 38.1132.

150. Chung Hsing, (c. 1600) ed., *Chin wen kuei* (reprint; Taipei: T'ai-wan shang-wu yin-shu-kuan, 1973), 4.13a.

151. *Ch'üan Chin wen* 80.1921.

152. De Crespigny, *Generals of the South,* p. 286.

153. This is the analysis of Liu Shu-fen, "Liu-ch'ao Chien-k'ang te ching-chi chi-ch'u," *Shih-huo yüeh-k'an* 12.10–11 (1983): 14.

154. Ch'en Shou, *San-kuo chih* 48.1158.

155. Li Yen-shou, *Nan-shih* 51.1278.

156. *Chin-shu* 94.2438.

157. *Ch'üan Chin wen* 80.1921. This must have been something of a Confucian truism. For nearly identical expressions, see Pan Ku, *Han-shu* 24.249, 72.895; Ch'en Shou, *San-kuo chih* 48.1158.

158. Mao Kuo-chin, *Chin-shih shan* 8.2a.

159. Wang Chung-lo, *Wei-Chin Nan-Pei-ch'ao shih,* p. 488.

160. *Sui-shu,* quoted in Hung Mai, *Jung-chai sui-pi,* hsü-pi, 1.221–222.

161. Chang Hua (232–300), *Po-wu chih* (reprint; Taipei: T'ai-wan chung-hua shu-chü, 1983), 1.2a. Straughair doubts the authenticity of the present text of this book (*Chang Hua,* p. 72, note 109).

162. The growth of shipping in the South Seas region during this period is surveyed in Li Tung-hua, "Han-Sui chien Chung-kuo Nan-hai chiao-t'ung chih yen-pien," *Shih-hsüeh chi-k'an* 11: especially page 50.

163. See Han Kuo-p'an, *Shih-kang,* p. 210.

164. Seng Yu, *Ch'u san-tsang chi-chi* 450.53a.

165. Elvin, *Pattern,* pp. 113–199.

166. Robert Temple, *The Genius of China: 3,000 Years of Science, Discovery, and Invention* (New York: Simon and Schuster, 1986). The greatest burst of Chinese technical creativity, as tabulated here, fell between the fourth century B.C. and the third century A.D., when fifty-six of the hundred discoveries cataloged in this book were made.

167. Mori Mikisaburō, *Seishin,* p. 239.

168. See Huang Cheng-fan and T'ien Tse-pin, "Tung-Chin men-fa cheng-chih san-lun," *Su-chou ta-hsüeh hsüeh-pao: Che-she-pan* 1990.1: 103.

4: The Institutional Machinery of Literati Ascendance

1. Yen Chih-t'ui, *Yen-shih chia-hsün* 3.7b, translated in Teng Ssu-yü, *Family Instructions,* p. 61. Compare *Analects* 14:25: "In ancient times, men learned with a view to their own improvement. Nowadays, men learn with a view to the approbation of others" (Legge, *Four Books,* p. 329).

2. In the eleventh century Shen Kua explicitly compared the status

distribution of the later Northern dynasties to the Indian caste system. See Denis Twitchett, "The Composition of the T'ang Ruling Class: New Evidence from Tunhuang," in *Perspectives on the T'ang*, edited by Arthur F. Wright and Denis Twitchett (New Haven: Yale University Press, 1973), pp. 54–56.

3. Mao Han-kuang, *Chung-ku she-hui*, pp. 33–35, 41.

4. For the formation of the literati class, see ibid., pp. 78–84.

5. Ebrey, *Aristocratic Families*, p. 4.

6. Patricia Ebrey, "The Economic and Social History of Later Han," in *The Cambridge History of China*, vol. 1: *The Ch'in and Han Empires, 221 B.C.– A.D. 220*, edited by Denis Twitchett and Michael Loewe (Cambridge: Cambridge University Press, 1986), pp. 643–646. Ebrey charts the diffusion of Confucianism among "ordinary" Chinese in "The Chinese Family and the Spread of Confucian Values," in *The East Asian Region: Confucian Heritage and its Modern Adaptation*, edited by Gilbert Rozman (Princeton: Princeton University Press, 1991).

7. Donald J. Munro, *The Concept of Man in Early China* (Stanford: Stanford University Press, 1969), pp. 115–116.

8. Ko Hung, *Pao p'u tzu* (c. 317; Taipei: T'ai-wan Chung-hua shu-chü, 1984), wai-p'ien, 15.4b. See also Jay Sailey, *The Master Who Embraces Simplicity: A Study of the Philosopher Ko Hung, A.D. 283–343* (San Francisco: Chinese Materials Center, 1978), p. 102.

9. Ku Yen-wu, *Jih-chih lu chi-shih* (17th century; Shanghai: Shang-hai ku-chi ch'u-pan-she, 1985), 13.11b.

10. H. G. Creel, "The Eclectics of Han Thought," in *The Making of China: Main Themes in Premodern Chinese History*, edited by Chun-shu Chang (Englewood Cliffs: Prentice-Hall, 1975), pp. 145–148.

11. Hirai Masashi, "Kandai ni okeru juka kanryō no kugyō-sō e no shinjun," *Rekishi ni okeru minshū to bunka—Sakai Tadao sensei koki shukuga kinen ronshū* (Tokyo: Kokusho kankokai, 1982), pp. 63–64. For the rise of the Han literati class, see also Hsü Cho-yün, "The Roles of the Literati and of Regionalism in the Fall of the Han Dynasty," in *The Collapse of Ancient States and Civilizations*, edited by Norman Yoffee and George L. Cowgill (Tucson: University of Arizona Press, 1988), pp. 176–187.

12. Higashi Shinji, "Go-Kan jidai no senkyo to chihō shakai," *Tōyōshi kenkyū* 46.2 (1987): 44. Higashi recognizes that this statement needs some qualification, and he adds on p. 45:

Of course, it probably cannot be denied that such things as economic power, the area of fields and land that one owns, the quantity of family members, and the number of servants and retainers had a great influence on the formation of this order, especially at the county level; but, in Later Han society, where the Confucian values system was firmly in operation, it can be supposed that the assessment of character and family status at the commandery and central levels was accomplished strictly according to the level of Confucian education and ability.

13. Something of the complexity of this subject can be appreciated by reading the recent work of Patricia Ebrey, "Toward a Better Understanding of the Late Han Upper Class," in *State and Society in Early Medieval China*, edited by Albert E. Dien (Stanford: Stanford University Press, 1990).

14. Hsing I-t'ien, "Tung-Han hsiao-lien te shen-fen pei-ching," in *Ti erh chieh Chung-kuo she-hui ching-chi shih yen-t'ao-hui lun-wen-chi*, edited by Hsü Cho-yün et al. (Taipei: Han-hsüeh yen-chiu tzu-liao chi fu-wu chung-hsin, 1983), p. 36.

15. Hsü Lien-ta and Lou Ching, "Han-T'ang k'o-chü i-t'ung lun," *Li-shih yen-chiu* 1990.5. For the Han dynasty examinations, see also Sailey, *Master*, pp. 393–395. On the late imperial examination system, see Ichisada Miyazaki, *China's Examination Hell: The Civil Service Examinations of Imperial China*, translated by Conrad Schirokauer (1963; New Haven: Yale University Press, 1981).

16. Yü Shih-nan (558–638) ed., *Pei-t'ang shu-ch'ao* (reprint; Taipei: Hung-yeh shu-chü, 1974), 79.348. Ko Hung (283–343) vigorously extolled the virtues of an examination system, while making it clear that the system had lapsed in the south in his own day. See Sailey, *Master*, pp. 97–105.

17. A lucid description of the Later Han selection system is available in English in Rafe de Crespigny, "The Recruitment System of the Imperial Bureaucracy of the Late Han," *Chung Chi Journal* 6.1 (1966). A similar treatment in Chinese can be found in Han Fu-chih, "Tung-Han te hsüan-chü," *Kuo-li T'ai-wan ta-hsüeh li-shih hsüeh-hsi hsüeh-pao* 4 (1977).

18. Fan Yeh, *Hou-Han shu* 4.176.

19. See Fan Shou-k'ang, *Wei-Chin chih ch'ing-t'an*, Shih-ti hsiao ts'ung-shu (Shanghai: Shang-wu yin-shu-kuan, 1936), p. 3.

20. Ch'en Shou, *San-kuo chih* 21.623.

21. Ch'ü T'ung-tsu, *Han Social Structure*, edited by Jack L. Dull (Seattle: University of Washington Press, 1972), p. 180.

22. Jack L. Dull, "The Evolution of Government in China," p. 66.

23. Yang Lien-sheng, "Great Families of Eastern Han," in *The Making of China: Main Themes in Premodern Chinese History*, edited by Chun-shu Chang (Englewood Cliffs: Prentice-Hall, 1975), p. 122.

24. Hsing I-t'ien, "Tung-Han," pp. 20–24, 37.

25. Fan Yeh, *Hou-Han shu* 67.2185. Ko Hung writes that in the days of emperors Ling and Hsien of Han (168–220), "eunuchs were in authority, and a crowd of villains held power, endangering the honest and virtuous" (*Pao p'u tzu*, wai-p'ien, 15.2a). Sailey regards such comments as

veiled criticism of the situation in Ko Hung's own time (*Master*, pp. 91, 444), but they also reflect the early medieval memory of the last days of Han. The latter has been vividly confirmed by Martin J. Powers with visual evidence from late Han mortuary art, illustrating the clash between the classical themes, simplicity, symmetry, and severity of the literati tombs with the obvious sensuality of the tombs of the eunuch-backed nouveaux riches (see *Art and Political Expression in Early China*).

26. Fan Yeh, *Hou-Han shu* 67.2187. See also T'ao Ch'ien (365–427), "Ch'ün fu lu," in *Pi-chi hsiao-shuo ta-kuan san-pien* (reprint; Taipei: Hsin-hsing shu-chü, 1974), p. 886. Interestingly, the terms "pure stream" *(ch'ing-liu)*, "pure criticism" *(ch'ing-i)*, and "public opinion" *(yü-lun)* were all reinvoked by a reform movement in the middle and lower ranks of the metropolitan bureaucracy at the end of the nineteenth century. See Mary Backus Rankin, "'Public Opinion' and Political Power: *Qingyi* in Late Nineteenth Century China," *Journal of Asian Studies* 41.3 (1982).

27. See Tanigawa Michio, "Kaiko," p. 215.

28. Ebrey, *Aristocratic Families*, p. 17.

29. Sato Tatsuro, "Sō-Gi Bun, Mei tei ki no seikai to meizokusō no dōkō—Chin Gun, Shiba I o chūshin ni," *Tōyōshi-kenkyū*, 52.1 (1993).

30. The word "womb" is borrowed from Yoshikawa Tadao, *Rikuchō seishin-shi kenkyū* (Kyoto: Dōhōsha, 1984), p. 185. Many scholars locate the genesis of medieval literati class self-consciousness in this period. Tanigawa Michio, for example, summarizing a main theme in Kawa-katsu Yoshio's early work, writes, "The public opinion that supported the political legitimacy of Pure Stream power qualified them [the heirs of late Han Pure Stream] as worthy of being rulers in the Wei, Chin, and after" (*Tankyū*, p. 259).

31. See Tsuzuki Akiko, "Nanjin kanmon, kanjin no shūkyōteki sōzō-ryoku ni tsuite—*Shinkō* o megutte," *Tōyōshi kenkyū* 47.2 (1988): 37.

32. Yü Ying-shih, "Han-Chin chih chi shih chih hsin tzu-chüeh yü hsin ssu-ch'ao," in *Shih yü Chung-kuo wen-hua* (Chung-kuo wen-hua shih ts'ung-shu; Shanghai: Shang-hai jen-min ch'u-pan-she, 1987), pp. 288, 307.

33. Ueda Sanae, "Kizokuteki kansei no seiritsu—shōkan no yurai to sono seikaku," in *Chūgoku chūsei-shi kenkyū*, edited by Utsunomiya Kiyo-yoshi (1970; Tokyo: Tōkai daigaku shuppansha, 1980), pp. 103–104; Watanabe Shinichirō, "Shō, aruiwa ni-shichi seiki Chūgoku ni okeru ichi *ideorogii*—keitai to kokka," *Kyōto fu-ritsu daigaku gakujutsu hōkoku, jinbun* 31 (1979).

34. Ch'en Shou, *San-kuo chih* 12.381.

35. Li Fang, *T'ai-p'ing yü-lan* 265.1372.

36. An excellent study of this system, available in French, is Donald Holzman, "Les débuts du système médiéval de choix et de classement des fonctionnaires: Les neuf categories et l'impartial et juste," in

Mélanges publiés par l'Institut des hautes études chinoises, vol. 1 (Paris: University of Paris, 1957). In Japanese, Miyazaki Ichisada's *Kyūhin kanjinhō no kenkyū: Kakyo zenshi* (Kyoto: Tōyōshi-kenkyū-kai, 1956) has attained the stature of a classic. Chinese-language studies are too numerous to review here. In English see, for example, Sailey, *Master,* pp. 399–407.

37. See Holzman, "Système médiéval," p. 394.

38. Ch'en Shou, *San-kuo chih* 1.32.

39. See Yoshimori Kensuke's article "San-ku kei-ji."

40. *Chin-shu* 45.1273.

41. See Mao Han-kuang, *Chung-ku she-hui,* pp. 9–10.

42. Shen Yüeh, *Sung-shu* 94.2301.

43. Ou-yang Hsiu, *Hsin T'ang-shu* 199.5677.

44. Patricia Ebrey writes that the most important effect of the Nine Ranks system in transforming the old Han great families into an "aristocracy" was the "thoroughness" of the rankings in establishing a formal, universal, hierarchy (*Aristocratic Families,* p. 18).

45. Chao I, *Nien-erh shih cha-chi* 12.253.

46. Ou-yang Hsiu, *Hsin T'ang-shu* 199.5677. The compilation of family genealogies became a significant literary activity beginning at the end of the fourth century, and it marks a milestone in the growth of aristocratic consciousness. See David Johnson, *Medieval Chinese Oligarchy,* p. 34 and passim.

47. *Chin-shu* 3.50.

48. James Legge, trans., *The Li Ki,* Sacred Books of the East, (Oxford: The Clarendon Press, 1885), vol. 27, p. 90.

49. Kamiya Noriko, "Shin jidai ni okeru irei shingi—sono genreishugi-teki seikaku," *Tōyō gakuhō* 67.3–4 (1986): 49. Chu Tsung-pin studies the convergence of Confucian ideals and the legal system during the Chin dynasty in "Lüeh-lun Chin-lü chih 'ju-chia-hua.' "

50. See Benjamin E. Wallacker, "Chang Fei's Preface to the Chin Code of Law," *T'oung Pao* 72.4–5 (1986): 253–254.

51. Wolfram Eberhard, *Conquerors and Rulers: Social Forces in Mediaeval China* (Leiden: E. J. Brill, 1952), p. 15.

52. Tu Yu, *T'ung-tien* 88.482. The incident is discussed in Ko Chien-p'ing, "Chia-t'ing lun-ch'ang," p. 73.

53. Liu Ch'ien-chih, "Chin-chi," in *Chin-chi chi-pen,* edited by T'ang Ch'iu (fifth century; Kuang-ya shu-chü ts'ung-shu, n.d.), p. 16b.

54. *Chin-shu* 90.2333.

55. See Nakamura Keiji, "'Shi-sho kubetsu' shōron—Nanchō kizokusei e no ichi shiten," *Shigaku zasshi* 88.2 (1979): 7. In the late fifth century Shen Yüeh brought an official accusation against Wang Yüan for arranging the marriage of his daughter beneath *shih* status. See Hsiao T'ung, *Wen-hsüan* 40.559–561.

56. See Okazaki Fumio, *Tsūshi,* pp. 590, 594–595.

57. Tu Yu, *T'ung-tien* 3.22.

58. Hsiao T'ung, *Wen-hsüan* 49.691.

59. *Chin-shu* 70.1871.

60. The current text of the *Chin-shu* (15.455) lists Nan-hsiang under Shun-yang Commandery and gives it a population of 20,100 households.

61. Hung Mai, *Jung-chai sui-pi* 11.145.

62. Yang Shang-hsi, quoted in Ssu-ma Kuang, *Tzu-chih t'ung-chien chin-chu*, vol. 9, 175.758–759.

5: Literati Culture

1. See, for example, Donald Holzman, *La vie et la pensée de Hi K'ang (223–262 Ap. J.-C.)* (Leiden: E. J. Brill, 1957), p. 77.

2. *Chin-shu* 14.414–415.

3. Hans Bielenstein, "The Census of China During the Period 2–742 A.D.," *Bulletin of the Museum of Far Eastern Antiquities* 19 (1947): 146, 154; Earl H. Pritchard, "Thoughts on the Historical Development of the Population of China," *Journal of Asian Studies* 23.1 (1963): 16–17. See also Hou Wai-lü, "Feng-chien she-hui," pp. 28–29.

4. *Chin-shu* 26.791. Ts'ai Hsüeh-hai, for example, counts at least 300,000 deaths resulting from the Wars of the Eight Princes in 291–306. See "Hsi-Chin chung-tsu pien-luan hsi-lun," *Kuo-li pien-i-kuan kuan-k'an* 15.2 (1986): 55.

5. Evidence for bacteriological infection in medieval China has not been thoroughly sorted out yet, but William H. McNeill offers some general observations in *Plagues and Peoples* (Garden City: Anchor Press, 1976), p. 118. For a specific example, see James R. Ware, trans., *Alchemy, Medicine, and Religion in the China of A.D. 320: The Nei P'ien of Ko Hung* (New York: Dover Publications, 1966), p. 159.

6. Sakuma Yoshinari, *Gi-Shin Nambokuchō suiri-shi kenkyū* (Tokyo: Kaimei shoin, 1980), p. 142.

7. These averages were obtained by simply adding the total ages together and dividing by the number of individuals. The raw data come from Chiang Liang-fu, ed., *Li-tai jen-wu nien li-pei chuan tsung-piao* (Hong Kong: Chung-hua shu-chü, 1976), pp. 14–21, 43–56.

8. Shen Yüeh, *Sung-shu* 93.2293–2294. A comparison with the medieval European quadrivium of arithmetic, music, geometry, and astronomy provides an interesting illustration of the humanistic orientation of China's traditional thought.

9. See Paul Demiéville, "Philosophy and Religion from Han to Sui," in *The Cambridge History of China*, vol. 1: *The Ch'in and Han Empires, 221 B.C.–A.D. 220*, edited by Denis Twitchett and Michael Loewe (Cambridge: Cambridge University Press, 1986), pp. 812–813; Sailey, *Master*, p. xvii. Timoteus Pokora ascribes the same eclectic tendencies to Yang Hsiung,

Huan T'an, and Wang Ch'ung, and associates all of them with the so-called Old Text school. ("The Life of Huan T'an," *Archiv Orientální* 31 [1963]: 40, 572).

10. See, for example, Mou Jun-sun, *Lun Wei-Chin i-lai chih ch'ung-shang t'an-pien chi ch'i ying-hsiang* (Hong Kong: Chinese University Press, 1966), p. 17 and passim.

11. See Liu Kuei-chieh, "Hsüan-hsüeh ssu-hsiang yü pan-jo ssu-hsiang chih chiao-jung," *Kuo-li pien-i-kuan kuan-k'an* 9.1 (1980): 109. The *Lun-heng* has been translated by Alfred Forke under the title *Lun-heng: Miscellaneous Essays of Wang Ch'ung* (reprint; New York: Paragon Book Gallery, 1962).

12. Sun Tao-sheng, "Ch'ing-t'an ch'i-yüan k'ao," *Tung-fang tsa-chih* 42.3 (1946): 20–21. See also Chang Hua, *Po-wu chih* 4.3b.

13. Forke, trans., *Lun-heng*, vol. 2, p. 368.

14. Tung Chung-shu, *Ch'un-ch'iu fan-lu*, Kuo-hsüeh chi-pen ts'ung-shu (2nd century B.C.; Taipei: T'ai-wan shang-wu yin-shu-kuan, 1968), 17.279. The term rendered here as "Heaven" *(t'ien)* appears to have originated in a religious context, possibly referring to "the sky in the very literal sense of the direction taken by the ashes of people burnt upon a pyre," and evolved from there into a somewhat indeterminate point of appeal for the entire Confucian philosophical agenda. See Robert Eno, *The Confucian Creation of Heaven: Philosophy and the Defense of Ritual Mastery* (Albany: State University of New York Press, 1990), pp. 2, 4, 23–28, 181–189. In the fourth century Lo Han wrote: "What is Heaven? It is a general name for all things" (*Ch'üan Chin wen* 131.2211).

15. Pokora suggests that Huan T'an could have exerted a significant influence on Wang Ch'ung ("Life," p. 9). For Huan's critique of teleology, see Pokora, *Hsin-lun (New Treatise) and Other Writings by Huan T'an (43 B.C.–28 A.D.)*, Michigan Papers in Chinese Studies, No. 20 (Ann Arbor: University of Michigan, Center for Chinese Studies, 1975), pp. xviii–xx, 50–51.

16. Huan T'an, *Huan tzu hsin-lun* (1st century A.D.; Taipei: T'ai-wan Chung-hua shu-chü, 1976), 26a. See Pokora, "Life," p. 538; *New Treatise*, pp. 80–81.

17. Pokora, "Life," pp. 575–576.

18. An excellent discussion of these aspects of Yen Tsun's thought can be found in Chu Jui-k'ai, *Liang-Han ssu-hsiang shih* (Shanghai: Shang-hai ku-chi ch'u-pan-she, 1989), pp. 204–206. I am grateful to Alan Berkowitz for help with sources concerning this fascinating figure.

19. Feng Yu-lan, *Chung-kuo che-hsüeh shih hsin-pien* (2 vols.; Peking: Jen-min ch'u-pan-she, 1964), vol. 2, pp. 245, 306; vol. 1, pp. 264, 266–267, 293. On the "naturalistic" philosophy of Lao Tzu, see Ch'en Ku-ying, *Lao Tzu: Text, Notes, and Comments*, translated by Rhett Y. W. Young and Roger T. Ames (San Francisco: Chinese Materials Center, 1977), p. 45

20. See Mou Tsung-san, *Ts'ai-hsing yü hsüan-li* (Taipei: Hsüeh-sheng shu-chü, 1975), pp. 6–7.

21. Michael Nylan and Nathan Sivin, "The First Neo-Confucianism: An Introduction to Yang Hsiung's 'Canon of Supreme Mystery' (T'ai hsuan ching, c. 4 B.C.)," in *Chinese Ideas about Nature and Society: Studies in Honour of Derk Bodde*, edited by Charles Le Blanc and Susan Blader (Hong Kong: Hong Kong University Press, 1987), p. 52.

22. Feng Yu-lan, *Hsin-pien*, vol. 1, pp. 55–60.

23. Wang, for example, described Taoist longevity exercises as "false." See Wang Ch'ung, *Lun-heng* (A.D. 82; Taipei: T'ai-wan Chung-hua shu-chü, 1981), 7.10b. For Yang Hsiung and Huan T'an, see Chang Hua, *Po-wu chih* 4.1a.

24. Sailey, *Master,* pp. xiv–xx.

25. *Chuang tzu tsuan-chien*, edited by Ch'ien Mu (revised ed.; Hong Kong: Tung-nan yin-wu ch'u-pan-she, 1956), nei-p'ien 6, p. 47.

26. *T'ai-p'ing ching ho-chiao*, edited by Wang Ming (Peking: Chung-hua shu-chü, 1960), 114.620. B. J. Mansvelt Beck concludes that the *T'ai-p'ing ching* is indeed "a genuine Later Han text" with some possible later alterations ("The Date of the *Taiping Jing*," *T'oung Pao* 66.4–5 [1980]: 175–176, 180). For the example from the Wei court, see Ch'en Shou, *San-kuo chih* 29.805, note 1.

27. Ssu-ma Ch'ien, *Shih-chi* 28.1369: "Tsou Yen made the succession of yin and yang apparent to the feudal lords, but the *fang-shih* on the coasts of Yen and Ch'i transmitted his arts without being able to understand them."

28. Juan Chi, in the third century, became the epitome of this kind of apolitical caution. See Mather, *Shih-shuo Hsin-yü*, p. 9, no. 15. The sequence of events is sketched in Ch'en Yin-k'o, "T'ao Yüan-ming chih ssu-hsiang yü ch'ing-t'an chih kuan-hsi," in *Ch'en Yin-k'o hsien-sheng wen-shih lun-chi* (1945; Hong Kong: Wen-wen ch'u-pan-she, 1972), vol. 1, p. 382.

29. See Donald Holzman, "Les sept sages de la forêt des bambous et la société de leur temps," *T'oung Pao* 44.4–5 (1956): 326–327.

30. Chin Kuan-t'ao and Liu Ch'ing-feng, "Hsing-sheng yü wei-chi," p. 229.

31. See Richard Mather, "The Controversy over Conformity and Naturalness during the Six Dynasties," *History of Religions* 9.2–3 (1969–70): 160; *Shih-shuo Hsin-yü*, p. xvii. Roger Ames favors "coherence" as a translation for *li*, instead of the more conventional "principle" (personal communication).

32. Fan Ning believes the political-intellectual controversy between the school of Names and that of Nature ended under the reign of the Ssu-ma ("Lun Wei-Chin shih-tai chih-shih fen-tzu te ssu-hsiang fen-hua chi ch'i she-hui ken-yüan," *Li-shih yen-chiu* 1955.4: 122–123). Indeed,

Brook Ziporyn thinks that the theoretical "harmonization of these two realms was high on the *xuanxue* [*hsüan-hsüeh*] agenda from the beginning." See "The Self-so and Its Traces in the Thought of Guo Xiang," *Philosophy East and West* 43.3 (1993): 511.

33. Li Heng, *Shao-hsing fu-chih* 63.1508.

34. Ch'en Shou, *San-kuo chih* 10.320, note 2.

35. Teng Ts'an (fourth century), "Chin-chi," in *Chin-chi chi-pen,* edited by T'ang Ch'iu (Kuang-ya shu-chü ts'ung-shu, n.d.), p. 6a.

36. Mather, *Shih-shuo Hsin-yü,* p. 372, no. 2, note 1; "Mei-tzu hsin-lun," p. 1a, in Ma Kuo-han, ed., *Yü-han shan-fang chi i-shu* (Ch'u-nan hsiang-yüan-t'ang, 1884); Teng Ts'an, "Chin chi," p. 5b. For Chang Han, see *Chin-shu* 92.2384.

37. Legge, *Li Ki,* vol. 27, pp. 12, 61, 414.

38. For the place of Confucianism in *hsüan-hsüeh* thought, see Horiike Nobuo, "Keikō ni okeru shinkō to shakai—Shō Shū to no 'yōjōron' ronsō o chūshin toshite," in *Rekishi ni okeru minshū to bunka—Sakai Tadao sensei koki shukuga kinen ronshū* (Tokyo: Kokusho kankokai, 1982), p. 115; Liu Hsiu-shih, "Wei-Chin ssu-hsiang lun," in *Wei-Chin ssu-hsiang: chia-pien wu-chung* (reprint; Taipei: Li-jen shu-chü, 1984), p. 22.

39. Chih Tun, "Shih-chia wen-fo hsiang tsan ping hsü," in *Chih Tun chi,* Shao-wu Hsü-shih ts'ung-shu, edited by Hsü Kan (Hangchow: 1884), 2.3a.

40. See T'ang Ch'ang-ju, "Wei-Chin hsüan-hsüeh chih hsing-ch'eng chi ch'i fa-chan," in *Wei-Chin Nan-Pei-ch'ao shih lun-ts'ung,* p. 320.

41. Mou Tsung-san, *Ts'ai-hsing yü hsüan-li,* pp. 244–245.

42. See T'ang Yung-t'ung, "Wei-Chin ssu-hsiang te fa-chan," *Hsüeh-yüan* 1.3 (1947): 3–4.

43. Ch'en Shou, *San-kuo chih* 10.319, note 2.

44. Shu Hsi, "Hsüan-chü shih," in Chung Hsing, ed., *Chin wen kuei,* 5.18a. For an expression of a similar opinion by Hsi K'ang, see Robert G. Henricks, trans., *Philosophy and Argumentation in Third-Century China: The Essays of Hsi K'ang* (Princeton: Princeton University Press, 1983), p. 51. For yet another contemporary example, see Lu Ching (247–277), "Tien-yü," pp. 2a–b, in Ma kuo-han, ed., *Yü-han shan-fang chi i-shu.*

45. Yang Hsiung, "T'ai-hsüan fu," in *Ch'üan Han wen* 52.408.

46. See Lu Chi, "Hao-shih fu hsü," in Chung Hsing, ed., *Chin wen kuei* 4.16a.

47. Chung Hsing, *Chin wen kuei,* 5.17a–19a. Also *Ch'üan Chin wen* 87.1964.

48. Seng Yu (435–518), *Hung ming chi* (reprint; Taipei: T'ai-wan chung-hua shu-chü, 1983), 2.14a.

49. "T'u-shan hui-chi shih," preface, in Chih Tun, *Chih Tun chi* 1.3b.

50. "Yung huai shih," no. 4, in Chih Tun, *Chih Tun chi* 1.2a.

51. Li Fang, ed., *T'ai-p'ing kuang-chi* (978; Peking: Chung-hua shu-chü, 1981), 8.55–56. See also Kobayashi Masayoshi, "The Celestial Masters under the Eastern Jin and Liu-Song Dynasties," *Taoist Resources* 3.2 (1992): 17, 21, 23–24.

52. Hsü Yün-lin (fl. c. 1616), ed., *Yü-chih-t'ang t'an-hui* (Ch'ien-yüan ts'ang-pan, 1875), 17.21a.

53. See Anna Seidel, "Taoist Messianism," *Numen: International Review for the History of Religions* 31.2 (1984): 173.

54. Tsuzuki Akiko, "Sōzōryoku," p. 49.

55. See Tanigawa Michio, *Local "Community"*, p. 96.

56. A. C. Graham, "'Being' in Western Philosophy Compared with *Shih/Fei* and *Yu/Wu* in Chinese Philosophy," *Asia Major,* new series 7.1–2 (1959): 81, 98. Reprinted in revised form in A. C. Graham, *Studies in Chinese Philosophy and Philosophical Literature* (Albany: State University of New York Press, 1990); See especially p. 324.

57. See Chu Jui-k'ai, *Liang-Han,* p. 204.

58. A. C. Graham, *Studies,* pp. 343–345, and *Disputers of the Tao: Philosophical Argument in Ancient China* (La Salle: Open Court, 1989), p. 411. Roger T. Ames, Chan Sin-wai, and Mau-sang Ng, eds., *Interpreting Culture through Translation: A Festschrift for D. C. Lau* (Hong Kong: The Chinese University Press, 1991), p. xix.

59. Aurelius Augustinus (354–430), *The Confessions and Letters of St. Augustin,* vol. 1 of *A Select Library of the Nicene and Post-Nicene Fathers of the Christian Church,* edited by Philip Schaff (New York: Charles Scribner's Sons, 1902), book 11, chapter 5, p. 165.

60. Roger Ames, "Introduction," in *Interpreting Culture through Translation,* p. xxiv.

61. Ariane Rump and Wing-tsit Chan, trans., *Commentary on the Lao Tzu, by Wang Pi,* Society for Asian and Comparative Philosophy (Honolulu: University Press of Hawaii, 1979), p. 1.

62. D. C. Lau, trans., *Lao Tzu: Tao Te Ching* (Harmondsworth: Penguin Books, 1963), p. 101.

63. See Alan K. L. Chan, *Two Visions of the Way: A Study of the Wang Pi and the Ho-Shang Kung Commentaries on the Lao-Tzu* (Albany: State University of New York Press, 1991), pp. 45–68. The quote is from p. 47. In contrast, Wing-tsit Chan argues that unlike ordinary Chinese, Taoists conceived of *wu* as more than just "the absence of something"—and that in the hands of Wang Pi *wu* became "the ultimate of all, or pure being." See Wing-tsit Chan, trans., *The Way of Lao Tzu (Tao-te ching)* (New York: Macmillan Publishing Company, 1963), pp. 7–8, 23.

64. Tao An (312–385), quoted in Ch'en Shu-liang, *Liu-ch'ao yen-shui, Ta wen-hsüeh shih-kuan ts'ung-shu* (Peking: Hsien-tai ch'u-pan-she, 1990), p. 35.

65. *Chuang tzu tsuan-chien,* wai-p'ien 15, p. 181. In a variation on this

theme, Ch'ü Yüan (c. 340–278 B.C.) allegedly asks: "Who handed down the stories of the beginning of antiquity? How could heaven and earth be examined before they had form?" Ch'ü Yüan and Liu Tsung-yüan (773–819), *T'ien-wen t'ien-tui chu* (Shanghai: Shang-hai jen-min ch'u-pan-she, 1973), p. 87 and notes, pp. 1–2.

66. On the antiquity of the *Lieh tzu*, see Feng Yu-lan, *Chung-kuo che-hsüeh-shih shih-liao hsüeh, San-sung t'ang ch'üan-chi*, vol. 6 (1962; Ho-nan jen-min ch'u-pan-she, 1989), pp. 420–425. A. C. Graham concludes firmly that the extant *Lieh tzu* was composed sometime after 285 as "a deliberate forgery" ("The Date and Composition of the Liehtzyy," *Asia Major*, new series 8.2 [1961]: 197).

67. Chang Chang (c. 370), ed., *Lieh tzu* (reprint; Taipei: T'ai-wan chung-hua shu-chü, 1982), 5.1a–b. Translated by A. C. Graham as *The Book of Lieh-tzu: A Classic of the Tao* (1960; New York: Columbia University Press, 1990). I accept Graham's reading of "Hsia Ke" as "Chi of Hsia" (p. 94).

68. Juan Chi, "Ta-Chuang lun," in *Ch'üan San-kuo wen* 45.1311.

69. *Chin-shu* 35.1046.

70. Hsi K'ang, "Yang-sheng lun," in *Ch'üan San-kuo wen* 48.1324.

71. For a discussion of the concept of *ch'i*, see Hu Fu-ch'en, *Wei-Chin shen-hsien tao-chiao: Pao p'u tzu nei-p'ien yen-chiu* (Peking: Jen-min ch'u-pan-she, 1989), pp. 221–223. Yung Sik Kim interprets *ch'i* to be "both the material basis of all the things of the world and the ultimate source of the nonphysical or nonmaterial qualities, including life" and the "spirit" ("Some Aspects of the Concept of *Ch'i* in Chu Hsi," *Philosophy East and West* 34.1 [1984]: 28, 30).

72. This is the discussant's view, which evidently expresses the pre-Buddhist consensus, in Hui Yüan's "Sha-men pu ching wang-che lun" (A.D. 404), in Seng Yu, *Hung ming chi* 5.9a.

73. Yang Ch'üan, "Wu-li lun," p. 6a. The same point is also made in the more famous *Pao p'u tzu*, nei-p'ien, 5.1a. This passage is translated in James R. Ware, *Alchemy*, pp. 98–99.

74. The most striking evidence of traditional Chinese belief in an afterlife is the magnificent tomb erected by the First Emperor of Ch'in. For Ch'in period attitudes, see Wu Hsiao-ch'iang, "*Jih-shu* so chien Ch'in-jen chih sheng-ssu kuan," *Ch'in-ling Ch'in-yung yen-chiu tung-t'ai* 1992, no. 2, especially pp. 21–23.

75. For a cogent analysis of this system of beliefs, see Yü Ying-shih, "'O Soul, Come Back!' A Study in the Changing Conceptions of the Soul and Afterlife in Pre-Buddhist China," *Harvard Journal of Asiatic Studies* 47.2 (1987): 369–378. See also Michael Loewe, *Chinese Ideas of Life and Death: Faith, Myth and Reason in the Han Period (202 B.C.–A.D. 220)* (London: George Allen and Unwin, 1982).

76. Li Yen-shou, *Nan-shih* 57.1421.

77. Yang Ch'üan, "Wu-li lun," p. 4b.

78. Chang Chan, *Lieh tzu* 1.14a.

79. This example is mentioned in *Ts'e-fu yüan-kuei*, edited by Wang Ch'in-jo (c. 1012; Taipei: T'ai-wan chung-hua shu-chü, 1981), 836.9917.

80. "Lai-hsiang chi," in *Ch'u-hsüeh chi*, edited by Hsü Chien (659–729) (reprint; Peking: Chung-hua shu-chü, 1962), 23.549–550. The work is undated, but the title refers to a Chin dynasty place name.

81. Huan T'an, "Hsin-lun hsing-shen," in Seng Yu, *Hung ming chi* 5.5b; Huan T'an, *Huan tzu hsin-lun* 25b; Pokora, *New Treatise*, pp. 76–81. On the modern reconstruction of the *Hsin-lun* from surviving fragments, see Pokora, "Life," pp. 15–16. Pokora rejects the Ssu-pu pei-yao edition (cited here) as inferior and himself prefers to work from the original fragments.

82. For Lieh-tzu's opinion, see Chang Chan, *Lieh tzu* 1.9b. Chuang-tzu's positive attitude toward death is well known.

83. *Chuang tzu tsuan-chien*, wai-p'ien, 10, p. 129.

84. Chang Chan, *Lieh tzu* 1.8a–b, note.

85. See ibid., 1.6a, note.

86. Chih Tun, "Shu-huai shih 2," in *Chih Tun chi* 1.3b.

87. "Yin-yang tzu-jan pien-hua lun," small fragments of which are preserved in *Yü-han shan-fang chi i-shu*, "Kan tzu," p. 2a.

88. Graham, *Book of Lieh-tzu*, pp. 21–22; "Date and Composition," pp. 156–157. Graham observes that *Lieh tzu*'s additions to an earlier chain of transformations in *Chuang tzu* obscure the original "evolutionary sequence," but Graham then concludes, quite correctly, that "in a Taoist context the significance of the idea is not that it explains the [evolutionary] origin of man, but that it shows that there is no absolute difference between one thing and another."

89. *Po-wu chih* 2.1b. On Chang Hua's alleged esoteric knowledge, see Straughair, *Chang Hua*, pp. 20, 58–63.

90. *Pao p'u tzu*, nei-p'ien, 16.1b; translated in Ware, *Alchemy*, p. 263.

91. See Li Chih-yung, ed., *Chung-kuo ch'i-kung shih* (Honan: Ho-nan k'o-hsüeh chi-shu ch'u-pan-she, 1988), pp. 9, 96–102.

92. "Yang-hsing yen-ming lu," in *Tao-tsang yang-sheng shu shih-chung*, edited by Li Shih-hua and Shen Te-hui (Peking: Chung-i ku-chi ch'u-pan-she, 1987), p. 14. Catherine Despeux dates this text to the mid-T'ang but dates the "P'eng tsu ching," which it is evidently quoting here, to the late Han ("Gymnastics: The Ancient Tradition," in *Taoist Meditation and Longevity Techniques*, edited by Livia Kohn [Ann Arbor: Center for Chinese Studies, University of Michigan, 1989], pp. 228–229).

93. *Pao p'u tzu*, nei-p'ien, 15.3a, 7b; translated in Ware, *Alchemy*, pp. 248, 260.

94. See Chu Jui-k'ai, *Liang-Han ssu-hsiang shih*, pp. 116–117. Compare Mencius' statement, centuries earlier, that "the will is commander of

ch'i, and *ch'i* is the substance of the body." *Meng tzu* (third century B.C.), annotated by Chao Ch'i, Ssu-pu ts'ung-k'an (Shanghai: Shang-hai shang-wu yin-shu-kuan, 1929), 3.6a–b.

95. *Ch'üan Chin wen* 48.1733.

96. *T'ai-p'ing ching ho-chiao* 18–34.25. For a discussion of this Taoist religious classic, see Max Kaltenmark, "The Ideology of the T'ai-p'ing ching," in *Facets of Taoism: Essays in Chinese Religion,* edited by Holmes Welch and Anna Seidel (New Haven: Yale University Press, 1979).

97. *T'ai-p'ing ching ho-chiao* 73–85.311.

98. The fusion of traditional Chinese beliefs in the spirit *(shen)* with the Indian Buddhist belief in reincarnation *(samsara)* resulted, by the early fifth century, in the idea of a spiritual "true-self" that was identical to the "Buddha-nature" within everyone. This sequence is sketched out in Richard Mather, *The Poet Shen Yüeh,* p. 142.

99. Tsung Ping, "Ming-fo lun," in Seng Yu, *Hung ming chi* 2.4a.

100. See Murakami Yoshimi, *Chūgoku no sennin—hōbokushi no shisō* (Kyoto: Heirakuji shōten, 1956), pp. 143–144.

101. *Pao p'u tzu,* nei-p'ien, 1.2b. Compare the rather different translation by Ware: "Truly the evocations of logical situations are as closely knitted to their sources as shadows and echoes. Being artifice and unreal, all these activities, when ended, leave a void" *(Alchemy,* p. 30).

102. Wang Pi, *Lun-yü shih-i.* This text is no longer extant, and the passage has been recovered from quotations elsewhere. See Liu Hsiu-shih, "Wei-Chin ssu-hsiang lun," p. 24.

103. Chang Chan, *Lieh tzu,* preface, 1b.

104. James Legge, trans., *The Yi King,* Sacred Books of the East (1882; Delhi: Motilal Banarsidass, 1966), vol. 16, p. 423. "Chou i," in *Shih-san ching chu-shu,* collated by Juan Yüan (1764–1849) (Taipei: Ta-hua shu-chü, 1982), 8.93.

105. See Huan T'an, *Huan tzu hsin-lun* 12a–b.

106. See Nylan and Sivin, "The First Neo-Confucianism," pp. 42, 59.

107. See Howard L. Goodman, "Exegetes and Exegeses of the Book of Changes in the Third Century A.D.: Historical and Scholastic Contexts for Wang Pi" (Ph.D. dissertation; Ann Arbor: University Microfilms International, 1985).

108. Edward H. Schafer, *Pacing the Void: T'ang Approaches to the Stars* (Berkeley: University of California Press, 1977), pp. 55–56.

109. Yang Ch'üan, "Wu-li lun," p. 2a.

110. *T'ai-p'ing ching ho-chiao* 18–34.27.

111. Chang Chan, *Lieh tzu* 5.2b–3a, note.

112. *Chuang tzu tsuan-chien,* wai-p'ien, 10, pp. 129–130; Henricks, *Philosophy and Argumentation in Third-Century China,* p. 167; Chih Tun, *Chih Tun chi* 2.6a.

113. *Po-wu chih* 7.2b–3a.

114. Chang P'u, ed., *Chin Wang yu-chün chi* 2.327.

115. *Pao p'u tzu*, nei-p'ien, 2.1a; translated in Ware, *Alchemy*, p. 33.

116. For Fo-t'u-teng, see Hui-chiao (c. 530), *Kao seng chuan*, 1 (reprint; Taipei: Hui-wen-t'ang ch'u-pan-she, 1987), 10.240–254.

117. See Mou Tsung-san, *Ts'ai-hsing*, preface to the third edition, p. 2.

118. Indeed, it is only with difficulty that Anselm's Ontological Argument can even be translated into Chinese. See Graham, *Disputers of the Tao*, pp. 411–413.

119. See, for example, de Bary, *Sources*, vol. 1, pp. 240, 243–244.

120. "Feng-fa yao," in Seng Yu, *Hung ming chi* 13.6b. See Zürcher, *Conquest*, p. 127, where Ch'ih Ch'ao is called Hsi Ch'ao.

121. "Yang-sheng lun," in *Ch'üan San-kuo wen* 48.1324–1325. The essay has been translated by Robert Henricks, in *Philosophy and Argumentation in Third-Century China*, pp. 21–30.

122. Religious Taoism did much the same thing—partially inspired, perhaps, by Buddhism. A fifth-century Taoist text, for example, "builds purpose back into the Tao" and "adds religious goals not found in" classical Taoism, as Donald J. Munro observes in the foreword to Livia Kohn, *Taoist Mystical Philosophy: The Scripture of Western Ascension* (Albany: State University of New York Press, 1991), pp. ix–xi.

123. For early Chinese Buddhist debate on the question of the immortality of the spirit, see T'ang Yung-t'ung, *Han Wei liang-Chin Nan-Pei-ch'ao Fo-chiao shih* (1938; Peking: Chung-hua shu-chü, 1983), pp. 303–306.

124. "Shen pu mieh lun," in Seng Yu, *Hung ming chi* 5.2a.

125. See Richard Mather, "The Conflict of Buddhism with Native Chinese Ideologies," *The Review of Religion* 20.1–2 (1955): 28.

126. Tsung Ping, "Ming Fo-lun," in Seng Yu, *Hung ming chi* 2.1b.

127. Tao Hsüan (596–667), *Shih-chia fang-chih* (reprint; Peking: Chung-hua shu-chü, 1983), p. 118.

128. See Li Chieh, *Wei-Chin Nan-Pei-ch'ao shih*, p. 312. The best English-language study of the life and work of Chih Tun remains Erik Zürcher's *The Buddhist Conquest of China*, especially pp. 116–130.

129. See Mather, *Shih-shuo Hsin-yü*, pp. 509, 586, 526.

130. Chih is cited a total of five times in the name index to the history of the Chin: Chang Ch'en-shih, ed., *Chin-shu jen-ming so-yin* (Peking: Chung-hua shu-chü, 1977), p. 248.

131. Hui-chiao, *Kao seng chuan* (c. 530), in *Hai-shan hsien-kuan ts'ung-shu*, edited by P'an Shih-ch'ung (1849), 4.8b–14a; or *Kao seng chuan*, 1 (reprint; Taipei: Hui-wen-t'ang ch'u-pan-she, 1987), 4.100–105. For a study of this important text, see Arthur F. Wright, "Biography and Hagiography: Hui-chiao's *Lives of Eminent Monks*," *Zinbun-kagaku-kenkyū-syo*, Silver Jubilee Volume (1954).

132. Hui-chiao, *Kao seng chuan* 4.8b.

133. See Kao Ssu-sun, *Shan lu* 3.14b–17b.

134. The location of Chih Tun at the time of his death is disputed. See Hui-chiao, *Kao seng chuan* 4.13b. Shih Su, ed., *K'uai-chi chih* (1201; Shaohsing: 1926), 6.29b, places Chih's tomb in Shan.

135. See Chih Tun, *Chih Tun chi,* foreword, p. 1a, citing the *Ssu-k'u weishou shu-mu t'i-yao.*

136. Leon Hurvitz, "Chih Tun's Notions of Prajñā," *Journal of the American Oriental Society* 88.2 (April–June, 1968). See also Zürcher, *Conquest,* p. 124.

137. Hui-chiao, *Kao seng chuan* 4.9a.

138. On the different fashions in north and south, see for example Kuwahara Jitsuzō, "Shin shitsu," p. 110; Wu Ch'eng-hsüeh, "Nan-peip'ai," p. 98.

139. See Fang Li-t'ien, *Wei-Chin Nan-Pei-ch'ao Fo-chiao lun-ts'ung* (Peking: Chung-hua shu-chü, 1982), p. 29.

140. The text of their commentary is translated in Mather, *Shih-shuo Hsin-yü,* p. 109, no. 32, note 2. See also I. Robinet, "Kouo Siang ou le monde comme absolu," *T'oung Pao* 69.1–3 (1983): 88–89.

141. See the interesting argument developed in Aramaki Noritoshi, "Nanchō zempanki ni okeru kyōsōhanshaku no seiritsu ni tsuite," in *Chūgoku chūsei no shūkyō to bunka,* edited by Fukunaga Mitsuji (Kyoto: Kyōto daigaku jinbun kagaku kenkyūsho, 1982), p. 249.

142. Hui-chiao, *Kao seng chuan* 4.9a.

143. Chih Tun, *Chih Tun chi,* supplement, pp. 11a–b.

144. Most Western scholars who have commented on Chih Tun's essay have misunderstood it slightly, perhaps following the lead of the usually reliable Paul Demiéville, who wrote: "Absurdité! se récriait Tche Touen. . . .Evadons-nous dans l'infini, comme le phénix-léviathan au vol prodigieux, comme le bouddhiste qui s'affranchit du monde!" ("La pénétration du bouddhisme dans la tradition philosophique chinoise," *Cahiers d'histoire mondiale 3* [1956–1957]: 27). This standard Western interpretation of Chih's essay is reasonable enough, but it does not agree with the original Chinese text, where Chih explicitly criticized the great bird for its failure to seek spiritual satisfaction "beyond the body" *(shih shih yü t'iwai)* as well as the little bird for its more obvious limitations. See Zürcher, *Conquest,* p. 129.

145. See Fang Li-t'ien, *Fo-chiao lun-ts'ung,* pp. 43–44.

146. Ch'en Yin-k'o, "Hsiao-yao-yu Hsiang Kuo i chi Chih Tun i t'anyüan," *Ch'ing-hua hsüeh-pao* 12.2 (1937): 312–313.

147. See Tsukamoto Zenryū, *Shina bukkyōshi kenkyū, hoku-Gi hen* (Tokyo: Kōbuntō shobō, 1942), p. 32; Liu Kuei-chieh, *Hsüan-hsüeh ssu-hsiang,* p. 113.

148. Chih Tun, *Chih Tun chi* 2.6b. See Zürcher, *Conquest,* p. 128.

149. See Zürcher, *Conquest*, p. 123.

150. The best quick reference for the study of these schools continues to be T'ang Yung-t'ung, *Fo-chiao shih*, pp. 165–167, and passim.

151. See Richard Mather's translation of the *Shih-shuo hsin-yü*, p. 111, no. 35, note 1.

152. A fine essay on Chinese interpretations of *śūnyatā* is included in Mori Mikisaburō, *Rōsōto Bukkyō* (Kyoto: Hōsōkan, 1986), pp. 133–157.

153. "Yü Lin fa-shih shu," in Tao-hsüan (596–667), *Kuang hung-ming chi*, Ssu-pu pei-yao edition (Shanghai: Chung-hua shu-chü, n.d.), 35.4b. Zürcher offers a different translation of this passage (*Conquest*, p. 134).

154. Whalen W. Lai, "The Early Prajñā Schools, Especially 'Hsin-wu,' Reconsidered," *Philosophy East and West* 33.1 (1983): 70–74. Lai offers, perhaps, the most penetrating English-language study of Chih Tun's "Matter Itself" thought, although Zürcher (*Conquest*) still provides the fullest and most rounded discussion of Chih's complete oeuvre.

155. *Se*, Indian *rūpa*, which Walter Liebenthal translates as "colour, matter or the phenomenal world" (*Chao Lun: The Treatises of Seng-chao* [2d edition; Hong Kong: University of Hong Kong Press, 1968], p. 138).

156. "Chi se lun, miao-kuan chang," in Chih Tun, *Chih Tun chi*, supplement, p. 11b; *Ch'üan Chin wen* 157.2366. See also Zürcher, *Conquest*, p. 123.

157. Quoted in T'ang Yung-t'ung, *Fo-chiao shih*, p. 184.

158. See Liebenthal, *Chao Lun*, pp. 24, 28 note 109, and 141.

159. This interpretation of Seng-chao's thought is derived from Mori, *Rōsō*, pp. 153–157. See also Zürcher, *Conquest*, p. 126.

160. *Ch'üan Chin wen* 164.2416.

161. See Kenneth Ch'en, *Buddhism in China: A Historical Survey* (Princeton: Princeton University Press, 1964), pp. 114–118.

162. See Chih Tun, *Chih Tun chi*, supplement, p. 4a, where he writes: "Coherence is not in change, and change is not in coherence. . . .A thousand changes and ten thousand transformations all lie outside of coherence. How could spirit move?" On Chih's use of the term *li*, or coherence, see Zürcher, *Conquest*, p. 125.

163. Chih Tun, *Chih Tun chi*, supplement, pp. 11a–b. The phrase is not entirely original: compare Kuan Tzu's "The gentleman uses things and is not used by things." *Kuan tzu* (attributed to Kuan Chung, d. 645 B.C.), Ssu-pu pei-yao edition (Taipei: T'ai-wan Chung-hua shu-chü, 1965), 16.3a.

164. Chih Tun, *Chih Tun chi*, supplement, pp. 2a–b. *Neng ch'i yü wu* is a possible bow in the direction of Chuang-tzu's *Ch'i-wu lun*.

165. Chih Tun, *Chih Tun chi*, supplement, p. 5a.

166. Ibid., 2.8a–b.

167. See Zürcher, *Conquest*, p. 91.

168. Hsi K'ang, *Hsi K'ang chi* (third century), in *Lu Hsün san-shih-nien chi*, vol. 5 (1923; Hong Kong: Hsin-i ch'u-pan-she, 1973), 6.81–82.

169. The "Feng-fa yao" is translated in Zürcher, *Conquest,* pp. 164–176.

170. "Feng-fa yao," in Seng Yu, *Hung ming chi* 13.6b–7a.

171. Hui-chiao, *Kao seng chuan* 4.11b.

172. "Mystery and more mystery. The door of all subtleties," writes Lao-tzu (Rump and Chan, trans., *Lao Tzu,* p. 2).

173. Presumably, the "two masters" refer to Lao-tzu and Chuang-tzu.

174. A reference to a somewhat obscure passage in the *Chuang tzu:*

The Yellow Emperor was traveling north of the Red River and ascended to the mound of K'un-lun. When he faced south to return, he left behind his mystic pearl [defined in a note as "Taoist truth"]. He sent Knowledge to find it without success; he sent Li-chu [a man famous for keen eyesight] to find it without success; he sent Quarrelsome to find it without success. Then he sent Imageless, and Imageless got it.

(*Chuang tzu tsuan-chien,* wai-p'ien, 5, p. 91)

175. Chih Tun, *Chih Tun chi* 1.1b. Also Tao-hsüan, *Kuang hung-ming chi* 39.3a. Slight variations in the text exist. In this translation I have relied heavily on the generous advice of Richard Mather.

176. Chih Tun, *Chih Tun chi* 1.2a.

6: "True Man"

1. See also *Chin-shu* 79.2072. Zürcher observes that the Chinese sources "show him [Chih Tun] conversing with some thirty-five persons, practically all well-known members of the highest gentry" (*Conquest,* p. 130).

2. Miyakawa Hisayuki, "Tō-Shin jidai no kizoku to bukkyō," *Shina bukkyō shigaku* 4.1–2 (1940), part 2, p. 60. For Chih's calligraphic skill, see Hui-chiao, *Kao seng chuan* 4.13b.

3. For Chih Tun, see *Chin-shu* 67.1805. For Hsü Hsün, see Kao Ssu-sun, ed., *Shan-lu* 3.6a.

4. Hui Chiao, *Kao seng chuan* 4.10b.

5. *Chin-shu* 67.1805.

6. Zürcher speaks of a handful of "gentlemen-monks," including Chih Tun, who were able to "preach their version of the doctrine with the authority of a Chinese scholar and the polished eloquence of a *ch'ing-t'an* adept" and who were instrumental in converting the Chinese elite to Buddhism (*Conquest,* p. 8).

7. *Chin-shu* 79.2076.

8. Hsieh's biography can be found in *Chin-shu* 79.2072–2077. Another important source of information concerning Hsieh is the trove of anec-

dotes in Mather, *Shih-shuo Hsin-yü*. See also Ishikawa Tadahisa, "Sha An to Kaikei no yū," *Tōkyō Shinagakuhō* 6 (1960); Ting Kuang-hsün, "Lüeh-lun Hsieh An," *Li-shih chiao-hsüeh wen-t'i* 1990.5; and Michael Rogers, "The Myth of the Battle of the Fei River."

9. Richard Madsen, *Morality and Power in a Chinese Village* (Berkeley: University of California Press, 1984), p. 244.

10. Rogers, "Battle of the Fei River," p. 56.

11. See, for example, Mather, *Shih-shuo Hsin-yü*, p. 89, no. 19; p. 107, no. 29; p. 175, no. 58.

12. Richard Curt Kraus, *Brushes With Power: Modern Politics and the Chinese Art of Calligraphy* (Berkeley: University of California Press, 1991), pp. x, 3–14.

13. *Chin-shu* 43.1238.

14. Chang P'u, *Chin Wang yu-chün chi* 1.81.

15. For the rise of a "Confucian exemplary" ideal of reclusive behavior, see Aat Vervoorn, *Men of the Cliffs and Caves: The Development of the Chinese Eremitic Tradition to the End of the Han Dynasty* (Hong Kong: The Chinese University Press, 1990). On the fashion for declining government appointments in the Chin dynasty, see Nomura Shigeo, "'Su' o tsūjite mita, Shin dai no jusha," *Tōhōgaku* 61 (1981): 58.

16. Wolfgang Bauer, "The Hidden Hero: Creation and Disintegration of the Ideal of Eremitism," in *Individualism and Holism: Studies in Confucian and Taoist Values,* edited by Donald J. Munro (Ann Arbor: Center for Chinese Studies, University of Michigan, 1985), pp. 166–172.

17. Li Heng, *Shao-hsing fu-chih* 63.1509.

18. This example comes from Wang Ch'in-jo, *Ts'e-fu yüan-kuei* 809.9623.

19. A representative example of Chinese scholarly opinion might be Lü Ssu-mien's statement that "the evil practice of esteeming literature" was one of the reasons for the loss of the north in the early fourth century. See *Lü Ssu-mien tu-shih cha-chi* (Shanghai: Shang-hai ku-chi ch'u-pan-she, 1982), p. 781. For a discussion of the role of *ch'ing-t'an* in the loss of the north, see Chou Shao-hsien, "Ch'ing-t'an wang Chin wen-t'i chih shang-ch'üeh," in *Ch'in-Han shih chi chung-ku shih ch'ien-ch'i yen-chiu lun-chi,* Ta-lu tsa-chih shih-hsüeh ts'ung-shu, 1.4 (1960); Ch'en Yin-k'o, "Ch'ing-t'an yü ch'ing-t'an wu-kuo," in *Ch'en Yin-k'o hsien-sheng lun-wen chi pu-pien,* Chiu-ssu ts'ung-shu 5 (Taipei: Fu-hsin hang yin-shua shih-yeh yu-hsien kung-ssu, 1977). "'The destruction of the state by *ch'ing-t'an*,' or 'the mismanagement of the state by *ch'ing-t'an*,' has seemingly already become a kind of established historical thesis" writes T'ien Wen-t'ang, in *Wei-Chin san ta ssu-ch'ao lun-kao* (Sian: Shan-hsi jen-min ch'u-pan-she, 1988), p. 1.

20. *Chin-shu* 35.1044.

21. Johnson, *Oligarchy,* p. 125.

22. Tanigawa, Local "Community," pp. xxii, xxiv.

23. See Yoshimori Kensuke, "'San-ku kei-ji,'" p. 139.

24. Thomas A. Metzger, "Was Neo-Confucianism 'Tangential' to the Elite Culture of Late Imperial China?" The American Asian Review 4.1 (1986): 2–3.

25. Legge, Four Books, p. 1002. See also pp. 338–339, 947.

26. Benjamin Schwartz, "Some Polarities in Confucian Thought," in Confucianism and Chinese Civilization, edited by Arthur F. Wright (Stanford: Stanford University Press, 1964), p. 5.

27. This was one opinion current at the end of Han, expressed in Ch'en Shou, San-kuo chih 15.468.

28. Legge, Four Books, pp. 4–7.

29. Ch'üan Chin wen 48.1733.

30. Shen Yüeh, Sung-shu 14.357.

31. Chuang tzu tsuan-chien, nei-p'ien, 7.62.

32. Roger T. Ames, "The Common Ground of Self-Cultivation in Classical Taoism and Confucianism," Ch'ing-hua hsüeh-pao, new series 17.1–2 (1985).

33. See, for example, Nakayashiki Hiroshi, Chūgoku ideorogii ron, pp. 102–103.

34. Kan Pao, "Chin-chi," in Chin-chi chi-pen, edited by T'ang Ch'iu (Kuang-ya shu-chü ts'ung-shu, n.d.), p. 25a. For Wang Hung, see Sung-shu 42.1314–1315.

35. Kohn, Mystical Philosophy, p. 11.

36. Tsung Ping (375–443), "Ming fo lun," in Seng Yu, Hung ming chi 2.14a–b.

37. Fung Yu-lan, A Short History of Chinese Philosophy, edited by Derk Bodde (New York: The Free Press, 1948), p. 8.

38. Julia Ching, "The Ancient Sages (sheng): Their Identity and Their Place in Chinese Intellectual History," Oriens Extremus 30 (1983–1986): 14.

39. Charles Le Blanc, Huai Nan Tzu: Philosophical Synthesis in Early Han Thought (Hong Kong: Hong Kong University Press, 1985), p. 206. See also pp. 192, 196. Confucius himself had shown that sagehood was "transcendent of rulership or government," according to Julia Ching, "Sages," p. 15.

40. Aramaki Noritoshi, "Kyōsōhanshaku," pp. 241, 264, 279. Yü Ying-shih ("Life and Immortality," p. 107), Li Feng-mao ("Liu-ch'ao hsien-ching ch'uan-shuo yü Tao-chiao chih kuan-hsi," Chung-wai wen-hsüeh 8.8 [1980]: 169, 185), and Kominami Ichirō (Chūgoku no shinwa to monoga-tari—ko shōsetsu-shi no tenkai [Tokyo: Iwanami shoten, 1984], p. 234) all make the observation that during the era of division the group of people who could properly aspire to "transcendent" status also swelled from royalty and fang-shih to include all literati.

41. *T'ai-p'ing ching ho-chiao* 94–95.403.

42. Seng Yu, *Ch'u san-tsang chi chi* 45.450.28a.

43. Tanigawa Michio, *Tankyū*, p. 123.

44. *Chin-shu* 43.1236.

45. Carlo Ginzburg, *The Cheese and the Worms: The Cosmos of a Sixteenth-Century Miller*, translated by John and Anne Tedeschi (Harmondsworth: Penguin Books, 1980), p. 17.

46. "Chou i," in Juan Yüan, *Shih-san ching chu-shu* 7.79. Translated in Legge, *Yi King*, 361–362. Burton Watson dates these commentaries to the late Chou or early Han (*Early Chinese Literature* [New York: Columbia University Press, 1962], pp. 151–152).

7: Epilogue

1. For a deft introduction to this great emperor, see Arthur F. Wright, "T'ang T'ai-tsung: The Man and The Persona," in *Essays on T'ang Society: The Interplay of Social, Political and Economic Forces*, edited by John Curtis Perry and Bardwell L. Smith (Leiden: E. J. Brill, 1976).

2. *Chin-shu* 3.82.

3. Mao Han-kuang, *Chung-ku she-hui*, pp. 88–90.

4. Okazaki Fumio, *Nanbokuchō ni okeru shakai keizai seido* (Tokyo: Kōbundō, 1955), p. 272. Dennis Grafflin, "The Great Family in Medieval South China," *Harvard Journal of Asiatic Studies* 41.1 (1981): 73. For a discussion of the longevity of the medieval aristocracy, see Helwig Schmidt-Glintzer, "Der Literatenbeamte und seine Gemeinde: oder Der Charakter der Aristokratie im chinesischen Mittelalter," *Zeitschrift der Deutschen Morgenländischen Gesellschaft* 139.2 (1989): 402–405.

5. See Mao Han-kuang, *Chung-ku she-hui*, pp. 21–24; Ebrey, *Aristocratic Families*, pp. 27–29.

6. Ssu-ma Kuang, *Tzu-chih t'ung-chien chin-chu*, vol. 9, 166.261.

7. Ibid., 176.802.

8. On the *fu-ping* system during the early T'ang dynasty, see Edwin G. Pulleyblank, *The Background of the Rebellion of An Lu-shan* (London: Oxford University Press, 1955), pp. 61–63. See also Ku Chi-kuang, *Fu-ping chih-tu k'ao-shih* (1962; Taipei: Hung-wen-kuan ch'u-pan-she, 1985).

9. See Tu Cheng-sheng, "'Pien-hu ch'i-min' te ch'u-hsien chi ch'i li-shih i-i: pien-hu ch'i-min te yen-chiu chih-i," *Chung-yang yen-chiu-yüan, Li-shih yü-yen yen-chiu-so chi-k'an* 54.3 (1983): 77–111.

10. For the decline of the Han dynasty conscription system, see Kao Min, "Ts'ao-Wei shih-chia chih-tu te hsing-ch'eng yü yen-pien," *Li-shih yen-chiu* 1989.5: 61.

11. Ssu-ma Kuang, *Tzu-chih t'ung-chien chin-chu*, vol. 9, 163.159; Ku Chi-kuang, *Fu-ping chih-tu*, pp. 23–29, 32–42.

12. Ssu-ma Kuang, *Tzu-chih t'ung-chien chin-chu*, vol. 9, 176.814–815.

13. Ibid., 176.775.

14. "Kuan wo sheng fu," in *Ch'üan Sui wen,* 13.4089, note. For Hou Ching, see his biography in Li Yen-shou, *Nan-shih* 80.1993–2017.

15. The Sui conquest of Ch'en is described in *Nan-shih* 10.308–310.

16. Miyazaki Ichisada, *China's Examination Hell,* p. 113.

17. The various Sui dynasty measures are described in Arthur F. Wright, *The Sui Dynasty* (New York: Alfred A. Knopf, 1978), pp. 101–103.

18. On the tax exemptions, see Kao Min, "Fu-i huo-mien," pp. 66, 68. For the Sui reforms, see Ssu-ma Kuang, *Tzu-chih t'ung-chien chin-chu,* vol. 9, 176.790–791.

19. Tu Yu, *T'ung-tien* 7.42.

20. Johnson, *Oligarchy,* pp. 132, 136. See also Mao Han-kuang, *Chung-ku she-hui,* pp. 42, 100–101.

21. On the Turkic elements in Western Wei, Northern Chou, Sui, and T'ang, see Edwin G. Pulleyblank, "The An Lu-shan Rebellion and The Origins of Chronic Militarism in Late T'ang China," in *Essays on T'ang Society: The Interplay of Social, Political and Economic Forces,* edited by John Curtis Perry and Bardwell L. Smith (Leiden: E. J. Brill, 1976), pp. 37–39. Arthur Wright observes that this Sino-Turkic elite "did little to perpetuate the great traditions of Chinese literature and scholarship" ("T'ang T'ai-tsung," pp. 20–21).

22. See Kawakatsu Yoshio, "La décadence de l'aristocratie chinoise sous les Dynasties du Sud," *Acta Asiatica* 21 (1971): 25. Chen's position in the Hsieh family genealogy is schematically diagramed by Wang I-t'ung in *Wu-ch'ao men-ti,* vol. 2, table 5. For Chen's biography, see Yao Ssu-lien, ed., *Ch'en-shu* (636; Peking: Chung-hua shu-chü, 1972), 32.426–429.

GLOSSARY

A-mi-t'o-fo hsiang tsan, ping hsü	阿彌陀佛像讚并序	Ch'ih Chien	郗鑒
An Shih-kao	安世高	Ching-chou	荆州
Ang Mountain	岬山	Ching-k'ou	京口
chan-t'ien	占田	Ch'ing-chou	青州
Chang Chan	張湛	ch'ing-i	清議
Chang Chin-chih	張進之	ch'ing-liu	清流
chang-chü	章句	ch'ing-t'an	清談
Chang Han	張翰	chiu-p'in chung-cheng	九品中正
Chang Hua	張華	Chou Chi	周纪
Chang Tao-ling	張道陵	chuang-yüan	莊園
Chao I	趙翼	chung-yang chi-ch'üan te feng-chien chuan-chih chu-i	中央集權的封建專制主義
chi-che	機者		
Chi-hsia (academy)	稷下		
Chi se lun	即色論		
Chiang-nan	江南	*Ch'ung-yu lun*	崇有論
Chiao Hsien	焦先	chün-t'ien	均田
ch'iao chün hsien chih-tu	僑郡縣制度	fan-ch'ang	反常
		Fan Chen	范縝
Chih Tun	支遁	Fan Ning	范甯
chih-wu-che wu-i neng sheng	至無者無以能生	Fan Wei	范蔚
		Feng-fa yao	奉法要
Ch'ih Ch'ao	郗超	Fo-t'u-teng	佛圖澄

187

Fu Chia	傅嘏	K'ung Ling-fu	孔靈符
Fu Hsüan	傅玄	Kuo Hsiang	郭象
fu-hua	浮華	kyōdōtai	共同体
fu-ping	府兵	Liu Fang	柳芳
Ho Hsün	賀循	Liu I	劉毅
Ho Yen	何晏	Liu Yü	劉裕
Hou Ching	侯景	Lu Chi	陸機
Hsi K'ang	嵇康	Lu Pao	魯褒
Hsiang Hsiu	向秀	Ma Jung	馬融
hsiao-yao yu	逍遙遊	Ma Tuan-lin	馬端臨
Hsieh An	謝安	mai shih chih feng	邁世之風
Hsieh Chen	謝貞	men-sheng	門生
hsing-ch'i	行氣	ming-li	名理
Hsü Hsün	許詢	Nan-hsiang	南鄉
hsüan-chü	選舉	Pei-fu ping	北府兵
hsüan-hsüeh	玄學	P'ei Wei	裴頠
Hsün Ts'an	荀粲	p'eng i ying-sheng	鵬以營生之
Hsün Yüeh	荀悅	chih lu k'uang,	路曠故失
Huan Hsüan	桓玄	ku shih shih yü	適於體外
Huan T'an	桓譚	t'i-wai	
Huan Wen	桓溫	Pien K'un	卞壼
huang-chi	黃籍	pu-ch'ü	部曲
Huang Tsung-hsi	黃宗羲	Seng-chao	僧肇
Hui-chiao	慧皎	Shan County	剡縣
Hui-yüan	慧遠	Shan Hsia	山遐
Hung Mai	洪邁	Shan T'ao	山濤
I-shan	嶧山	Shang-yü	上虞
jen-tzu	任子	Shen Ching	沈警
Juan Chi	阮籍	shen-se pu-pien	神色不變
Juan Fang	阮放	Shen Yüeh	沈約
Kan Pao	干寶	*Shih-ssu lun*	釋私論
Ko Hung	葛洪	shih-ta-fu	士大夫
k'o-t'ien	課田	Shih Tao-an	釋道安
K'uai-chi	會稽	Shih-tsu	士族
Kuang-ling	廣陵	shou-i	守一
kuei-tsu	貴族	Shu Hsi	束皙
k'ung chung hsing	空中行空	shu-jen	庶人
k'ung		Ssu-ma Jui	司馬睿

Ssu-ma Tao-tzu	司馬道子	Wang Seng-ta	王僧達
Ssu-ma Yü	司馬昱	Wang Tao	王導
Su Chün	蘇峻	Wang Tun	王敦
Sun En	孫恩	Wei Kuan	衛瓘
Sun T'ung	孫統	wei-ts'ai shih-chü	唯才是舉
Ta-hsiao p'in tui-pi	大小品對比	Wen Ch'iao	溫嶠
yao-ch'ao hsü	要抄序	Wu-ch'ang	武昌
t'ai-fu	太傅	wu-hu	五胡
t'ai pao	太保	Wu-ning	吳寧
T'ao Ch'ien	陶潛	wu wu wu chih wu	無無無之無
Tiao Hsieh	刁協	Yang-chou	揚州
Ts'ao Chiung	曹冏	Yang Ch'üan	楊泉
ts'eng-tzu	傖子	Yang Chün	楊俊
Tsu T'i	祖逖	Yang Hsiung	揚雄
ts'un-ssu	存思	Yen Chih-t'ui	顏之推
Tsung Ping	宗炳	yen pu chin i	言不盡意
t'u-tuan	土斷	Yen Tsun	嚴遵
t'un-t'ien	屯田	yin-pi	蔭庇
tzu-jan	自然	Yü Ch'un	庾純
Wang Ch'eng	王澄	Yü Kun	庾袞
Wang Ch'ia	王洽	Yü Liang	庾亮
Wang Hsi-chih	王羲之	yü-lun	輿論
Wang Hsien-chih	王獻之	Yü-yao	餘姚
Wang Jung	王戎	Yüan-k'ang	元康
Wang Pi	王弼	Yün-meng	雲夢
Wang Piao-chih	王彪之		

SELECT BIBLIOGRAPHY

Classical Chinese Sources

Chang Chan (c. 370), ed. *Lieh tzu* (The Book of Lieh-tzu). Reprint; Taipei: T'ai-wan Chung-hua shu-chü, 1982.

Chang Hua (232–300). *Po-wu chih* (An Account of Many Things). Reprint; Taipei: T'ai-wan Chung-hua shu-chü, 1983.

Chang Ju-yü (c. 1200), ed. *Shan-t'ang (hsien-sheng ch'ün-shu) k'ao-so* ([The Genleman] from the Mountain Hall's Examination [of Many Books]). Reprint; Yüan-sha shu-yüan edition, 1320.

Chang P'u (c. 1635), ed. *Chin Wang yu-chün chi* (The Collected Works of General of the Right Wang [Hsi-chih] of the Chin). Photocopy of 1892 edition; Taipei: Hsüeh-sheng shu-chü, 1979.

Chao I. *Nien-erh shih cha-chi* (Notes to Twenty-two Histories). 1795; Taipei: Hua-shih ch'u-pan-she, 1977.

Ch'en Shou (233–297). *San-kuo chih* (Chronicles of the Three Kingdoms). Reprint; Peking: Chung-hua shu-chü, 1959.

Chih Tun (314–366). *Chih Tun chi* (Collected Works of Chih Tun). Shao-wu Hsü-shih ts'ung-shu. Edited by Hsü Kan. Hangchow, 1884.

Chin-shu. See Fang Hsüan-ling, ed.

Chou Chi (1781–1839), ed. *Chin lüeh* (An Outline of the Chin). Reprint; Wei-chün chai, 1876.

Chu Ming-p'an (1852–1893), ed. *Nan-ch'ao Sung hui-yao* (Institutes of Southern Dynasties Sung). Taipei: Hung-wen-kuan ch'u-pan-she, 1986.

Chuang tzu tsuan-chien (Collected Commentaries on the *Chuang tzu*) (3d century B.C.). Edited by Ch'ien Mu. Revised ed.; Hong Kong: Tung-nan yin-wu ch'u-pan-she, 1956.

Ch'üan Chin wen, Ch'üan Han wen, Ch'üan Hou-Han wen, Ch'üan San-kuo wen, Ch'üan Sui wen. See Yen K'o-chün, ed., *Ch'üan Shang-ku San-tai Ch'in Han San-kuo Liu-ch'ao wen.*

Chung Hsing (c. 1600), ed. *Chin wen kuei* (Return to Chin Literature). Reprint; Taipei: T'ai-wan shang-wu yin-shu-kuan, 1973.

Fan Yeh (398–445). *Hou-Han shu* (History of the Later Han). Reprint; Peking: Chung-hua shu-chü, 1965.

Fang Hsüan-ling, ed. *Chin-shu* (History of the Chin). 644; Peking: Chung-hua shu-chü, 1974.

Ho Fa-sheng (5th century). "Chin chung-hsing shu" (History of the Chin Restoration). In *Huang-shih i-shu k'ao,* edited by Huang Shih. Ts'ung-shu ching-hua. I-wen yin-shu-kuan, 1934.

Hsi K'ang (223–262). *Hsi K'ang chi* (Collected Works of Hsi K'ang). *Lu Hsün san-shih-nien chi,* vol. 5. 1923; Hong Kong: Hsin-i ch'u-pan-she, 1973.

Hsiao T'ung (501–531), ed. *Wen-hsüan* (Selections of Refined Literature). Reprint; Tainan: T'ai-nan pei-i ch'u-pan-she, 1974.

Hsü Chien (659–729), ed. *Ch'u-hsüeh chi* (Record for Initial Study). Reprint; Peking: Chung-hua shu-chü, 1962.

Hsü T'ien-lin (13th century), ed. *Tung-Han hui-yao* (Institutes of the Eastern Han). Shanghai: Shang-hai ku-chi ch'u-pan-she, 1978.

Hsü Yüan-mei, ed. *Shan-yin hsien chih* (Chronicles of Shan-yin County). Shan-yin, 1803.

Huan T'an (43 B.C.–A.D. 28). *Huan tzu hsin-lun* (Huan tzu's New Discourse). Reprint; Taipei: T'ai-wan Chung-hua shu-chü, 1976.

Hui-chiao. *Kao seng chuan* (Lives of Eminent Monks) (c. 530). In *Hai-shan hsien-kuan ts'ung-shu,* edited by P'an Shih-ch'ung. 1849.

———. *Kao seng chuan.* Vol. 1. Reprint; Taipei: Hui-wen-t'ang ch'u-pan-she, 1987.

Hung Mai (1123–1202). *Jung-chai sui-pi* (Miscellaneous Notes from a Capacious Studio). Reprint; Taipei: Ta-li ch'u-pan-she, 1981.

Juan Yüan (1764–1849), collator. *Shih-san ching chu-shu* (Commentaries on the Thirteen Classics). Taipei: Ta-hua shu-chü, 1982.

Kan Pao (early 4th century). "Chin-chi" (Annals of the Chin). In *Chin-chi chi-pen,* edited by T'ang Ch'iu. Kuang-ya shu-chü ts'ung-shu, n.d.

Kao Ssu-sun (early 13th century), ed. *Shan lu* (Records of Shan [County]). Reprint; Sheng County Yamen, 1828.

Ko Hung. *Pao p'u tzu* (Master Embracing Simplicity). C. 317; Taipei: T'ai-wan Chung-hua shu-chü, 1984.

Ku Yen-wu (1613–1682). *Jih-chih lu chi-shih* (Collected Explanations to a Record of Daily Knowledge). Reprint; Shanghai: Shang-hai ku-chi ch'u-pan-she, 1985.

Li Fang, ed. *T'ai-p'ing kuang-chi* (Extensive Records [Assembled during] the T'ai-p'ing Era [976–984]). 978; Peking: Chung-hua shu-chü, 1981.

———. *T'ai-p'ing yü-lan* ([Encyclopedia Assembled for] Imperial Inspection during the T'ai-p'ing Era). 983; Taipei: T'ai-wan shang-wu yin-shu-kuan, 1980.

Li Heng, ed. *Shao-hsing fu-chih* (Chronicles of Shao-hsing Prefecture). Chung-kuo fang-chih ts'ung-shu 221. 1792; Taipei: Ch'eng-wen ch'u-pan-she, 1975.

Li Yen-shou, ed. *Nan-shih* (History of the Southern Dynasties). C. 629; Peking: Chung-hua shu-chü, 1975.

Liu Ch'ien-chih (5th century). "Chin-chi" (Annals of the Chin). In *Chin-chi chi-pen,* edited by T'ang Ch'iu. Kuang-ya shu-chü ts'ung-shu, n.d.

Lu I-t'ung, ed. *Yu-chün nien-p'u* (Annual Register of the General of the Right [Wang Hsi-chih]). Mei-shu ts'ung-shu 4.9 (1855); Taipei: I-wen yin-shu-kuan, n.d.

Ma Kuo-han, ed. *Yü-han shan-fang chi i-shu* (Compiled Lost Works of the Jade-Sheath Mountain Home). Ch'u-nan hsiang-yüan-t'ang, 1884.

Ma Tuan-lin (13th century). *Wen-hsien t'ung-k'ao* (Thorough Examination of Literary Offerings). Wan-yu wen-k'u 2. Reprint; Shanghai: Shang-wu yin-shu-kuan, 1936.

Mao Kuo-chin, ed. *Chin shih shan* (Parings from Chin History). C. 1600.

Ou-yang Hsiu (1007–1072). *Hsin T'ang-shu* (New History of the T'ang). Reprint; Peking: Chung-hua shu-chü, 1975.

Pan Ku (A.D. 39–92). *Han-shu* (History of the Han). Pai-na pen, Erh-shih-ssu shih edition. Reprint; Taipei: T'ai-wan shang-wu yin-shu-kuan, 1988.

Seng Yu (435–518). *Ch'u san-tsang chi chi* (Collected Records from the Tripitika). Reprint of Sung dynasty Ch'i-sha ts'ang-ching edition; Shanghai, 1934–1936.

———. *Hung ming chi* (Collection of Expanding Brilliance). Reprint; Taipei: T'ai-wan Chung-hua shu-chü, 1983.

Shen Yüeh (441–513). *Sung-shu* (History of the [Southern Dynasties Liu-] Sung). Reprint; Peking: Chung-hua shu-chü, 1974.

Shih Su, ed. *K'uai-chi chih* (Chronicles of K'uai-chi). 1201; Shao-hsing, 1926.

Ssu-ma Ch'ien (145–c. 90 B.C.). *Shih-chi* (Records of the Grand Historian of China). Reprint; Peking: Chung-hua shu-chü, 1959.

Ssu-ma Kuang (1019–1086). *Tzu-chih t'ung-chien chin-chu* (New Annotations to the *Comprehensive Mirror for Aid in Governance*). Chung-hua ts'ung-shu. Reprint; Taipei: T'ai-wan shang-wu yin-shu-kuan, 1966.

Sun Sheng (c. 302–373). "Chin yang-ch'iu" (Spring and Autumn of the Chin). In *Chin yang-ch'iu chi-pen,* edited by T'ang Ch'iu. Kuang-ya shu-chü ts'ung-shu, 1920.

T'ai-p'ing ching ho-chiao (Collated Scripture of Great Peace) (2d century). Edited by Wang Ming. Peking: Chung-hua shu-chü, 1960.

T'an Tao-luan (5th century). "Hsü Chin yang-ch'iu" (Continued Spring and Autumn of the Chin). *Chin yang-ch'iu chi-pen,* edited by T'ang Ch'iu. Kuang-ya shu-chü ts'ung-shu, 1920.

T'ao Ch'ien (365–427). "Ch'ün fu lu" (Record of the Many Ministers). In *Pi-chi hsiao-shuo ta-kuan san-pien.* Reprint; Taipei: Hsin-hsing shu-chü, 1974.

Tao-hsüan, ed. (596–667). *Kuang hung-ming chi* (Extended Collection of Expanding Brilliance). Ssu-pu pei-yao edition. Shanghai: Chung-hua shu-chü, n.d.

——. *Shih-chia fang-chih* (Local Annals of the Buddha's Clan). Reprint; Peking: Chung-hua shu-chü, 1983.

Tao-tsang yang-sheng shu shih-chung (Ten Sorts of Nourishment of Life Writings from the Taoist Canon). Edited by Li Shih-hua and Shen Te-hui. Peking: Chung-i ku-chi ch'u-pan-she, 1987.

Teng Ts'an (4th century). "Chin-chi" (Annals of the Chin). In *Chin-chi chi-pen,* edited by T'ang Ch'iu. Kuang-ya shu-chü ts'ung-shu, n.d.

Tsang Jung-hsü (late 5th century). "Chin-shu" (History of the Chin). In *Chiu-chia chiu Chin-shu chi-pen,* edited by T'ang Ch'iu. Kuang-ya shu-chü ts'ung-shu, n.d.

Tu Yu (735–812). *T'ung-tien* (Comprehensive Canons). Reprint; Peking: Chung-hua shu-chü, 1984.

Wang Ch'in-jo, ed. *Ts'e-fu yüan-kuei* (The Great Tortoise of Archives). C. 1012; Taipei: T'ai-wan Chung-hua shu-chü, 1981.

Wang Ch'ung. *Lun-heng* (Balancing of Essays). A.D. 82; Taipei: T'ai-wan Chung-hua shu-chü, 1981.

Wang Ying-lin (1223–1296), ed. *K'un-hsüeh chi-wen* (Recorded Tidings of Difficult Learning). Annotated by Weng Yüan-ch'i. Kuo-hsüeh chi-pen ts'ung-shu. Reprint; Shanghai: Shang-wu yin-shu-kuan, 1935.

Yang Ch'üan (3d century). "Wu-li lun" (Essay on the Principles of Things). In *Lung-hsi ching-she ts'ung-shu,* edited by Cheng Kuo-hsün. Reprint; Shanghai: Shang-hai ku-chi shu-tien, 1962.

Yao Ssu-lien, ed. *Ch'en-shu* (History of the Ch'en). 636; Peking: Chung-hua shu-chü, 1972.

Yen Chih-t'ui (c. 531–591). *Yen-shih chia-hsün* (Family Instructions for the Yen Clan). Reprint; Taipei: T'ai-wan Chung-hua shu-chü, 1974.

Yen K'o-chün (1762–1843), ed. *Ch'üan Shang-ku San-tai Ch'in Han San-kuo Liu-ch'ao wen* (Complete Literature from High Antiquity, the Three Dynasties, Ch'in, Han, the Three Kingdoms, and the Six Dynasties). Reprint; Kyoto: Chūbun shuppansha, 1981.

Yü Shih-nan (558–638). *Pei-t'ang shu-ch'ao* (Northern Hall Documents). Reprint; Taipei: Hung-yeh shu-chü, 1974.

Modern Scholarship:
Studies of China, Han through T'ang

Aramaki Noritoshi. "Nanchō zempanki ni okeru kyōsōhanshaku no sei-ritsu ni tsuite" (Concerning the Emergence of Doctrinal Distinctions in the First Half of the Southern Dynasties). In *Chūgoku chūsei no shū-kyō to bunka,* edited by Fukunaga Mitsuji. Kyoto: Kyōto daigaku jin-bun kagaku kenkyūsho, 1982.

Balazs, Etienne. *Chinese Civilization and Bureaucracy.* Translated by H. M. Wright. New Haven: Yale University Press, 1964.

Beck, B. J. Mansvelt. "The Date of the *Taiping Jing.*" *T'oung Pao* 66.4–5 (1980).

Bielenstein, Hans. "The Census of China during the Period 2–742 A.D." *Bulletin of the Museum of Far Eastern Antiquities* 19 (1947).

————. "Lo-yang in Later Han Times." *Bulletin of the Museum of Far East-ern Antiquities* 48 (1976).

————. "The Restoration of the Han Dynasty, Vols. 3–4." *Bulletin of the Museum of Far Eastern Antiquities* 39.2 (1967) and 51 (1979).

Bodde, Derk. "Some Chinese Tales of the Supernatural: Kan Pao and His *Sou-shen chi,*" *Harvard Journal of Asiatic Studies* 6 (1941).

Chan, Alan K. L. *Two Visions of the Way: A Study of the Wang Pi and the Ho-Shang Kung Commentaries on the Lao-Tzu.* Albany: State University of New York Press, 1991.

Chang Ch'un-shu. "Ku-tai t'un-t'ien chih-tu te yüan-shih yü Hsi-Han ho-hsi, hsi-yü pien-sai shang t'un-t'ien chih-tu chih fa-chan kuo-ch'eng" (The Beginnings of the Ancient T'un-t'ien System, and the Process of Development of the T'un-t'ien System in Western Han West of the Yellow River, in the Western Regions Frontier Passes). In *Ch'ü Wan-li hsien-sheng ch'i-chih jung-ch'ing lun-wen chi.* Taipei: Lien-ching ch'u-pan shih-yeh kung-ssu, 1978.

Chang Hsing-lang. "Tao-chia hsien-ching chih yen-pien chi ch'i so shou ti-li chih ying-hsiang" (Progressive Changes in the Taoist Paradise and the Geographic Influences Acting on It). *Chung-kuo hsüeh-pao* 1.3–4 (1944).

Chang Jen-ch'ing. "Liu-ch'ao jen te ai-mei hsin-li" (The Aesthetic Incli-nations of People in the Six Dynasties). *Tung-fang tsa-chih,* fu-k'an 17.1 (1983.7).

Chang, Kang-i Sun. *Six Dynasties Poetry.* Princeton: Princeton University Press, 1986.

Chang Pin-sheng. *Wei-Chin Nan-Pei-ch'ao cheng-chih shih* (A Political His-tory of the Wei, Chin, and Northern and Southern Dynasties). Taipei: Chung-kuo wen-hua ta-hsüeh, 1983.

Chappell, David W., ed. *Buddhist and Taoist Practice in Medieval Chi-*

nese Society. Buddhist and Taoist Studies, 2. Honolulu: University of Hawaii Press, 1987.

Ch'en Ch'i-yün. "A Confucian Magnate's Idea of Political Violence: Hsun Shuang's (128–190 A.D.) Interpretation of the Book of Changes." *T'oung Pao* 54.1–3 (1968).

————. *Hsün Yüeh (A.D. 148–209): The Life and Reflections of an Early Medieval Confucian.* Cambridge: Cambridge University Press, 1975.

————. *Hsün Yüeh and the Mind of Late Han China.* Princeton: Princeton University Press, 1980.

————. "Wei-Chin Nan-Pei-ch'ao shih-ch'i Chung-kuo chih-shih fen-tzu te t'e-se" (The Special Characteristics of Chinese Intellectuals in the Wei, Chin, and Northern and Southern Dynasty Period). *Kuo-chi Han-hsüeh hui-i lun-wen chi: Li-shih k'ao-ku tsu* 1981.10. Taipei: Chung-yang yen-chiu-yüan, 1981.

Ch'en Hsiao-chiang. "San-kuo shih-tai te jen-k'ou i-tung" (Movements of Population in the Three Kingdoms Period). *Shih-huo pan-yüeh k'an* 1.3 (1935).

Ch'en, Kenneth. "Neo-Taoism and the Prajñā School during the Wei and Chin Dynasties." *Chinese Culture* 1.2 (1957).

Ch'en Lin-kuo. "Shu-tsu, su-tsu ho han-men" (Commoner Families, Ordinary Families, and Cold Gates). *Chung-kuo shih yen-chiu* 21.1 (1984).

Ch'en Shih-hsiang, trans. *Biography of Ku K'ai-chih.* Berkeley: University of California Press, 1953.

Ch'en Shu-liang. *Liu-ch'ao yen-shui* (Six Dynasties Misty Waters). Ta wen-hsüeh shih-kuan ts'ung-shu. Peking: Hsien-tai ch'u-pan-she, 1990.

Ch'en Yin-k'o. *Ch'en Yin-k'o, Wei-Chin Nan-Pei-ch'ao shih chiang-yen lu* (Notes from Ch'en Yin-k'o's Lectures [1947–1948] on Wei, Chin, and Northern and Southern Dynasties History). Edited by Wan Sheng-nan. Ho-fei: Huang-shan shu-she, 1987.

————. "Ch'ing-t'an yü ch'ing-t'an wu-kuo" (Pure Conversation and Mismanagement of the State Due to Pure Conversation). *Ch'en Yin-k'o hsien-sheng lun-wen chi pu-pien.* Chiu-ssu ts'ung-shu 5. Taipei: Fu-hsin hang yin-shua shih-yeh yu-hsien kung-ssu, 1977.

————. "Hsiao-yao-yu Hsiang Kuo i chi Chih Tun i t'an-yüan" (An Inquiry into the Origins of the Hsiang and Kuo Interpretations of "Free and Easy Wandering" and Chih Tun's Interpretation). *Ch'ing-hua hsüeh-pao* 12.2 (1937).

————. "Shu Tung-Chin Wang Tao chih kung-yeh" (A Statement of Wang Tao's Achievements in the Eastern Chin). *Ch'en Yin-k'o wen-chi* 2. Chin-ming-kuan ts'ung-kao edition. 1956; Shanghai: Shang-hai ku-chi ch'u-pan-she, 1980.

————. "T'ao Yüan-ming chih ssu-hsiang yü ch'ing-t'an chih kuan-hsi"

(The Relationship between T'ao Yüan-ming's Thought and Pure Converstaion). *Ch'en Yin-k'o hsien-sheng wen-shih lun-chi* 1. 1945; Hong Kong: Wen-wen ch'u-pan-she, 1972.

———. "T'ien-shih tao yü pin-hai-yü chih kuan-hsi" (The Way of the Heavenly Masters and Its Relationship to the Region Near the Sea). *Ch'en Yin-k'o hsien-sheng wen-shih lun-chi* 1. Hong Kong: Wen-wen ch'u-pan-she, 1972.

Ch'en Yung. "Liu Yü yü Chin-Sung chih chi te han-men shih-tsu" (Liu Yü and the Cold Gate Literati at the Time of Transition from Chin to Sung). *Li-shih yen-chiu* 1984.6.

Cheng Ch'in-jen. "Chiu-p'in kuan-jen fa—Liu-ch'ao te hsüan-chü chih-tu" (The Nine Ranks of Officials Law—the Selection System of the Six Dynasties). *Chung-kuo wen-hua hsin-lun (chih-tu p'ien)*, 1982.6.

Chiang Fu-ya. "Tung-Chin Nan-ch'ao te ta-t'u-ti so-yu-chih" (The Large Landholding System of the Eastern Chin and Southern Dynasties). *Chiang-hai hsüeh-k'an* 1992.2.

Chiang Po-ch'in. "Chung-kuo t'ien-k'o-chih, pu-ch'ü-chih yü Ying-kuo wei-lan-chih te pi-chiao yen-chiu" (A Comparative Study of China's T'ien-k'o and Pu-ch'ü Systems with English Villenage). *Li-shih yen-chiu* 1984.4.

Chiang Wei-ch'iao. "Liu-ch'ao wen-hsüeh yü Fo-chiao ying-hsiang" (Six Dynasties Literature and Buddhist Influence). *Kuo-hsüeh lun-heng* 1935.6.

Chien Po-tsan. "Ch'in-Han li-shih shang te jo-kan wen-t'i" (Several Problems in Ch'in-Han History). *Li-shih hsüeh* 1 (1979).

Ch'ien Mu. *Ch'in-Han shih* (A History of Ch'in and Han). Ts'ang-hai ts'ung-k'an. 1957; Taipei: Tung-ta t'u-shu kung-ssu, 1985.

———. "Lüeh lun Wei-Chin Nan-Pei-ch'ao hsüeh-shu wen-hua yü tang-shih men-ti chih kuan-hsi" (A Brief Discussion of Wei, Chin, and Northern and Southern Dynasties Scholarly Culture and Its Relation to Social Position at That Time). *Hsin-ya hsüeh-pao* 5.2 (1963).

———. "Yüan Hung cheng-lun yü shih-hsüeh" (Yüan Hung's Essay on Politics and Historical Studies). *Chung-kuo hsüeh-shu ssu-hsiang shih lun-ts'ung* 3. 1955; Taipei: Tung-ta t'u-shu t'ou-fen yu-hsien kung-ssu, 1985.

Chin Chia-jui. "Tung-Chin Nan-ch'ao ta ti-chu te t'u-ti chan-yu yü lao-tung-li te pien-chih" (The Occupation of Land and Organization of Labor by Great Landlords in the Eastern Chin and Southern Dynasties). *Shih-hsüeh yüeh-k'an* 1957.1.

Chin Fa-ken. *Yung-chia luan hou pei-fang te hao-tsu* (Northern Magnates after the Yung-chia Disturbances [307–313]). Taipei: T'ai-wan shang-wu yin-shu-kuan, 1964.

Chin, Frank Fa-ken. "The Element of Regionalism in Medieval China:

Observations on the Founding of the Eastern Chin." In International Congress of Orientalists, *Actes du XXIXe congrès. Chine ancienne.*
Paris, 1977.

Ch'in-Han ching-chi ssu-hsiang shih (A History of Ch'in-Han Economic
Thought). Written by Shang-hai she-hui k'o-hsüeh yüan, ching-chi
yen-chiu-so, ching-chi ssu-hsiang shih yen-chiu shih. Peking: Chung-
hua shu-chü, 1989.

Chou I-liang. "Liang-Chin Nan-ch'ao te ch'ing-i" (Pure Criticism in the
Two Chin and Southern Dynasties). In *Wei-Chin Sui-T'ang shih lun-chi*
2. Edited by Huang Lieh. Peking: Chung-kuo she-hui k'o-hsüeh
ch'u-pan-she, 1983.

————. "Nan-ch'ao ching-nei chih ko chung jen chi cheng-fu tui-tai
chih cheng-ts'e" (The Kinds of People within the Borders of the
Southern Dynasties and the Government's Policies for the Treatment of Them). In *Wei-Chin Nan-Pei-ch'ao shih lun-chi.* Peking:
Chung-hua shu-chü, 1963.

Chou Nien-ch'ang. "Tung-Chin Pei-fu-ping te chien-li chi ch'i t'e-tien"
(The Establishment of the Eastern Chin Northern Palace Army and
Its Special Characteristics). In *Wei-Chin Sui-T'ang shih lun-chi* 2.
Edited by Huang Lieh. Peking: Chung-kuo she-hui k'o-hsüeh ch'u-
pan-she, 1983.

Chou Shao-hsien. "Ch'ing-t'an wang Chin wen-t'i chih shang-ch'üeh"
(A Discussion of the Question of Chin's Destruction by Pure Conversation). In *Ch'in-Han shih chi chung-ku shih ch'ien-ch'i yen-chiu lun-chi*
(Collected Essays on the Study of Ch'in-Han History and Early Medieval History). Ta-lu tsa-chih shih-hsüeh ts'ung-shu, 1.4. 1960.

Chu I-yün. *Wei-Chin feng-ch'i yü Liu-ch'ao wen-hsüeh* (The Wei-Chin Style
and Six Dynasties Literature). Taipei: Wen-shih-che ch'u-pan-so,
1980.

Chu Jui-k'ai. *Liang-Han ssu-hsiang shih* (A History of Thought in the Two
Han). Shanghai: Shang-hai ku-chi ch'u-pan-she, 1989.

Chu Shao-hou. *Wei-Chin Nan-Pei-ch'ao t'u-ti chih-tu yü chieh-chi kuan-hsi*
(The Land System and Class Relations of the Wei, Chin, and Northern and Southern Dynasties). Chengchow, Honan: Chung-chou ku-
chi ch'u-pan-she, 1988.

Chu Ta-wei. "Nan-ch'ao shao-shu-min-tsu kai-k'uang chi ch'i yü Han-tsu
te jung-ho" (The General Condition of Minorities in the Southern
Dynasties and Their Mixing with the Han People). *Chung-kuo shih
yen-chiu* 1980.1.

————. "Wei-Chin Nan-Pei-ch'ao wen-hua te chi-pen t'e-cheng" (The
Basic Characteristics of Wei, Chin, Northern and Southern Dynasty
Culture). *Wen-shih-che* 1993.3.

Chu Tsung-pin. "Lüeh-lun Chin-lü chih 'ju-chia-hua'" (A Brief Essay on
the "Confucianization" of Chin Law). *Chung-kuo shih yen-chiu* 1985.2.

Chu Yung-chia. "Lun Ts'ao Ts'ao te i-chih hao-ch'iang chi ch'i fa-chia ssu-hsiang" (On Ts'ao Ts'ao's Restraint of Magnates and His Legalist Thought). In *Ts'ao Ts'ao lun-chi*, edited by Kuo Mo-jo. Hong Kong: Sheng-huo tu-shu hsin-chih san-lien shu-tien, 1979.

Ch'ü, T'ung-tsu. *Han Social Structure*. Edited by Jack L. Dull. Seattle: University of Washington Press, 1972.

Chung Ch'i-chieh. "Nan-Pei-ch'ao shih-ch'i hsing-ch'eng pei-ch'iang nan-jo chü-mien chih tsai-hsi" (A Reanalysis of the Formation of Conditions of Northern Strength and Southern Weakness in the Northern and Southern Dynasties Period). *Pei-fang lun-ts'ung* 1992.3.

Creel, H. G. "The Eclectics of Han Thought." In *The Making of China: Main Themes in Premodern Chinese History*, edited by Chun-shu Chang. Englewood Cliffs, N. J.: Prentice-Hall, 1975.

Crowell, William G. "Northern Émigrés and the Problems of Census Registration Under the Eastern Jin and Southern Dynasties." In *State and Society in Early Medieval China*, edited by Albert E. Dien. Stanford: Stanford University Press, 1990.

————. "Social Unrest and Rebellion in Jiangnan during the Six Dynasties." *Modern China* 9.3 (1983).

Cutter, Robert Joe. "The Incident at the Gate: Cao Zhi, the Succession, and Literary Fame." *T'oung Pao* 71.4–5 (1985).

De Crespigny, Rafe. "The Chinese War-lord in Fact and Fiction: A Study of Ts'ao Ts'ao." *Chung-kuo li-shih hsüeh-hui shih-hsüeh chi-k'an* 4 (1972).

————. *Generals of the South: The Foundation and Early History of the Three Kingdoms State of Wu*. Faculty of Asian Studies Monographs No. 16. Canberra: Australian National University, 1990.

————. "Political Protest in Imperial China: The Great Proscription of Later Han, 167–184." *Papers in Far Eastern History* 11 (1975).

————. "Politics and Philosophy under the Government of Emperor Huan, 159–168 A.D." *T'oung Pao* 66.1–3 (1980).

————. "Prefectures and Population in South China in the First Three Centuries A.D." *Chung-yang yen-chiu-yüan, li-shih yü-yen yen-chiu-so chi-k'an* 40 (1968).

————. "The Recruitment System of the Imperial Bureaucracy of the Late Han." *The Chung Chi Journal* 6.1 (1966).

————, trans. *The Last of the Han: Being the Chronicle of the Years 181–220 A.D. as Recorded in Chapters 58–68 of the Tzu-chih T'ung-Chien of Ssu-ma Kuang*. Canberra: Australian National University, 1969.

Demiéville, Paul. "La pénétration du bouddhisme dans la tradition philosophique chinoise." *Cahiers d'histoire mondiale* 3 (1956–1957).

————. "Philosophy and Religion from Han to Sui." In *The Cambridge History of China*, vol. 1: *The Ch'in and Han Empires, 221 B.C.–A.D. 220*, edited by Denis Twitchett and Michael Loewe. Cambridge: Cambridge University Press, 1986.

DeWoskin, Kenneth, trans. *Doctors, Diviners, and Magicians of Ancient China: Biographies of Fang-shih.* New York: Columbia University Press, 1983.

Dien, Albert E., ed. *State and Society in Early Medieval China.* Stanford: Stanford University Press, 1990.

————. "Yen Chih-t'ui (531–591+): A Buddho-Confucian." In *Confucian Personalities,* edited by Arthur F. Wright and Denis Twitchett. Stanford: Stanford University Press, 1962.

————. "The *Yüan-hun chih* (Accounts of Ghosts with Grievances): A Sixth-Century Collection of Stories." In *Wen-lin: Studies in the Chinese Humanities,* edited by Chow Tse-tsung. Madison: University of Wisconsin, 1968.

Dohi, Yoshikazu. "A Study of a Fragmentary Tun-Huang District Land Allotment Record from the T'ien-pao Period of the T'ang Dynasty with Regard to the Problem of Land Reallotment." *Memoirs of the Research Department of the Toyo Bunko* 42 (1984).

Dubs, Homer H. "The Beginnings of Alchemy." *Isis* 38.1–2 (1947).

Eberhard, Wolfram. *Conquerors and Rulers: Social Forces in Mediaeval China.* Leiden: E. J. Brill, 1952.

————. "The Political Function of Astronomy and Astronomers in Han China." In *Chinese Thought and Institutions,* edited by John K. Fairbank. Chicago: University of Chicago Press, 1957.

Ebrey, Patricia B. *The Aristocratic Families of Early Imperial China: A Case Study of the Po-Ling Ts'ui Family.* Cambridge: Cambridge University Press, 1978.

————. "Estate and Family Management in the Later Han as Seen in the *Monthly Instructions for the Four Classes of People*." *Journal of the Economic and Social History of the Orient* 17.2 (1974).

————. "Towards a Better Understanding of the Late Han Upper Class." In *State and Society in Early Medieval China,* edited by Albert E. Dien. Stanford: Stanford University Press, 1990.

Edwards, E. D. " 'Principles of Whistling'—*Hsiao chih*—Anonymous." *Bulletin of the School of Oriental and African Studies* 20 (1957).

————. "Some Aspects of the Conflicts of Religion in China during the Six Dynasties and T'ang Periods." *Bulletin of the School of Oriental Studies* 7.4 (1935).

Fan Ning. "Lun Wei-Chin shih-tai chih-shih fen-tzu te ssu-hsiang fen-hua chi ch'i she-hui ken-yüan" (On the Differentiation of the Thought of Intellectuals in the Wei-Chin Period and Its Social Origins). *Li-shih yen-chiu* 1955.4.

Fan Shou-k'ang. *Wei-Chin chih ch'ing-t'an* (Wei and Chin Pure Conversation). Shih-ti hsiao ts'ung-shu. Shanghai: Shang-wu yin-shu-kuan, 1936.

Fang, Achilles, trans. *The Chronicle of the Three Kingdoms (220–265): Chapters 69–78 from the* Tzu Chih T'ung Chien *of Ssu-ma Kuang (1019–1086),* 2. Harvard-Yenching Institute Studies 6. Cambridge: Harvard University Press, 1965.

Fang Hsün. "T'ang-tai Chung-kuo ho Ya-chou ko-tsu te wen-hua chiao-liu" (Cultural Exchange between China and All the Peoples of Asia during the T'ang Dynasty). In *Sui-T'ang shih yen-chiu lun-chi, hsüeh-shu wen-hua p'ien,* edited by Ho Kuan-piao. 1956; Hong Kong: Shih-hsüeh yen-chiu-hui, 1979.

Fang Li-t'ien. *Wei-Chin Nan-Pei-ch'ao Fo-chiao lun-ts'ung* (Collected Essays on Wei, Chin, and Northern and Southern Dynasties Buddhism). Peking: Chung-hua shu-chü, 1982.

Fang Pei-ch'en. "Shih chiu-p'in chung-cheng chih-tu chih i-p'in hsü-she wen-t'i" (An Explanation of the Problem of the Unused Provision for Rank One in the Nine Ranks and Arbiters System). *Hsü-ch'ang shih-chuan hsüeh-pao: She-k'o-pan* 1989.1.

Fang P'eng-ch'eng, ed. *San-kuo liang-Chin jen-wu hsiao-chuan nien-piao* (Short Biographies and Chronological Tables of Personalities in the Three Kingdoms and Two Chin Dynasties). Taipei: T'ai-wan shang-wu yin-shu-kuan, 1981.

Feifel, Eugene, trans. *"Pao-p'u tzu Nei-p'ien."* *Monumenta Serica* 6.1–2 (1941), 9 (1944), 11 (1946).

Fogel, Joshua A. "A New Direction in Japanese Sinology." *Harvard Journal of Asiatic Studies* 44.1 (1984).

Forke, Alfred, trans. *Lun-heng: Miscellaneous Essays of Wang Ch'ung.* Reprint; New York: Paragon Book Gallery, 1962.

Frankel, Hans H. "The K'ung Family of Shan-yin." *Ch'ing-hua hsüeh-pao,* new series 2.2 (1961).

Frodsham, J. D. "Hsieh Ling-yün's Contribution to Medieval Chinese Buddhism." In International Association of Historians of Asia, *Proceedings of the Second Biennial Conference.* Taipei, 1962.

———. *The Murmuring Stream: The Life and Works of the Chinese Nature Poet Hsieh Ling-yün (385–433), Duke of K'ang-lo.* Kuala Lumpur: University of Malaya Press, 1967.

Fu Chao-chün. "Liu-ch'ao ch'eng-shih ching-chi te t'e-tian chi ch'i tsai hsin ching-chi-ch'ü fa-chan chung te tso-yung" (The Special Features of the Urban Economy in the Six Dynasties and Its Function in the Development of New Economic Zones). *Hsüeh-shu yüeh-k'an* 1992.11.

Fu K'o-hui. "Wei-Chin Nan-ch'ao huang-chi chih yen-chiu" (A Study of the Yellow Registers in the Wei, Chin, and Southern Dynasties). *Shan-tung ta-hsüeh hsüeh-pao: Che-she pan,* 1989.1.

Fu Lo-ch'ung. *Han-T'ang shih lun-chi* (Collected Essays on Han through T'ang History). Taipei: Lien-ching ch'u-pan shih-yeh kung-ssu, 1977.

Fu Mao-mien. "Lun Chin-tai te in-i ssu-hsiang ho yin-i shih-jen" (On Reclusive Thought and Recluse-Poets in the Chin Dynasty). *Shantung ta-hsüeh hsüeh-pao: Wen-shih-che* 1958.4.

Fukui, Fumimasa-Bunga, "Buddhism and the Structure of *Ch'ing-t'an* ('Pure Discourses')—A Note on Sino-Indian Intercourse." *Chinese Culture* 10.2 (1969).

Grafflin, Dennis. "The Great Family in Medieval South China." *Harvard Journal of Asiatic Studies* 41.1 (1981).

———. "The Onomastics of Medieval South China: Patterned Naming in the Lang-yeh and T'ai-yüan Wang." *Journal of the American Oriental Society* 103.2 (1983).

———. "Reinventing China: Pseudobureaucracy in the Early Southern Dynasties." In *State and Society in Early Medieval China,* edited by Albert E. Dien. Stanford: Stanford University Press, 1990.

Graham, A. C. " 'Being' in Western Philosophy Compared with *Shih/Fei* and *Yu/Wu* in Chinese Philosophy." *Asia Major,* new series 7.1–2 (1959). Reprinted, with some revisions, in *Studies in Chinese Philosophy and Philosophical Literature.* Albany: State University of New York Press, 1990.

———. "The Date and Composition of Liehtzyy." *Asia Major,* new series 8.2 (1961).

———, trans. *The Book of Lieh-tzu: A Classic of Tao.* New York: Columbia University Press, 1960.

Han Fu-chih. "Tung-Han te hsüan-chü" ([Bureaucratic] Selection in the Eastern Han). *Kuo-li T'ai-wan ta-hsüeh li-shih hsüeh-hsi hsüeh-pao* 4 (1977).

Han Kuo-p'an. *Nan-ch'ao ching-chi shih-t'an* (Probing the Southern Dynasty Economy). Shanghai: Shang-hai jen-min ch'u-pan-she, 1963.

———. *Pei-ch'ao Sui-T'ang te chün-t'ien chih-tu* (The Equal Fields System of the Northern Dynasties, Sui and T'ang). Shanghai: Shang-hai jen-min ch'u-pan-she, 1984.

———. *Wei-Chin Nan-Pei-ch'ao shih-kang* (An Outline of Wei, Chin, and Northern and Southern Dynasties History). Peking: Jen-min ch'u-pan-she, 1983.

Hashimoto, Hokei. "The Philosophic Influence of *Vimalakīrti-nirdeśa sūtra* upon Chinese Culture." *Actes du XXIXe congrès international des orientalistes. Chine ancienne.* Paris, 1977.

Henderson, Keith M. "The Han-Sui Bureaucratic System in Ancient China." *Philippine Journal of Public Administration* 9.3 (1965).

Henricks, Robert G., trans. *Philosophy and Argumentation in Third-Century China: The Essays of Hsi K'ang.* Princeton: Princeton University Press, 1983.

Henry, Eric. "Chu-ko Liang in the Eyes of His Contemporaries." *Harvard Journal of Asiatic Studies* 52.2 (1992).

Herbert, P. A. "Civil Service Selection in China in the Latter Half of the Seventh Century." *Papers on Far Eastern History* 13 (1976).

―――. "Perceptions of Provincial Officialdom in Early T'ang China." *Asia Major*, third series 2.1 (1989).

Higashi Shinji. "Go-Kan jidai no senkyo to chihō shakai" (The [Bureaucratic] Selection and Local Society of Later Han Times). *Tōyōshi kenkyū* 46.2 (1987).

Hirai Masashi. "Kandai ni okeru juka kanryō no kugyō-sō e no shinjun" (The Infiltration of Confucian Officials into the High Ranks of Officialdom in the Han Dynasty). *Rekishi ni okeru minshū to bunka—Sakai Tadao sensei koki shukuga kinen ronshū.* Tokyo: Kokusho kankokai, 1982.

Ho Ch'ang-ch'ün. *Han T'ang chien feng-chien te kuo-yu t'u-ti chih yü chün-t'ien chih* (The Feudal System of State Landownership and the Equal Fields System between Han and T'ang). Shanghai: Shang-hai jen-min ch'u-pan-she, 1958.

―――. *Wei-Chin ch'ing-t'an ssu-hsiang ch'u-lun* (A Preliminary Essay on the Thought of Wei-Chin Ch'ing-t'an). Shanghai: Shang-wu yin-shu-kuan, 1947.

Ho Ch'i-min. "Han-Chin pien-chü chung te chung-yüan shih-feng" (The Literati Style in the Central Plain amid the Changing Circumstances from Han to Chin). *Chung-kuo li-shih hsüeh-hui shih-hsüeh chi-k'an* 5. Taipei, 1973.

―――. "Wei-Chin ssu-hsiang yü shih-tsu hsin-t'ai" (Wei-Chin Thought and Literati Attitudes). *Kuo-li cheng-chih ta-hsüeh li-shih hsüeh-pao* 1.3 (1983).

―――. *Wei-Chin ssu-hsiang yü t'an-feng* (Wei-Chin Thought and Conversational Style). Taipei: T'ai-wan hsüeh-sheng shu-chü, 1982.

Ho, Peng-yoke. "The Search for Perpetual Youth in China, with Special Reference to Chinese Alchemy." *Papers on Far Eastern History* 7 (1973).

Ho, Ping-yü, and Joseph Needham. "Elixir Poisoning in Medieval China." *Janus* 48 (1959).

Ho, Tzu-ch'üan. "Early Development of Manorial Economy in Wei and Tsin." In *Chinese Social History,* edited by E-Tu Zen Sun and John DeFrancis. Washington, D.C.: American Council of Learned Societies, 1956.

―――. "Liang-Han hao-tsu fa-chan te san ko shih-ch'i" (The Three Periods in the Development of Magnates in the Two Han). *Ch'in-Han shih lun-ts'ung* 3. Sian: Shan-hsi jen-min ch'u-pan-she, 1986.

―――. "Nan-Pei-ch'ao shih-ch'i nan-pei ju-hsüeh feng-shang pu t'ung te yüan-yüan" (The Origins of the Difference between Confucian Fashions in North and South in the Northern and Southern Dynasties Period). In *Chi-nien Ch'en Yin-k'o hsien-sheng tan-ch'en pai-nien hsüeh-shu lun-wen-chi,* edited by Pei-ching ta-hsüeh Chung-kuo chung-ku-shih yen-chiu chung-hsin. 1983; Peking: Pei-ching ta-hsüeh ch'u-pan-she, 1989.

———. "San-kuo shih-ch'i nung-ts'un ching-chi te p'o-huai yü fu-hsing" (The Destruction and Revival of the Village Economy during the Three Kingdoms Period). *Shih-huo pan-yüeh k'an* 1.5 (1935).

———. "Wei-Chin shih-ch'i chuang-yüan ching-chi te ch'u-hsing" (The Incipient Manorial Economy of the Wei and Chin Period). *Shih-huo pan-yüeh k'an* 1.1 (1934).

Holcombe, Charles. "The Bonds of Empire: Liberty in Early Medieval China." *The Historian* 54.4 (1992).

———. "The Exemplar State: Ideology, Self-Cultivation, and Power in Fourth-Century China." *Harvard Journal of Asiatic Studies* 49.1 (1989).

Holmgren, Jennifer. "The Lu Clan of Tai Commandery and Their Contribution to the T'o-Pa State of Northern Wei in the Fifth Century." *T'oung Pao* 69.4–5 (1983).

———. "The Making of an Élite: Local Politics and Social Relations in Northeastern China during the Fifth Century A.D." *Papers on Far Eastern History* 30 (1984).

———. "Northern Wei as a Conquest Dynasty: Current Perceptions; Past Scholarship." *Papers on Far Eastern History* 40 (1989).

Holzman, Donald. "Les débuts du système médiéval de choix et de classement des fonctionnaires: Les neuf categories et l'impartial et juste." *Mélanges publiés par l'Institut des hautes études chinoises,* vol. 1. Paris: University of Paris, 1957.

———. *Poetry and Politics: The Life and Works of Juan Chi, A.D. 210–263.* Cambridge: Cambridge University Press, 1976.

———. "Les sept sages de la forêt des bambous et la société de leur temps." *T'oung Pao* 44.4–5 (1956).

———. "Ts'ao Chih and the Immortals." *Asia Major,* third series 1.1 (1988).

———. *La vie et la pensée de Hi K'ang (223–262 Ap. J.-C.)* Leiden: E.J. Brill, 1957.

Horiike Nobuo. "Keikō ni okeru shinkō to shakai—Shō Shū to no 'Yōjō-ron' ronsō o chūshin toshite" (Belief and Society in Hsi K'ang—Centering on His Dispute with Hsiang Hsiu over the "Essay on Nourishing Life"). *Rekishi ni okeru minshū to bunka—Sakai Tadao sensei koki shukuga kinen ronshū.* Tokyo: Kokusho kankokai, 1982.

Hou Hsü-tung. "Chin-nien li-yung Tun-huang T'u-lu-fan wen-shu yen-chiu Wei-Chin Nan-Pei-ch'ao shih kai-k'uang" (The General Situation in Recent Years Regarding the Use of Texts from Tunhuang and Turfan in Studying Wei, Chin, and Northern and Southern Dynasties History). *Chung-kuo shih yen-chiu tung-t'ai* 1992.5.

Hou Wai-lü. "Chung-kuo feng-chien she-hui t'u-ti so-yu-chih hsing-shih te wen-t'i: Chung-kuo feng-chien she-hui fa-chan kuei-lü shang-tui chih-i" (The Problem of the Form of Landownership in Chinese Feudal Society: An Exchange Concerning the Laws of Development of Chinese Feudal Society). *Li-shih yen-chiu* 1954.1.

Hsing I-t'ien. "Tung-Han hsiao-lien te shen-fen pei-ching" (The Social Status Background of the "Filial and Upright" in the Eastern Han). In *Ti erh chieh Chung-kuo she-hui ching-chi shih yen-t'ao-hui lun-wen-chi,* edited by Hsü Cho-yün et al. Taipei: Han-hsüeh yen-chiu tzu-liao chi fu-wu chung-hsin, 1983.

Hsing T'ieh. "Liang Chin Nan-Pei-ch'ao shih-ch'i te hu-teng chih-tu" (The Household Ranking System of the Two Chin and Northern and Southern Dynasties Period). *Ho-pei shih-yüan hsüeh-pao: She-k'o-pan* 1991.4.

Hsiung Te-chi. "Wei-Chin Nan-Pei-ch'ao shih-ch'i chieh-chi chieh-kou yen-chiu chung te chi-ko wen-t'i" (Several Problems in the Study of Class Structure in the Wei, Chin, and Northern and Southern Dynasties Period). In *Wei-Chin Sui-T'ang shih lun-chi* 1, edited by Huang Lieh. Peking: Chung-kuo she-hui k'o-hsüeh ch'u-pan-she, 1981.

Hsü, Cho-yün. *Han Agriculture: The Formation of Early Chinese Agrarian Economy (206 B.C.–A.D. 220).* Edited by Jack L. Dull. Seattle: University of Washington Press, 1980.

———. "The Roles of the Literati and of Regionalism in the Fall of the Han Dynasty." In *The Collapse of Ancient States and Civilizations,* edited by Norman Yoffee and George L. Cowgill. Tucson: University of Arizona Press, 1988.

Hsü Hui. "Lun Liu-ch'ao shih-ch'i Ch'ang-chiang liu-yü ching-chi te cheng-t'i k'ai-fa" (On the Economic Development of the Entire Yangtze River Valley in the Six Dynasties Period). *Chiang-hai hsüeh-k'an* 1992.4.

Hsü Lien-ta and Lou Ching. "Han-T'ang k'o-chü i-t'ung lun" (On the Similarities and Differences between the Examination Systems of Han and T'ang). *Li-shih yen-chiu* 1990.5.

Hu A-hsiang. "Shih-lun liang-Chin Nan-ch'ao shih-ch'i te t'u-tuan" (An Experimental Essay on Residence Determination in the Two-Chin and Southern Dynasties Period). *Nan-ching shih chih* 1992.5.

Hu Fu-ch'en. *Wei-Chin shen-hsien tao-chiao: Pao-p'u-tzu nei-p'ien yen-chiu* (Immortality Taoism of Wei and Chin: Studies of the Inner Chapters of the *Pao-p'u-tzu*). Peking: Jen-min ch'u-pan-she, 1989.

Hu Ju-lei. *Chung-kuo feng-chien she-hui hsing-t'ai yen-chiu* (Studies on the Form of Chinese Feudal Society). Peking: Sheng-huo, tu-shu, hsin-chih san-lien shu-tien, 1979.

Hu, Shih. "Buddhistic Influence on Chinese Religious Life." *Chinese Social and Political Science Review* 9.1 (1925).

———. "The Establishment of Confucianism as a State Religion During the Han Dynasty." *Journal of the North China Branch of the Royal Asiatic Society* 60 (1929).

———. "The Indianization of China: A Case Study in Cultural Borrowing." In *Independence, Convergence, and Borrowing in Institutions, Thought, and Art*, Harvard Tercentenary Conference of Arts and Sciences. Cambridge: Harvard University Press, 1937.

Hua Chih-sun. "Wei-Chin Nan-Pei-ch'ao chih ching-chi chuang-k'uang" (Economic Conditions in the Wei, Chin, and Northern and Southern Dynasties). *Chung-kuo ching-chi* 2.9 (1934).

Huang Cheng-fan and T'ien Tse-pin. "Tung-Chin men-fa cheng-chih san-lun" (Scattered Thoughts on Eastern Chin Great Family Politics). *Su-chou ta-hsüeh hsüeh-pao: Che-she-pan* 1990.1.

Huang Lieh. "Wei-Chin Nan-Pei-ch'ao min-tsu kuan-hsi te chi ko li-lun wen-t'i" (Several Theoretical Problems in Ethnic Relations during the Wei, Chin, and Northern and Southern Dynasties). *Li-shih yen-chiu* 1985.3.

Hughes, E. R. *The Art of Letters: Lu Chi's 'Wen Fu,'* A.D. *302.* New York: Pantheon Books, 1951.

Hulsewé, A. F. P. "Han China—A Proto 'Welfare State'? Fragments of Han Law Discovered in North-West China." *T'oung Pao* 73.4–5 (1987).

Hung Hsiu-p'ing. "Fo-chiao pan-jo ssu-hsiang te ch'uan-ju ho Wei-Chin hsüan-hsüeh te ch'an-sheng" (The Introduction of Buddhist Prajñā Thought and the Birth of Wei and Chin Hsüan-hsüeh). *Nan-ching ta-hsüeh hsüeh-pao (che-hsüeh she-hui k'o-hsüeh)* 1985, supplement.

Hurvitz, Leon. "Chih Tun's Notions of Prajñā." *Journal of the American Oriental Society* 88.2 (1968).

———. " 'Render unto Caesar' in Early Chinese Buddhism." *Sino-Indian Studies*, Liebenthal festschrift, 5.3–4 (1957).

Ikeda On. "Chūgoku rekidai boken ryakukō" (A Brief Examination of Chinese Tomb Deeds through the Ages). *Tōyō bunka kenkyūsho kiyō: Sōritsu yon-jū shūnen kinen ronshū* 1, 86 (1981).

———. "T'ang Household Registers and Related Documents." In *Perspectives on the T'ang*, edited by Arthur F. Wright and Denis Twitchett. New Haven: Yale University Press, 1973.

Inaba Ichirō. "Kandai ni okeru minkan chitsujo no keisei—iwayuru gōzoku no chūshin to suru" (The Formation of Private Order in the Han Dynasty—Centering on the So-called Magnates). In *Chūgoku kizokusei shakai no kenkyū*, edited by Kawakatsu Yoshio and Tonami Mamoru. Kyoto: Kyōto daigaku jinbun kagaku kenkyūsho, 1987.

Ishikawa Tadahisa. "Sha An to Kaikei no yū" (Hsieh An and Travels in K'uai-chi). *Tōkyō Shinagakuhō* 6 (1960).

Jen Chi-yü. *Han-T'ang Fo-chiao ssu-hsiang lun-chi* (Collected Essays on

Han through T'ang Buddhist Thought). 1963; Peking: Jen-min ch'u-pan-she, 1973.

Johnson, David G. *The Medieval Chinese Oligarchy.* Boulder: Westview Press, 1977.

Kaltenmark, Max. "The Ideology of the T'ai-p'ing ching." In *Facets of Taoism: Essays in Chinese Religion,* edited by Holmes Welch and Anna Seidel. New Haven: Yale University Press, 1979.

Kamiya Noriko. "Shin jidai ni okeru irei shingi—sono genreishugiteki seikaku" (An Investigation of Violations of *Li* in Chin Times—Its Character of Strict Ritualism). *Tōyō gakuhō* 67.3–4 (1986).

———. "Shin jidai ni okeru ōhō to karei" (Royal Law and Family Ritual in Chin Times). *Tōyō gakuhō* 60.1–2 (1978).

Kanō Naosada. "Go-Kan matsu chihō gōzoku no dōkō—chihō bunken-ka to gōzoku" (The Trend toward Local Magnates at the End of the Later Han—Local Separatism and Magnates). In *Chūgoku chūsei-shi kenkyū—Rikuchō Zui Tō no shakai to bunka,* edited by Utsunomiya Kiyoyoshi. Tokyo: Tōkai daigaku shuppankai, 1970.

———. "Kan Bō to sono shūhen—Kōnan bunka no ichi kōsatsu" (Kan Pao and His Environment—an Investigation of Chiang-nan Culture). *Kodaigaku* 18.1 (1972).

Kao Chih-hsin. "Hsi-Chin k'o-t'ien k'ao shih" (An Explanation of *K'o-t'ien* [Dutied Fields] in the Western Chin). In *Wei-Chin Sui-T'ang shih lun-chi* 1. Peking: Chung-kuo she-hui k'o-hsüeh ch'u-pan-she, 1981.

Kao Min. *Ch'in-Han Wei-Chin Nan-Pei-ch'ao t'u-ti chih-tu yen-chiu* (Studies on the Land System of Ch'in, Han, Wei, Chin, and the Northern and Southern Dynasties). Kaifeng: Chung-chou ku-chi ch'u-pan-she, 1986.

———. "Kuan-yü hsi-Chin chan-t'ien, k'o-t'ien chih te chi-ko wen-t'i" (Several Problems Concerning the Western Chin *Chan-t'ien* [Occupation of Fields] and *K'o-t'ien* [Dutied Fields] Systems). *Li-shih yen-chiu* 1983.3.

———. "Shih-lun liang-Chin shih-ch'i she-hui chu-yao mao-tun te yen-pien kuo-ch'eng" (An Experimental Essay on the Process of Change in the Principal Social Contradictions of the Two Chin Period). *Shih-hsüeh shih-yen-chiu* 1989.2.

———. "Ts'ao-Wei shih-chia chih-tu te hsing-ch'eng yü yen-pien" (The Formation and Changes in the Ts'ao-Wei System of *Shih-chia* [Military Families]). *Li-shih yen-chiu* 1989.5.

———. "Wei-Chin Nan-Pei-ch'ao fu-i huo-mien te tui-hsiang yü t'iao-chien" (The Subjects and Conditions of Tax and Labor Exemptions in the Wei, Chin, and Northern and Southern Dynasties). *Chiang-Han lun-t'an* 1990.6.

———. "Wei-Chin Nan-Pei-ch'ao shih pu-fen" (Section on Wei, Chin, and Northern and Southern Dynasties History). In *Chung-kuo ku-tai-shih tao-tu* (Reader's Guide to Ancient Chinese History), edited by Hsiao Li and Li Kuei-hai. Shanghai: Wen-hui ch'u-pan-she, 1991.

Kawakatsu, Yoshio. "L'aristocratie et la société féodale au début des six dynasties." *Zinbun* 17 (1981).

―――. *Chūgoku no rekishi*, 3: *Gi Shin nanbokuchō* (Chinese History, [volume] 3: the Wei, Chin, and Northern and Southern Dynasties). Tokyo: Kōdansha, 1981.

―――. "La décadence de l'aristocratie chinoise sous les Dynasties du Sud." *Acta Asiatica* 21 (1971).

―――. *Rikuchō kizokusei shakai no kenkyū* (Studies in Six Dynasties Aristocratic Society). Tokyo: Iwanami shoten, 1982.

―――. "Sie Ling-yun et le *che-chouo sin-yu.*" *Mélanges de sinologie, offerts à Monsieur Paul Demiéville* 2. Paris: Institut des hautes études chinoises, 1974.

―――. "Tō Shin kizokusei no kakuritsu katei—gunjiryoku to no kanren no moto ni" (The Process of Establishment of the Eastern Chin Aristocratic System—on the Basis of Its Relationship to Military Strength). *Tōhō gakuhō* 52 (1980).

Kim Minsoo. "Tōshin seiken no seiritsu katei—Shiba-Ei (Gen-tei) no furyō o chūshin toshite" (The Process of Formation of Eastern Chin Political Authority—Centering on Ssu-ma Jui's [Emperor Yüan's] Administration). *Tōyōshi kenkyū* 48.2 (1989).

Kimura, Eiichi. "The New Confucianism and Taoism in China and Japan from the Fourth to the Thirteenth Centuries A.D." *Cahiers d'histoire mondiale* 5.4 (1960).

Kitamura Yoshikazu. "Zenkan matsu no kairei ni tsuite" (Concerning Changes in Ritual at the End of the Former Han). *Nippon-Chūgoku-gakkai-hō* 33 (1981).

Knechtges, David R., trans. *Wen xuan, or Selections of Refined Literature.* Edited by Xiao Tong (501–531). 2 vols. Princeton: Princeton University Press, 1982–1987.

Ko Chien-p'ing. "Tung-Chin Nan-ch'ao she-hui chung te chia-t'ing lun-ch'ang" (Family Ethics in Eastern Chin and Southern Dynasty Society). *Chung-shan ta-hsüeh hsüeh-pao (che-hsüeh she-hui k'o-hsüeh pan)* 1990.3.

K'o Yu-ken. "Shih-tsu ti-chu shih Ts'ao Ts'ao chi-t'uan te chu-yao chieh-chi chi-ch'u" (Hereditary Landlords Were the Principal Class Base for Ts'ao Ts'ao's Organization). *Hsia-men ta-hsüeh hsüeh-pao: Che-hsüeh she-hui k'o-hsüeh pan* 1983.2.

Kobayashi, Masayoshi. "The Celestial Masters under the Eastern Jin and Liu-Song Dynasties." *Taoist Resources* 3.2 (1992).

Kohn, Livia. "Philosophy as Scripture in the Taoist Canon." *Journal of Chinese Religions* 20 (1992).

———. *Taoist Mystical Philosophy: The Scripture of Western Ascension*. Albany: State University of New York Press, 1991.

———, ed. *Taoist Meditation and Longevity Techniques*. Ann Arbor: Center for Chinese Studies, University of Michigan, 1989.

Kominami Ichirō. *Chūgoku no shinwa to monogatari—ko shōsetsu-shi no ten-kai* (Chinese Myths and Legends—a Development of the History of Ancient Fiction). Tokyo: Iwanami shoten, 1984.

———. "Dōkyō shinkō to shisha no kyūsai" (Taoist Faith and the Salvation of the Dead). *Tōyō gakujutsu kenkyū* 27, supplement (1987).

———. "Rikuchō Zui Tō shōsetsu-shi no tenkai to Bukkyō shinkō" (The Development of Fiction in the Six Dynasties, Sui, and T'ang, and Buddhist Belief). *Chūgoku chūsei no shūkyō to bunka* 1982.3.

Ku Chi-kuang. *Fu-ping chih-tu k'ao-shih* (An Explanation of the Fu-ping [Government Troops] System). 1962; Taipei: Hung-wen-kuan ch'u-pan-she, 1985.

———. "Liu-ch'ao men-fa" (Six Dynasties Great Families). *Kuo-li Wu-han ta-hsüeh wen-che chi-k'an* 5.4 (1936).

Ku Ming-chien [Ku Chieh-kang]. *Ch'in-Han te fang-shih yü ju-sheng* (*Fang-shih* [Sorcerers] and Confucian Scholars of the Ch'in and Han). 1933; Taipei: Li-jen shu-chü, 1985.

Kuang Li-an [Kuang Shih-yüan]. "Wei-Chin men-ti shih-li chuan-i yü chih-luan chih kuan-hsi" (The Transferral of Social Status and Power in Wei and Chin and Its Relationship to Order and Disorder). *Shih-hsüeh hui-k'an* 8 (1977).

Kuang Shih-yüan. "Ts'ao-Wei t'un-t'ien k'ao" (An Examination of Ts'ao-Wei *T'un-t'ien* [Agricultural Colonies]). In *Wei-Chin Nan-Pei-ch'ao yen-chiu lun-chi*. Taipei: Wen-shih-che ch'u-pan-she, 1984.

Kubozoe Yoshifumi. "Gi-Shin Nanbokuchō ni okeru chihōkan no hon-sekichi nin'yō ni tsuite" (Concerning the Employment of Local Officials in Their Original Places of Registration in the Wei, Chin, and Northern and Southern Dynasties). *Shigaku zasshi* 83.1 (1974).

———. "1970–1989 nien Jih-pen te Wei-Chin Nan-Pei-ch'ao shih yen-chiu" (Japanese Studies of Wei, Chin, and Northern and Southern Dynasties History from 1970 to 1989). *Chung-kuo shih yen-chiu tung-t'ai* 1991.12.

Kuo Hsi-wei. "Hsüan-hsüeh yü Tung-Chin Nan-ch'ao cheng-chih" (*Hsüan-hsüeh* and Eastern Chin, Southern Dynasty Politics). *Wen shih chih-shih* 6 (1989).

Kuo Lin-ko. "Wei-Chin feng-liu" (Wei and Chin Fashions). *Chung-kuo hsüeh-pao* 1.6 (1944).

Kuo, Mo-jo. "A Reappraisal of the Case of Ts'ao Ts'ao." *Chinese Studies in History and Philosophy* 1.4 (1968).

———, ed. *Chung-kuo shih kao*, 3 (A Sketch of Chinese History). Peking: Jen-min ch'u-pan-she, 1979.

Kuwahara Jitsuzō. "Shin shitsu no nan-to to nampō no kaihatsu" (The Passage South of the House of Chin and the Development of the South). In *Tōyōshi setsuen*. Kyoto: Kōbundo insatsu-bu, 1927.

Lai, Whalen W. "The Early Prajñā Schools, Especially 'Hsin-wu,' Reconsidered." *Philosophy East and West* 33.1 (1983).

————. "Emperor Wu of Liang on the Immortal Soul, *Shen Pu Mieh*." *Journal of the American Oriental Society* 101.2 (1981).

Lancaster, Lewis R. "The Chinese Translation of the *Aṣṭasāhasrikā-Prajñāpāramitā-sūtra* Attributed to Chih Ch'ien." *Monumenta Serica* 28 (1969).

Lao Kan. *Ch'in-Han shih* (A History of Ch'in and Han). Taipei: Chung-kuo wen-hua ta-hsüeh ch'u-pan-pu, 1986.

————. "Population and Geography in the Two Han Dynasties." In *Chinese Social History*, edited by E-tu Zen Sun and John DeFrancis. Washington, D.C.: American Council of Learned Societies, 1956.

————. *Wei-Chin Nan-Pei-ch'ao shih* (A History of the Wei, Chin, and Northern and Southern Dynasties). Taipei: Chung-kuo wen-hua ta-hsüeh, 1980.

Le Blanc, Charles. *Huai Nan Tzu: Philosophical Synthesis in Early Han Thought*. Hong Kong: Hong Kong University Press, 1985.

Ledderose, Lothar. "Some Taoist Elements in the Calligraphy of the Six Dynasties." *T'oung Pao* 70.4–5 (1984).

Lee, John. "The Original Equal Field: The Regulations." *Early Medieval China Group, Newsletter* 1 (1988).

Leslie, Daniel. "Les théories de Wang Tch'ong sur la causalité." *Mélanges de sinologie, offerts à Monsieur Paul Demiéville* 2. Paris: Institut des hautes études chinoises, 1974.

Li, Chi. "The Changing Concept of the Recluse in Chinese Literature." *Harvard Journal of Asiatic Studies* 24 (1962–1963).

Li Chieh. *Wei-Chin Nan-Pei-ch'ao shih* (A History of the Wei, Chin, and Northern and Southern Dynasties). Taipei: Chiu-ssu ch'u-pan yu-hsien kung-ssu, 1978.

Li Feng-mao. "Hsi K'ang yang-sheng ssu-hsiang chih yen-chiu" (A Study of Hsi K'ang's Thought on Nourishing Life). *Ching-i wen-li hsüeh-yüan hsüeh-pao* 2 (1979).

————. "Kuo P'u yu-hsien shih pien-ch'uang shuo chih t'i-ch'u chi ch'i i-i" (The Proposal for a Renovated View of Kuo P'u's Wandering Immortals Poetry and Its Significance). In *Ku-tien wen-hsüeh* 6. Taipei: Hsüeh-sheng shu-chü, 1984.

————. "Liu-ch'ao ching chien ch'uan-shuo yü tao-chiao fa-shu ssu-hsiang" (Six Dynasties Legends of Mirrors and Swords, and Taoist Supernatural Thought). *Chung-kuo ku-tien hsiao-shuo yen-chiu chuan-chi* 2. Taipei: Lien-ching ch'u-pan shih-yeh kung-ssu, 1980.

———. "Liu-ch'ao hsien-ching ch'uan-shuo yü Tao-chiao chih kuan-hsi" (Six Dynasties Legends of Lands of Immortals and Their Relationship to Taoism). *Chung-wai wen-hsüeh* 8.8 (1980).

———. "Shen-hsien san-p'in shuo te yüan-shih chi ch'i yen-pien—i Liuch'ao Tao-chiao wei chung-hsin te k'ao-ch'a" (The Origin and Evolution of the Theory of Three Classes of Spirits—an Investigation Centering on Six Dynasties Taoism). In *Han-hsüeh lun-wen-chi* 2. Taipei, 1983.

Li Hsing. "Tung-Chin ching-lüeh chung-yüan chih ching-kuo" (The Eastern Chin Experience at Putting the Central Plain in Order). *Wen-shih tsa-chih* 1.7 (1941).

Li Hsü. "Wei-Chin Nan-Pei-ch'ao shih cheng-chih ching-chi chung-hsin te chuan-i" (The Transfer of Political and Economic Centers in Wei, Chin, and Northern and Southern Dynasties Times). *Shih-huo panyüeh k'an* 1.1 (1934).

Li Shih-chieh. "Tung-Chin shih-tai chih Fo-chiao ssu-hsiang" (Buddhist Thought in the Eastern Chin Period). In *Wei-Chin Nan-Pei-ch'ao Fo-chiao hsiao-shih*, edited by Huang Ch'an-hua. Taipei: Ta-ch'eng wen-hua ch'u-pan-she, 1979.

Li T'ang. *Nan-Pei-ch'ao* (The Northern and Southern Dynasties). Hong Kong: Hung-yeh shu-chü, 1978.

———. *Tung-Chin* (The Eastern Chin). Hong Kong: Hung-yeh shu-chü, 1974.

Li Tung-hua. "Han-Sui chien Chung-kuo nan-hai chiao-t'ung chih yen-pien." (The Evolution of Chinese Communications with the South Seas from Han to Sui). *Shih-hsüeh chi-k'an* 11.

Li Yüan-ch'eng. "Liang-Chin Nan-ch'ao she-hui chieh-chi k'ao" (An Investigation of Social Classes in the Two Chin and Southern Dynasties). *Wen-shih tsa-chih* 5.5–6 (1945).

Liao Wei-ch'ing. "Chang Hua yü Hsi-Chin cheng-chih chih kuan-hsi" (Chang Hua and His Connection with Western Chin Politics). *Kuo-li T'ai-wan ta-hsüeh wen-shih-che hsüeh-pao* 22 (1973).

Liebenthal, Walter. "A Biography of Chu Tao-sheng." *Monumenta Nipponica* 11.3 (1955).

———. *Chao Lun: The Treatises of Seng-chao*. 2d edition; Hong Kong: University of Hong Kong Press, 1968.

———. "Chinese Buddhism during the 4th and 5th Centuries." *Monumenta Nipponica* 11.1 (1955).

———. "The Immortality of the Soul in Chinese Thought." *Monumenta Nipponica* 8.1–2 (1952).

Lin Chien-ming. "Ch'in-Han shih pu-fen" (Section on Ch'in and Han History). In *Chung-kuo ku-tai-shih tao-tu* (Reader's Guide to Ancient Chinese History), edited by Hsiao Li and Li Kuei-hai. Shanghai: Wen-hui ch'u-pan-she, 1991.

Lin Chien-ming et al. *Ch'in-Han she-hui wen-ming* (Ch'in and Han Society and Civilization). Sian: Hsi-pei ta-hsüeh ch'u-pan-she, 1985.

Lin Jui-han and Lu Yao-tung. "Chin hui-yao, 3" (Institutes of Chin, [Part] 3). *Kuo-li T'ai-wan ta-hsüeh li-shih hsüeh-hsi hsüeh-pao* 7 (1980).

Lin Kan-ch'üan. "Lun Ch'in-Han feng-chien kuo-chia te nung-yeh cheng-ts'e: Kuan-yü cheng-chih ch'üan-li yü ching-chi fa-chan kuan-hsi te k'ao-ch'a" (On the Agricultural Policies of the Feudal State in Ch'in and Han: An Investigation into the Relationship between Political Authority and Economic Development). In *Ti shih-liu chieh kuo-chi li-shih k'o-hsüeh ta-hui: Chung-kuo hsüeh-che lun-wen-chi*, edited by Chang Lien-fang. Peking: Chung-hua shu-chü, 1985.

Lin, Tien-wai. "Some Thoughts on the Development of the Chuang-yuan System in the [*sic*] Medieval China." *Chinese Culture* 18.1 (1977).

Link, Arthur E., and Tim Lee. "Sun Ch'o's *Yü-Tao-Lun:* A Clarification of the Way." *Monumenta Serica* 25 (1966).

Liu Hsiu-shih. "Wei-Chin ssu-hsiang lun" (On Wei-Chin Thought). *Wei-Chin ssu-hsiang: Chia-pien wu-chung*. Reprint; Taipei: Li-jen shu-chü, 1984.

Liu Kuei-chieh. "Hsüan-hsüeh ssu-hsiang yü pan-jo ssu-hsiang chih chiao-jung" (The Blending of *Hsüan-hsüeh* and Prajñā Thought). *Kuo-li pien-i-kuan kuan-k'an* 9.1 (1980).

Liu, Ming-wood. "Fan Chen's *Treatise on the Destructibility of the Spirit* and Its Buddhist Critics." *Philosophy East and West* 37.4 (1987).

Liu P'an-sui. "Liu-ch'ao ch'eng Yang-chou (chin chih Nan-ching) wei shen-chou k'ao" (An Investigation into the Six Dynasty Labeling of Yang-chou [Modern Nanking] as Shen-chou). *Yü-kung pan-yüeh-k'an* 1.9 (1934).

Liu Shu-fen. "Liu-ch'ao Chien-k'ang te ching-chi chi-ch'u" (The Economic Foundations of Six Dynasties Chien-k'ang [Nanking]). *Shih-huo yüeh-k'an* 12.10–11 (1983).

Liu Yü-huang. "Lun Han-Chin Nan-ch'ao te feng-chien chuang-yüan chih-tu" (On the Feudal Manorial System of Han, Chin, and the Southern Dynasties). *Li-shih yen-chiu* 1962.3.

Lo, Chin-t'ang. "Popular Stories of the Wei and Chin Periods." *Journal of Oriental Studies* 17.1–2 (1979).

Lo, Kuan-chung. *Three Kingdoms: China's Epic Drama*. Translated by Moss Roberts. 14th century; New York: Pantheon Books, 1976.

Loewe, Michael. *Chinese Ideas of Life and Death: Faith, Myth, and Reason in the Han Period (202 B.C.-A.D. 220)*. London: George Allen and Unwin, 1982.

———. *Crisis and Conflict in Han China: 104 B.C. to A.D. 9*. London: George Allen and Unwin, 1974.

————. "K'uang Heng and the Reform of Religious Practices (31 B.C.)." *Asia Major* 17.1 (1971).

Lü Ssu-mien. *Liang-Chin Nan-Pei-ch'ao shih* (A History of the Two Chin and the Northern and Southern Dynasties). Reprint; Shanghai: Shang-hai ku-chi ch'u-pan-she, 1983.

————. *Lü Ssu-mien tu-shih cha-chi* (Lü Ssu-mien's Commentaries on Historical Readings). Shanghai: Shang-hai ku-chi ch'u-pan-she, 1982.

Makita, Tairyō. "Hui-yüan—His Life and Times." Translated by Philip Yampolsky. *Zinbun* 6 (1962).

Mao Han-kuang. *Chung-kuo chung-ku she-hui shih-lun* (Essays on Medieval Chinese Social History). Taipei: Lien-ching ch'u-pan shih-yeh kung-ssu, 1988.

————. *Liang-Chin Nan-Pei-ch'ao shih-tsu cheng-chih chih yen-chiu* (Studies of Literati Politics in the Two Chin and Northern and Southern Dynasties). Taipei: T'ai-wan shang-wu yin-shu-kuan, 1966.

————. "San-kuo cheng-ch'üan te she-hui chi-ch'u" (The Social Foundation of Political Authority in the Three Kingdoms). *Chung-yang yen-chiu-yüan, li-shih yü-yen yen-chiu-so chi-k'an* 46.1 (1974).

————. "Ts'ung chung-cheng p'ing-p'in yü kuan-chih chih kuan-hsi lun Wei-Chin Nan-ch'ao chih she-hui chia-kou" (A Discussion of Wei, Chin, and Southern Dynasties Social Structure through the Relationship between the Critical Evaluations of the Arbiters and Official Positions). *Chung-yang yen-chiu-yüan, li-shih yü-yen yen-chiu-so chi-k'an* 46.4 (1975).

————. "Wu-ch'ao chün-ch'üan chuan-i chi ch'i tui cheng-chü chih ying-hsiang" (The Transfer of Military Authority during the Five Dynasties and Its Influence on the Political Situation). *Ch'ing-hua hsüeh-pao*, new series 8.1–2 (1970).

Marney, John. *Liang Chien-Wen Ti.* Boston: Twayne Publishers, 1976.

Mather, Richard. "The Conflict of Buddhism with Native Chinese Ideologies." *The Review of Religion* 20.1–2 (1955).

————. "The Controversy over Conformity and Naturalness during the Six Dynasties." *History of Religions* 9.2–3 (1969–1970).

————. "Individualist Expressions of the Outsiders during the Six Dynasties." In *Individualism and Holism: Studies in Confucian and Taoist Values,* edited by Donald J. Munro. Ann Arbor: Center for Chinese Studies, University of Michigan, 1985.

————. "K'ou Ch'ien-chih and the Taoist Theocracy at the Northern Wei Court, 425–451." In *Facets of Taoism: Essays in Chinese Religion,* edited by Holmes Welch and Anna Seidel. New Haven: Yale University Press, 1979.

————. "The Landscape Buddhism of the Fifth-Century Poet Hsieh Ling-yün." *Journal of Asian Studies* 18.1 (1958).

————. "The Mystical Ascent of the T'ien T'ai Mountains: Sun Cho's *Yu-t'ien-t'ai-shan fu.*" *Monumenta Serica* 20 (1961).

————. "A Note on the Dialects of Lo-yang and Nanking during the Six Dynasties." In *Wen-lin: Studies in the Chinese Humanities,* edited by Chow Tse-tsung. Madison: University of Wisconsin Press, 1968.

————. *The Poet Shen Yüeh (441–513): The Reticent Marquis.* Princeton: Princeton University Press, 1988.

————. "Vimalakīrti and Gentry Buddhism." *History of Religions* 8.1 (1968).

————, trans. *Shih-shuo Hsin-yü: A New Account of Tales of the World.* Minneapolis: University of Minnesota Press, 1976.

Mekata, Makoto. "The Ruin of the Land of Enchantment." *Acta Asiatica* 21 (1971).

Meng Hui. "Tung-Chin te hao-tsu" (The Eastern Chin Magnates). *Nan-feng* 1.4–5 (1945).

Meng Mo and Sun Ta-jen. "Kuan-yü Chung-kuo feng-chien t'u-ti so-yu-chih te hsing-shih wen-t'i" (Concerning the Problem of the Form of Feudal Landownership in China). *Li-shih yen-chiu* 1961.1.

Meng Ssu-ming. "Liu-ch'ao shih-tsu hsing-ch'eng te ching-kuo" (The Process of Formation of the Six Dynasties Great Families). *Wen-shih tsa-chih* 1.9 (1941).

Miao Yüeh. "Ch'ing-t'an yü Wei-Chin cheng-chih" (*Ch'ing-t'an* [Pure Conversation] and Wei and Chin Politics). *Chung-kuo wen-hua yen-chiu hui-k'an* 8 (1948).

Michaud, Paul. "The Yellow Turbans." *Monumenta Serica* 17 (1958).

Miyakawa, Hisayuki. "The Confucianization of South China." In *The Confucian Persuasion,* edited by Arthur F. Wright. Stanford: Stanford University Press, 1960.

————. "Local Cults around Mount Lu at the Time of Sun En's Rebellion." In *Facets of Taoism: Essays in Chinese Religion,* edited by Holmes Welch and Anna Seidel. New Haven: Yale University Press, 1979.

————. *Rikuchō shi kenkyū: Seiji shakai hen* (Studies in Six Dynasties History: Political and Social Section). Tokyo: Nihon gakujutsu shinkō kai, 1956.

————. "Tō-Shin jidai no kizoku to bukkyō" (The Aristocracy and Buddhism in the Eastern Chin Period). *Shina bukkyō shigaku* 4.1–2 (1940).

Miyazaki Ichisada. "Chūgoku ni okeru sonsei no seiritsu—kodai teikoku hōkai no ichimen" (The Formation of the Village System in China—One Aspect of the Collapse of the Ancient Empire). *Tōyōshi kenkyū* 18.4 (1960).

————. *Kyūhin kanjinhō no kenkyū: Kakyo zenshi* (Studies of the Nine Ranks of Officials Law: A Prehistory of the Examination System). Kyoto: Tōyōshi-kenkyū-kai, 1956.

Mori Mikisaburō. "Chūgoku shisō ni okeru chōetsu to naizai" (Transcendence and Immanence in Chinese Thought). *Tōyō gakujutsu kenkyū* 23.2 (1984).

―――. "Rikuchō shidaifu no seishin" (The Spirit of Six Dynasties Literati). *Ōsaka daigaku bungakubu kiyō* 3 (1954).

―――. *Rikuchō shidaifu no seishin.* Kyoto: Dōbōsha, 1986.

―――. *Rōsō to Bukkyō* (Lao [-tzu]–Chuang [-tzu] and Buddhism). Kyoto: Hōsōkan, 1986.

Mou Jun-sun. *Lun Wei-Chin i-lai chih ch'ung-shang t'an-pien chi ch'i yinghsiang* (On the Esteem for Discussion since Wei and Chin, and Its Influence). Hong Kong: Chinese University Press, 1966.

Mou Tsung-san. *Ts'ai-hsing yü hsüan-li* (The Property of Talent and Abstruse Principles). Taipei: Hsüeh-sheng shu-chü, 1975.

Mugitani Kunio. "Dōkyōteki seiseiron no keisei to tenkai: 'Ki no shisō' horon" (The Formation and Development of Taoist Theories of Creation: A Supplemental Study of "*Ch'i* Thought"). *Tōdai-Chūtetsubungakkai hō* 4 (1979).

―――. "Shoki Dōkyō ni okeru kyūsai shisō" (Salvationist Thought in Early Taoism). *Tōyō bunka* 57 (1977).

Murakami Yoshimi. *Chūgoku no sennin—hōbokushi no shisō* (China's Immortals—the Thought of *Pao p'u tzu*). Kyoto: Heirakuji shōten, 1956.

―――. "Initsu—Tō Shin jidai" (Eremitism—the Eastern Chin Period). *Shirin* 39.6 (1956).

―――. "Kizoku shakai no bunka" (The Culture of Aristocratic Society). In *Kizoku shakai,* edited by Sotoyama Gunji. Osaka: Sōgensha, 1981.

―――. "Tō Shin chūki no shōkō—sansui bungaku, sansui e hassei no seijiteki haikei" (The Lull in the Middle Period of the Eastern Chin —the Political Background for the Appearance of Landscape Literature and Landscape Painting). *Chūgoku tetsugakushi no tembō to mosaku.* Tokyo: Sōbunsha, 1976.

Na, Tsung Shun. "A Historical Study of Juan Chi." *Chinese Culture* 22.1 (1981).

Naba Toshisada. "O-shu kō" (An Investigation of Castellans). *Tōa jinbun gakuhō* 2.4 (1943).

Nakamura Keiji. " 'Kyōri' no ronri: Rikuchō kizoku shakai no *ideorogii*" (The Logic of "Home": The Ideology of Six Dynasties Aristocratic Society). *Tōyōshi kenkyū* 41.1 (1982).

―――. "Kyūhin kanjin hō ni okeru kyōhin ni tsuite" (Concerning Local Rankings in the Nine Ranks of Officials Law). *Jinbun kenkyū* 36.9 (1984).

―――. " 'Shi-sho kubetsu' shōron—Nanchō kizokusei e no ichi shiten" (A Brief Discussion of the "Distinction between Literati and Commoners"—a Viewpoint on the Southern Dynasty Aristocratic System). *Shigaku zasshi* 88.2 (1979).

Ni Chin-sheng. "Wu-hu luan-Hua ch'ien-yeh te Chung-kuo ching-chi" (The Chinese Economy on the Eve of the Invasions of the Five Northern Tribes). *Shih-huo pan-yüeh k'an* 1.7 (1935).

————. "Wu-hu luan-Hua ming-jih te Chung-kuo ching-chi" (The Chinese Economy in the Aftermath of the Invasions of the Five Northern Tribes). *Shih-huo pan-yüeh k'an* 1.8 (1935).

Nomura Shigeo. " 'Su' o tsūjite mita, Shin dai no jusha" (The Chin Dynasty Confucians as Observed through the Term "Plain"). *Tōhō gaku* 61 (1981).

Nylan, Michael, and Nathan Sivin. "The First Neo-Confucianism: An Introduction to Yang Hsiung's 'Canon of Supreme Mystery' (T'ai hsuan ching, c. 4 B.C.)." In *Chinese Ideas about Nature and Society: Studies in Honour of Derk Bodde*, edited by Charles Le Blanc and Susan Blader. Hong Kong: Hong Kong University Press, 1987.

Ōba Osamu. *Ch'in-Han fa-chih shih yen-chiu* (Studies in the History of the Ch'in-Han Legal System). Translated from the Japanese by Lin Chien-ming et al. Shanghai: Shang-hai jen-min ch'u-pan-she, 1991.

Ochi Shigeaki. "Gi-Shin Nanchō no tonden" (The Agricultural Colonies of Wei, Chin, and the Southern Dynasties). *Shigaku zasshi* 70.3 (1961).

————. "Hoku-Gi no kinden-sei o megutte" (Concerning the Northern Wei Equal Fields System). *Shien* 108 (1972).

————. "Nanchō no kizoku to gōzoku" (The Aristocrats and Magnates of the Southern Dynasties). *Shien* 69 (1956).

————. "Seigi to kyōron" (Pure Criticism and Local Opinion). *Tōyō gakuhō* 48.1 (1965).

————. "Thoughts on the Understanding of the Han and the Six Dynasties." *Memoires of the Research Department of the Toyo Bunko* 35 (1977).

————. "Tō Shin Nanchō no mura to gōzoku" (The Villages and Magnates of the Eastern Chin and Southern Dynasties). *Shigaku zasshi* 79.10 (1970).

————. "Tō Shin Nanchō no zokumon-sei ni tsuite" (Concerning the Family System of the Eastern Chin and the Southern Dynasties). *Kodaigaku* 18.1 (1972).

————. "Tō Shin no kizoku-sei to Nanboku no 'chi-en' sei" (The Aristocratic System of the Eastern Chin and the Nature of Northern and Southern "Regional Affinity"). *Shigaku zasshi* 67.8 (1958).

Ōkawa Fujio. "Rikuchō zenki no Gokō gun no gōzoku—tokuni Bukō no Shin shi o megutte" (The Magnates of Wu-hsing Commandery in the First Part of the Six Dynasties—Especially Concerning the Shen Family of Wu-k'ang). In Risshō daigaku shigakukai, *Shūkyō shakai shi kenkyū*. Tokyo: Yūzankaku Publishing Co., 1977.

Okazaki Fumio. *Gi-Shin Nanbokuchō tsūshi* (A Comprehensive History of the Wei, Chin, and Northern and Southern Dynasties). 1932; Tokyo: Kōbundō shobō, 1943.

————. *Nanbokuchō ni okeru shakai keizai seido* (The Socioeconomic System in the Northern and Southern Dynasties). 1935; Tokyo: Kōbundō, 1955.

Paper, Jordan D., trans. *The Fu-Tzu: A Post-Han Confucian Text.* Leiden: E. J. Brill, 1987.

Pearce, Scott. "Status, Labor, and Law: Special Service Households under the Northern Dynasties." *Harvard Journal of Asiatic Studies* 51.1 (1991).

————. "A Survey of Recent Research on the History of Early Medieval China." *Studies in Chinese History (Chūgoku shigaku),* 2 (1992).

Pelliot, Paul. "Les classiques gravés sur pierre sous les Wei en 240–248." *T'oung Pao* 23 (1924).

Pokora, Timoteus. *Hsin-lun (New Treatise) and Other Writings by Huan T'an (43 B.C.–28 A.D.).* Michigan Papers in Chinese Studies, No. 20. Ann Arbor: University of Michigan, Center for Chinese Studies, 1975.

————. "The Life of Huan T'an." *Archiv Orientální* 31 (1963).

Powers, Martin J. *Art and Political Expression in Early China.* New Haven: Yale University Press, 1991.

Pulleyblank, Edwin G. "The An Lu-shan Rebellion and the Origins of Chronic Militarism in Late T'ang China." In *Essays on T'ang Society: The Interplay of Social, Political and Economic Forces,* edited by John Curtis Perry and Bardwell L. Smith. Leiden: E. J. Brill, 1976.

————. *The Background of the Rebellion of An Lu-shan.* London: Oxford University Press, 1955.

————. "Registration of Population in China in the Sui and T'ang Periods." *Journal of the Economic and Social History of the Orient* 4.3 (1961).

Robinet, I. "Kouo Siang ou le monde comme absolu." *T'oung Pao* 69.1–3 (1983).

Rogers, Michael C., trans. *The Chronicle of Fu Chien: A Case of Exemplar History.* Berkeley: University of California Press, 1968.

————. "The Myth of the Battle of the Fei River (A.D. 383)." *T'oung Pao* 54.1–3 (1968).

Rump, Ariane, and Wing-tsit Chan, trans. *Commentary on the Lao Tzu, by Wang Pi.* Society for Asian and Comparative Philosophy. Honolulu: University Press of Hawaii, 1979.

Sa Meng-wu. "Nan-Pei-ch'ao Fo-chiao liu-hsing te yüan-yin" (The Causes of the Spread of Buddhism in the Northern and Southern Dynasties). *Ta-lu tsa-chih* 2.10 (1951).

Sa Shih-chiung. "Wei-Chin Nan-Pei-ch'ao shih-tai te ti-fang chih-tu" (The Local System of the Wei, Chin, and Northern and Southern Dynasties). *Tung-fang tsa-chih* 41.17 (1945).

Sailey, Jay. *The Master Who Embraces Simplicity: A Study of the Philosopher Ko Hung, A.D. 283–343.* San Francisco: Chinese Materials Center, 1978.

Sakanishi, Shio. *The Spirit of the Brush: Being the Outlook of Chinese Painters on Nature from Eastern Chin to Five Dynasties, A.D. 317–960.* London: John Murray, 1939.

Sakuma Yoshinari. *Gi-Shin Nanbokuchō suiri-shi kenkyū* (Studies in the History of Water Conservancy in the Wei, Chin, and Northern and Southern Dynasties). Tokyo: Kaimei shoin, 1980.

Satō Tatsurō. "Sō-Gi Bun, Mei tei ki no seikai to meizokusō no dōkō—Chin Gun, Shiba I o chūshin ni" (The Political World in the Time of Emperors Wen and Ming of the Ts'ao-Wei [Dynasty], and Tendencies in the Class of Famous Families: Centering on Ch'en Ch'ün and Ssu-ma I). *Tōyōshi kenkyū* 52.1 (1993).

Schafer, Edward H. *Pacing the Void: T'ang Approaches to the Stars.* Berkeley: University of California Press, 1977.

———. *The Vermilion Bird: T'ang Images of the South.* Berkeley: University of California Press, 1967.

Schmidt-Glintzer, Helwig. "Der Literatenbeamte und seine Gemeinde: oder Der Charakter der Aristokratie im chinesischen Mittelalter." *Zeitschrift der Deutschen Morgenländischen Gesellschaft* 139.2 (1989).

Seidel, Anna. "Taoist Messianism." *Numen: International Review for the History of Religions* 31.2 (1984).

———. "Tokens of Immortality in Han Graves." *Numen: International Review for the History of Religions* 29.1 (1982).

Shigezawa Toshirō. "Bunken mokuroku o tōshite mita rikuchō no rekishi ishiki" (The Historical Consciousness of the Six Dynasties as Seen through Literary Catalogs). *Tōyōshi kenkyū* 18.1 (1959).

Shih Feng-yü. "T'ang-tai Tao-chiao t'u-shih yin-shih te chüeh-ch'i: Lun Li Po yin-i ch'iu-hsien huo-tung te cheng-chih she-hui pei-ching" (The Precipitous Rise of Taoist-style Scholars in Retirement in the T'ang Dynasty—on the Political and Social Background for Li Po's Eremitic and Immortality-Seeking Activities). *Ch'ing-hua hsüeh-pao,* new series 16.1–2 (1984).

Shih, Vincent Yu-chung, trans. *The Literary Mind and the Carving of Dragons: A Study of Thought and Pattern in Chinese Literature.* New York: Columbia University Press, 1959.

Shin Un-chol. "Plagiarism and Originality in Kuo Hsiang's Commentary on the Chuang-Tzu." *Asian Thought and Society* 8.22–23 (1983).

Shryock, J. K. *The Origin and Development of the State Cult of Confucius.* New York: The Century Co., 1932.

———, trans. *The Study of Human Abilities: The Jen Wu Chih of Liu Shao.* New Haven: American Oriental Society, 1937.

Sivin, Nathan. "Chinese Alchemy and the Manipulation of Time." In *Sci-*

ence and Technology in E. Asia. New York: Science History Publications, 1977.

―――. *Chinese Alchemy: Preliminary Studies.* Cambridge: Harvard University Press, 1968.

Somers, Robert M. "The Society of Early Imperial China: Three Recent Studies." *Journal of Asian Studies* 38.1 (1978).

―――. "Time, Space, and Structure in the Consolidation of the T'ang Dynasty (A.D. 617–700)." *Journal of Asian Studies* 45.5 (1986).

Sotoyama Gunji. "Seiji" (Politics). In *Kizoku shakai,* edited by Sotoyama Gunji. Osaka: Sōgensha, 1981.

Spade, Beatrice. "The Education of Women in China during the Southern Dynasties." *Journal of Asian History* 13.1 (1979).

Spiro, Audrey. *Contemplating the Ancients: Aesthetic and Social Issues in Early Chinese Portraiture.* Berkeley: University of California Press, 1990.

Stein, Rolf A. "Religious Taoism and Popular Religion from the Second to Seventh Centuries." In *Facets of Taoism: Essays in Chinese Religion,* edited by Holmes Welch and Anna Seidel. New Haven: Yale University Press, 1979.

Straughair, Anna. *Chang Hua: A Statesman-Poet of the Western Chin Dynasty.* Faculty of Asian Studies Occasional Paper 15. Canberra: Australian National University, 1973.

Strickmann, Michel. "The Mao Shan Revelations: Taoism and the Aristocracy." *T'oung Pao* 63.1 (1977).

―――. "On the Alchemy of T'ao Hung-ching." In *Facets of Taoism: Essays in Chinese Religion,* edited by Holmes Welch and Anna Seidel. New Haven: Yale University Press, 1979.

―――. "Review Article: History, Anthropology, and Chinese Religion." *Harvard Journal of Asiatic Studies* 40.1 (1980).

Su Shao-hsing. *Liang-Chin Nan-ch'ao te shih-tsu* (Literati of the Two Chin and Southern Dynasties). Taipei: Lien-ching ch'u-pan shih-yeh kung-ssu, 1987.

Sun Tao-sheng. "Ch'ing-t'an ch'i-yüan k'ao" (An Examination of the Origins of Pure Conversation). *Tung-fang tsa-chih* 42.3 (1946).

Sung Yen. "Wei-Chin Nan-Pei-ch'ao shih-tsu ti-chu cheng-ch'üan te yen-pien" (The Evolution of the Political Authority of Wei, Chin, and Northern and Southern Dynasty Great Family Landlords). *Li-shih chiao-hsüeh wen-t'i* 6 (1957).

Takahashi Tetsu. "Rikuchō-ki Kōnan no ko-nōmin" (The Small Farmers of Chiang-nan in the Six Dynasties Period). *Shichō* 107 (1969).

T'an Ch'i-hsiang. *Chung-kuo li-shih ti-t'u chi,* vol. 4: *Tung-Chin Shih-liu-kuo, Nan-Pei-ch'ao shih-ch'i* (Historical Atlas of China: The Eastern Chin, Sixteen Kingdoms, and Northern and Southern Dynasties Period). Shanghai: Ti-t'u ch'u-pan-she, 1982.

————. "Lun liang-Han Hsi-Chin hu-k'ou" (On the Population of the Two Han and Western Chin). *Yü-kung pan-yüeh-k'an* 1.7 (1934).

T'ang Ch'ang-ju. "Nan-ch'ao te t'un, ti, pieh-shu chi shan-tse chan-ling" (Camps, Lodges, Villas, and the Occupation of Mountains and Fens in the Southern Dynasties). *Li-shih yen-chiu* 1954.3.

————. *San chih liu shih-chi Chiang-nan ta t'u-ti so-yu-chih te fa-chan* (The Development of a System of Large Landholding in Third- through Sixth-Century Chiang-nan). 1957; Taipei: Pai-shu ch'u-pan-she, n.d.

————. *Wei-Chin Nan-Pei-ch'ao shih-lun shih-i* (Overlooked Essays on the History of the Wei, Chin, and Northern and Southern Dynasties). Peking: Chung-hua shu-chü, 1983.

————. *Wei-Chin Nan-Pei-ch'ao shih lun-ts'ung* (Collected Essays on the History of the Wei, Chin, and Northern and Southern Dynasties). 1955; Peking: Sheng-huo, tu-shu, hsin-chih san-lien shu-tien, 1978.

T'ang Hsi-yü [T'ang Yung-t'ung]. "Wei-Chin hsüan-hsüeh lun-kao" (Draft Essay on Wei and Chin *Hsüan-hsüeh* [Mysterious Studies]). In *Wei-Chin ssu-hsiang: Chia-pien wu-chung*. Reprint; Taipei: Li-jen shu-chü, 1984.

T'ang I-chieh. *Kuo Hsiang yü Wei-Chin hsüan-hsüeh* (Kuo Hsiang and Wei and Chin *Hsüan-hsüeh* [Mysterious Studies]). Chung-ho [Taipei]: Ku-feng ch'u-pan-she, 1987.

T'ang Yung-t'ung. *Han Wei liang-Chin Nan-Pei-ch'ao Fo-chiao shih* (A History of Buddhism in the Han, Wei, Two Chin, and Northern and Southern Dynasties). 1938; Peking: Chung-hua shu-chü, 1983.

————. "Wang Pi's New Interpretation of the *I ching* and *Lun-yü*." Translated by Walter Liebenthal. *Harvard Journal of Asiatic Studies* 10.2 (1947).

————. "Wei-Chin ssu-hsiang te fa-chan" (The Development of Wei and Chin Thought). *Hsüeh-yüan* 1.3 (1947).

Tanigawa Michio. "Bokuchō kizoku no seikatsu rinri" (The Northern Dynasty Aristocracy's Ethics of Life). In *Chūgoku chūsei-shi kenkyū— Rikuchō Zui Tō no shakai to bunka* (Studies in Medieval Chinese History: Six Dynasties, Sui, and T'ang Society and Culture), edited by Utsunomiya Kiyoyoshi. Tokyo: Tōkai daigaku shuppankai, 1970.

————. *Chūgoku chūsei no tankyū: Rekishi to ningen* (The Search for a Chinese Middle Ages: History and Humanity). Tokyo: Nihon edeitā sukūru shuppanbu, 1987.

————. "Kinden-sei no rinen to dai-tochi shoyū" (The Ideal of the Equal Fields System and Large Landownership). *Tōyōshi kenkyū* 25.4 (1967).

————. *Medieval Chinese Society and the Local "Community."* Translated by Joshua A. Fogel. Berkeley: University of California Press, 1985.

————. "Nei-t'eng Hu-nan te liu-ch'ao lun chi ch'i tui Jih-pen hsüeh-shu-chieh te ying-hsiang" (Naitō Konan's Six Dynasty Theories and

Their Influence on the Japanese Academic World). *Shan-hsi shih-ta hsüeh-pao: Che-she-pan* 1993.1.

————. "Nihon ni okeru Gi-Shin Nanbokuchō shi kenkyū no kaiko" (A Retrospective on Wei, Chin, and Northern and Southern Dynasties Historical Study in Japan). *Studies in Chinese History (Chūgoku shigaku)*, 2 (1992).

————. "Problems Concerning the Japanese Periodization of Chinese History." Translated by Joshua A. Fogel. *Journal of Asian History* 21.2 (1987).

T'ao Hsi-sheng and Shen Chü-ch'en. *Ch'in-Han cheng-chih chih-tu* (The Ch'in and Han Political System). Shih-ti hsiao ts'ung-shu. Shanghai: Shang-wu yin-shu-kuan, 1936.

T'ao Hsi-sheng and Wu Hsien-ch'ing. *Nan-Pei-ch'ao ching-chi shih* (An Economic History of the Northern and Southern Dynasties). 1937; Taipei: Shih-huo ch'u-pan-she, 1979.

Teng Shih-liang. *Liang-Chin shih lun* (On Poetry in the Two Chin). Hong Kong: Chung-wen ta-hsüeh, 1972.

Teng, Ssu-yü, trans. *Family Instructions for the Yen Clan: Yen-Shih Chia-Hsün.* Leiden: E.J. Brill, 1968.

T'ien Yü-ch'ing. *Tung-Chin men-fa cheng-chih* (Eastern Chin Great Family Politics). Peking: Pei-ching ta-hsüeh ch'u-pan-she, 1989.

Ting Kuang-hsün. "Lüeh-lun Hsieh An" (A Brief Essay on Hsieh An). *Li-shih chiao-hsüeh wen-t'i* 1990.5.

Ts'ai Hsüeh-hai. "Hsi-Chin chung-tsu pien-luan hsi-lun" (An Analysis of Ethnic Strife in the Western Chin). *Kuo-li pien-i-kuan kuan-k'an* 15.2 (1986).

Ts'en Chung-mien. "Chiu chan-t'ien k'o-t'ien wen-t'i tsai shuo chi chü hua" (A Few Words More Concerning the Problem of *Chan-t'ien* [Occupation of Fields] and *K'o-t'ien* [Dutied Fields]). *Chung-hsüeh li-shih chiao-hsüeh* 1957.11.

————. "Hsi-Chin chan-t'ien ho k'o-t'ien chih-tu chih tsung-ho shuo-ming" (A Synthetic Explanation of the Western Chin *Chan-t'ien* [Occupation of Fields] and *K'o-t'ien* [Dutied Fields] Systems). *Chung-hsüeh li-shih chiao-hsüeh* 1957.8.

Tsukamoto, Zenryū. "The Early Stages in the Introduction of Buddhism into China (Up to the Fifth Century A.D.)." *Cahiers d'histoire mondiale* 5.3 (1960).

————. *Shina Bukkyōshi kenkyū, Hoku-Gi hen* (Studies in Chinese Buddhist History, the Northern Wei Section). Tokyo: Kōbuntō shobō, 1942.

Tsuzuki Akiko. "Nanjin kanmon, kanjin no shūkyōteki sōzōryoku ni tsuite—*Shinkō* o megutte" (On the Religious Imagination of Southern Nonaristocratic Families and Individuals—Regarding the *Chenkao* [Declarations of the Perfected]). *Tōyōshi kenkyū* 47.2 (1988).

Tu Shou-su. "Wei-Chin Nan-Pei-ch'ao te she-hui ching-chi chi ch'i ssu-hsiang tung-hsiang" (The Social Economy of the Wei, Chin, and Northern and Southern Dynasties, and Their Trends of Thought). *Wen-hsün yüeh-k'an* 8.4 (1948).

Tung Ch'u. "San-kuo liang-Chin shih-tai te Fo-chiao" (The Buddhism of the Three Kingdoms and Two Chin Dynasties). In *Wei-Chin Nan-Pei-ch'ao Fo-chiao hsiao-shih,* edited by Huang Ch'an-hua. Taipei: Ta-ch'eng wen-hua ch'u-pan-she, 1979.

T'ung Ch'ao. "Chung-kuo ta-lu te Wei-Chin Nan-Pei-ch'ao shih yen-chiu" (Mainland Chinese Studies of Wei, Chin, and Northern and Southern Dynasties History). *Studies in Chinese History (Chūgoku shigaku),* 2 (1992).

Twitchett, Denis. "The Composition of the T'ang Ruling Class: New Evidence from Tunhuang." In *Perspectives on the T'ang,* edited by Arthur F. Wright and Denis Twitchett. New Haven: Yale University Press, 1973.

———. *Financial Administration under the T'ang Dynasty.* Cambridge: Cambridge University Press, 1963.

———, ed. *The Cambridge History of China,* vol. 3: *Sui and T'ang China, 589–906, Part 1.* Cambridge: Cambridge University Press, 1979.

Twitchett, Denis, and Michael Loewe, eds. *The Cambridge History of China,* vol. 1: *The Ch'in and Han Empires, 221 B.C.–A.D. 220.* Cambridge: Cambridge University Press, 1986.

Uchida Gifu. "Kizoku shakai no kōzō" (The Structure of Aristocratic Society). In *Kizoku shakai,* edited by Sotoyama Gunji. Osaka: Sōgen-sha, 1981.

Uchiyama Toshihiko. "Chū-chō Tō—Go-Kan matsu ichi chishikijin no shisō to kōdō" (Chung-ch'ang T'ung—the Thought and Behavior of an Intellectual at the End of the Later Han). *Nippon Chūgoku gakkai hō* 36 (1984).

Ueda Sanae. "Kizokuteki kansei no seiritsu—shōkan no yurai to sono seikaku" (The Formation of Aristocratic Governmental Organization—the Origin of Pure Offices and Their Character). In *Chūgoku chūsei-shi kenkyū,* edited by Utsunomiya Kiyoyoshi. 1970; Tokyo: Tōkai daigaku shuppansha, 1980.

Vervoorn, Aat. *Men of the Cliffs and Caves: The Development of the Chinese Eremitic Tradition to the End of the Han Dynasty.* Hong Kong: The Chinese University Press, 1990.

Waley, Arthur. "The Fall of LoYang." *History Today* 1 (1951).

———. "Life under the Han Dynasty: Notes on Chinese Civilization in the First and Second Centuries A.D." *History Today* 3.2 (1953).

———. "Notes on Chinese Alchemy." *Bulletin of the School of Oriental Studies* 6.1 (1930).

Wallacker, Benjamin E. "Chang Fei's Preface to the Chin Code of Law." *T'oung Pao* 72.4–5 (1986).

――――. "Han Confucianism and Confucius in Han." In *Ancient China: Studies in Early Civilization*, edited by David T. Roy and Tsuen-hsuin Tsien. Hong Kong: The Chinese University Press, 1978.

Wan, Kuo-ting. "The System of Equal Land Allotments in Medieval Times." In *Chinese Social History*, edited by E-Tu Zen Sun and John DeFrancis. Washington, D.C.: American Council of Learned Societies, 1956.

Wan Sheng-nan. *Wei-Chin Nan-Pei-ch'ao shih lun-kao* (Draft Essays on Wei, Chin, and Northern and Southern Dynasties History). Ho-fei: An-hui chiao-yü ch'u-pan-she, 1983.

Wang Chung-lo. "Chung-kuo feng-chien she-hui te t'e-tien" (The Special Characteristics of Chinese Feudal Society). *Li-shih yen-chiu* 1985.1.

――――. *Tse-hua shan-kuan ts'ung-kao* (Collected Manuscripts from the Tse-hua Mountain Academy). 1987; Taipei: T'ai-wan shang-wu yin-shu-kuan, 1990.

――――. *Wei-Chin Nan-Pei-ch'ao shih* (A History of the Wei, Chin, and the Northern and Southern Dynasties). Shanghai: Shang-hai jen-min ch'u-pan-she, 1980.

Wang I-t'ung [Wang Yi-t'ung]. *Wu-ch'ao men-ti* (Social Position in the Five [i.e., Six] Dynasties). Reprint; Hong Kong: Chung-wen ta-hsüeh ch'u-pan-she, 1978.

Wang Yen-wu. "Hsüan-tse te kuo-ch'eng—Wei Chin Nan-Pei-ch'ao shih-tai t'e-cheng" (The Process of Selection—a Special Feature of the Wei, Chin, and Northern and Southern Dynasties Era). *Chung-nan min-tsu hsüeh-yüan hsüeh-pao: Che-she pan* 1989.4.

Wang, Yi-t'ung. "Slaves and Other Comparable Social Groups during the Northern Dynasties (386–618)." *Harvard Journal of Asiatic Studies* 16.3–4 (1953).

Wang, Yü-ch'üan. "The Central Government of the Former Han Dynasty." In *The Making of China: Main Themes in Premodern Chinese History*, edited by Chang Chun-shu. Englewood Cliffs, N.J.: Prentice-Hall, 1975.

Wang Yün-wu. *Chin-T'ang cheng-chih ssu-hsiang* (Political Thought from Chin to T'ang). Taipei: T'ai-wan shang-wu yin-shu-kuan, 1969.

Ware, James R. "Wei Shou on Buddhism." *T'oung Pao* 30 (1933).

――――, trans. *Alchemy, Medicine, and Religion in the China of A.D. 320: The Nei P'ien of Ko Hung*. Reprint; New York: Dover Publications, 1966.

Watanabe Shinichirō. "Shō—aruiwa ni-shichi seiki Chūgoku ni okeru ichi *ideorogii*—keitai to kokka" (Purity, a Possible Ideology in Second- to Seventh-Century China—Form and Nation). *Kyōto fu-ritsu daigaku gakujutsu hōkoku, jinbun* 31 (1979).

Watanabe Yoshihiro. "Kan-Gi kōtaiki no shakai" (Society in the Period of Transition from Han to Wei). *Rekishigaku kenkyū* 626 (1991.11).

Wechsler, Howard J. *Offerings of Jade and Silk: Ritual and Symbol in the*

Legitimation of the T'ang Dynasty. New Haven: Yale University Press, 1985.

Wilhelm, Hellmut. "A Note on Sun Ch'o and His *Yü-Tao-Lun.*" *Sino-Indian Studies,* Liebenthal festschrift, 5.3–4 (1957).

———. "Shih Ch'ung and His Chin-ku-Yüan." *Monumenta Serica* 18 (1959).

Wright, Arthur F. "Biography and Hagiography: Hui-chiao's *Lives of Eminent Monks.*" In the *Silver Jubilee Volume of the Zinbun-kagaku-kenkyusyo.* Kyoto: Kyoto University, Institute for Research in the Humanities, 1954.

———. "Buddhism and Chinese Culture: Phases of Interaction." *Journal of Asian Studies* 17.1 (1957).

———. "The Formation of Sui Ideology, 581–604." In *Chinese Thought and Institutions,* edited by John K. Fairbank. Chicago: University of Chicago Press, 1957.

———. "Fu I and the Rejection of Buddhism." *Journal of the History of Ideas* 12.1 (1951).

———. *The Sui Dynasty.* New York: Alfred A. Knopf, 1978.

———. "T'ang T'ai-tsung: The Man and the Persona." In *Essays on T'ang Society: The Interplay of Social, Political and Economic Forces,* edited by John Curtis Perry and Bardwell L. Smith. Leiden: E. J. Brill, 1976.

Wu Chu-chu. "Hao-men cheng-chih tsai nan-fang te i-chih: Wang Tao te 'k'uei-k'uei chih cheng'" (The Transplantation of Magnate Politics to the South: The "Confused Government" of Wang Tao). *Fu-chien shih-fan ta-hsüeh hsüeh-pao: Che-she-pan* 1992.2.

Wu Hsien-ch'ing. "Hsi-Chin mo te liu-min pao-tung" (Refugee Riots at the End of the Western Chin). *Shih-huo pan-yüeh k'an* 1.6 (1935).

———. "Nan-ch'ao ta-tsu te ting-sheng yü shuai-lo" (The Prosperity and Decline of Southern Dynasties Great Families). *Shih-huo pan-yüeh k'an* 1.10 (1935).

———. "Wei-Chin shih-ch'i she-hui ching-chi te chuan-pien" (Social and Economic Changes in the Wei and Chin Period). *Shih-huo pan-yüeh k'an* 1.2 (1934).

Wu, Lu-ch'iang, and Tenny L. Davis. "An Ancient Chinese Treatise on Alchemy Entitled *Ts'an T'ung Ch'i.*" *Isis* 18.2 (1932).

Wu Tse. "Liu-ch'ao she-hui ching-chi cheng-chih te fa-chan kuei-lü ho t'e-tien" (The Laws of Development and Special Characteristics of Society, Economics, and Politics in the Six Dynasties). *Su-chou ta-hsüeh hsüeh-pao: Che-she-pan* 1990.3.

Xiong, Victor Cunrui. "Sui Yangdi and the Building of Sui-Tang Luoyang." *Journal of Asian Studies* 52.1 (1993).

Yang Hsiang-k'uei. "Shih-lun Tung-Han Pei-Wei chih chi Chung-kuo feng-chien she-hui te t'e-cheng" (An Examination of the Special Characteristics of Chinese Feudal Society between the Eastern Han and the Northern Wei [A.D. 25–534]). In *Ching-shih-chai hsüeh-shu wen-chi*. 1953; Shanghai: Shang-hai jen-min ch'u-pan-she, 1983.

Yang Kuang-hui. "Kuan-p'in, feng-chüeh yü men-fa shih-tsu" (Official Rank, Appointment to the Nobility, and Hereditary Great Families). *Hang-chou ta-hsüeh hsüeh-pao: Che-she-pan* 1990.4.

Yang, Lien-sheng. "Great Families of Eastern Han." In *The Making of China: Main Themes in Premodern Chinese History*, edited by Chun-shu Chang. Englewood Cliffs, N.J.: Prentice-Hall, 1975.

———. "Notes on the Economic History of the Chin Dynasty." In id., *Studies in Chinese Institutional History*. Cambridge: Harvard University Press, 1961.

Yang Shu-fan. "Wei-Chin chiu-p'in chung-cheng chih-tu chi ch'i tui cheng-feng chih ying-hsiang" (The Nine Ranks and Arbiters System of Wei and Chin, and Its Influence on Governmental Style). *Ta-lu tsa-chih* 19.8 (1959).

Yang T'ing-hsien. "Nan-Pei-ch'ao chih shih-tsu" (The Literati of the Northern and Southern Dynasties). *Tung-fang tsa-chih* 36.7 (1939).

Yang, V. T. "About *Shih Shuo Hsin Yü*." *Journal of Oriental Studies* 2.2 (1955).

Yang Yün-ju. *Chiu-p'in chung-cheng yü liu-ch'ao men-fa* (The Nine Ranks and Arbiters [System] and Six Dynasties Great Families). Chung-kuo li-shih ts'ung-shu. Shanghai: Shang-wu yin-shu-kuan, 1930.

Yano Chikara. "Dotan to hakuseki—Nanchō no seiritsu" (Residence Determination and White Registers—the Establishment of the Southern Dynasties). *Shigaku zasshi* 79.8 (1970).

Yao Ta-chung. *Nan-fang te fen-ch'i* (The Rise of the South). Taipei: San-min shu-chü, 1981.

Yasuda Jirō. "'Shinan ō Shi Kun no hanran' ni tsuite—Nanchō mon-batsu kizoku taisei to gōzoku dogō" (Concerning the "Rebellion of Prince Tzu-hsün of Chin-an"—the Southern Dynasties Great Family–Aristocratic Establishment and Local Magnates). *Tōyōshi kenkyū* 25.4 (1967).

———. "Shin-Sō kakumei to Yōshū (Jōyō) no kyōmin—gunsei shihai kara minsei shihai e" (The Chin-Sung Revolution and the Emigrants of Yung-chou (Hsiang-yang)—from Rule by Military Govern-ment to Rule by Civilian Government). *Tōyōshi kenkyū* 42.1 (1983).

Yoshida Fudōmaro. "Shindai ni okeru tochi shoyū keitai to nōgyō mon-dai" (The Form of Landownership in the Chin Dynasty and Agricul-tural Problems). *Shigaku zasshi* 43.2 (1932)

Yoshikawa Tadao. *Rikuchō seishin-shi kenkyū* (Studies in the Spiritual His-tory of the Six Dynasties). Kyoto: Dōhōsha, 1984.

Yoshimori Kensuke. "'San-ku kei-ji' no kenkyū: Sei-Shin shoki no ribu senyō" (Studies of the "Mountain Duke's Announcements": Employ-ment by the Board of Civil Office in the First Part of the Western

Chin). In *Chūgoku kizokusei shakai no kenkyū*, edited by Kawakatsu Yoshio and Tonami Mamoru. Kyoto: Kyōto daigaku jinbun kagaku kenkyūsho, 1987.

———. "Shin-Sō kakumei to Kōnan shakai" (The Chin-Sung Revolution and Chiang-nan Society). *Shirin* 63.2 (1980).

Yü Ying-shih. *Chung-kuo chih-shih chieh-ts'eng shih-lun (ku-tai p'ien)* (Essays in the History of the Chinese Intellectual Class [the Ancient Period]). Taipei: Lien-ching ch'u-pan shih-yeh kung-ssu, 1980.

———. "Han-Chin chih chi shih chih hsin tzu-chüeh yü hsin ssu-ch'ao" (The New Self-Consciousness and New Currents of Thought of the Literati in the Time between Han and Chin). In *Shih yü Chung-kuo wen-hua*, edited by Chou Ku-ch'eng. Chung-kuo wen-hua shih ts'ung-shu. Shanghai: Shang-hai jen-min ch'u-pan-she, 1987.

———. "Individualism and the Neo-Taoist Movement in Wei-Chin China." In *Individualism and Holism: Studies in Confucian and Taoist Values*, edited by Donald J. Munro. Ann Arbor: Center for Chinese Studies, University of Michigan, 1985.

———. "Life and Immortality in the Mind of Han China." *Harvard Journal of Asiatic Studies* 25 (1965).

———. "Ming-chiao ssu-hsiang yü Wei-Chin shih-feng te yen-pien" (The Thought of the School of Names and the Evolution of Wei and Chin Literati Style). In *Shih yü Chung-kuo wen-hua*, edited by Chou Ku-ch'eng. Chung-kuo wen-hua shih ts'ung-shu. Shanghai: Shang-hai jen-min ch'u-pan-she, 1987.

———. " 'O Soul, Come Back!' A Study in the Changing Conceptions of the Soul and Afterlife in Pre-Buddhist China." *Harvard Journal of Asiatic Studies* 47.2 (1987).

———. *Trade and Expansion in Han China: A Study in the Structure of Sino-Barbarian Economic Relations*. Berkeley: University of California Press, 1967.

Ziporyn, Brook. "The Self-so and Its Traces in the Thought of Guo Xiang." *Philosophy East and West* 43.3 (1993).

Zürcher, Erik. *The Buddhist Conquest of China: The Spread and Adaptation of Buddhism in Early Medieval China*. Leiden: E. J. Brill, 1959.

———. "Buddhist Influence on Early Taoism: A Survey of Scriptural Evidence." *T'oung Pao* 66.1–3 (1980).

———. " 'Prince Moonlight': Messianism and Eschatology in Early Medieval Chinese Buddhism." *T'oung Pao* 68.1–3 (1982).

Tertiary Sources:
Studies on Topics Other Than China in the Han through T'ang

Ames, Roger T. "The Common Ground of Self-Cultivation in Classical Taoism and Confucianism." *Ch'ing-hua hsüeh-pao*, new series 17.1–2 (1985).

Ames, Roger T., Sin-wai Chan, and Mau-sang Ng, eds. *Interpreting Culture through Translation: A Festschrift for D. C. Lau.* Hong Kong: The Chinese University Press, 1991.

An Tso-chang. "Ts'ung Shui-hu-ti Ch'in mu chu-chien k'an Ch'in-tai te nung-yeh ching-chi" (The Agricultural Economy of the Ch'in Dynasty as Seen from the Bamboo Tablets in the Ch'in Grave at Shui-hu-ti). In *Ch'in-Han shih lun-ts'ung*, 1. Sian: Shan-hsi jen-min ch'u-pan-she, 1981.

Anderson, Benedict. *Imagined Communities: Reflections on the Origin and Spread of Nationalism.* Revised ed.; London: Verso, 1991.

Arendt, Hannah. "On Violence." In id., *Crises of the Republic.* New York: Harcourt Brace Jovanovich, 1969.

Barfield, Thomas J. *The Perilous Frontier: Nomadic Empires and China, 221 B.C. to A.D. 1757.* Cambridge, U.K.: Blackwell Publishers, 1989.

Bauer, Wolfgang. "The Hidden Hero: Creation and Disintegration of the Ideal of Eremitism." In *Individualism and Holism: Studies in Confucian and Taoist Values*, edited by Donald J. Munro. Ann Arbor: Center for Chinese Studies, University of Michigan, 1985.

Bestor, Theodore C. *Neighborhood Tokyo.* Stanford: Stanford University Press, 1989.

Birch, Cyril, ed. *Anthology of Chinese Literature: From Early Times to the Fourteenth Century.* New York: Grove Press, 1965.

Bodde, Derk. "Feudalism in China." In *Feudalism in History*, edited by Rushton Coulborn. Princeton: Princeton University Press, 1956.

Chang, Chun-shu. "The Periodization of Chinese History: A Survey of Major Schemes and Hypotheses." In *The Making of China: Main Themes in Premodern Chinese History*, edited by Chun-shu Chang. Englewood Cliffs, N.J.: Prentice-Hall, 1975.

Chang Chün-mai. *Chung-kuo chuan-chih chün-chu cheng-chih chih p'ing-i* (A Critical Evaluation of China's System of Government by Autocratic Monarchs). Taipei: Hung-wen-kuan ch'u-pan-she, 1986.

Chang Po-ch'üan. "'Chung-hua i-t'i' lun" (On the "Unity of China"). *Chi-lin ta-hsüeh she-hui k'o-hsüeh hsüeh-pao* 1986.5.

Chao Kang. *Man and Land in Chinese History: An Economic Analysis.* Stanford: Stanford University Press, 1986.

Chao Shih-ch'ao. *Chou-tai kuo-yeh chih-tu yen-chiu* (Studies of the Chou Dynasty State and Wilderness System). Sian: Shan-hsi jen-min ch'u-pan-she, 1991.

Ch'en, Kenneth. *Buddhism in China: A Historical Survey.* Princeton: Princeton University Press, 1964.

Ch'en Kuang-chung and Tsang Jung, eds. *Ch'u-chi chung-hsüeh k'o-pen: Chung-kuo li-shih*, vol. 1 (Introductory Middle School Text Book: Chinese History). 1981; Peking: Jen-min chiao-yü ch'u-pan-she, 1985.

Chiang Ta-ch'un. "Li-shih li-lun" (Historical Theories). In *Chung-kuo li-shih hsüeh ssu-shih nien, 1949–1989,* edited by Hsiao Li. Peking: Shu-mu wen-hsien ch'u-pan-she, 1989.

Chin Kuan-t'ao and Liu Ch'ing-feng. *Hsing-sheng yü wei-chi: Lun Chung-kuo feng-chien she-hui te ch'ao wen-ting chieh-kou* (Prosperity and Crisis: On the Super Stable Structure of Chinese Feudal Society). 1982; Taipei: T'ien-shan ch'u-pan-she, 1987.

Ching, Julia. "The Ancient Sages *(sheng):* Their Identity and Their Place in Chinese Intellectual History." *Oriens Extremus* 30 (1983–1986).

Chou Tao-chi. "Wo-kuo min-pen ssu-hsiang te fen-hsi yü t'an-t'ao" (An Analysis and Discussion of Our Country's Thought Concerning the Primacy of the People). In *Chung-kuo shih-hsüeh lun-wen hsüan-chi* 5, edited by Wang Shou-nan. Taipei: Yu-shih wen-hua shih-yeh kung-ssu, 1984.

Ch'ü, T'ung-tsu. "Chinese Class Structure and Its Ideology." In *Chinese Thought and Institutions,* edited by John K. Fairbank. Chicago: University of Chicago Press, 1957.

De Bary, Wm. Theodore, et al., eds. *Sources of Chinese Tradition,* vol. 1. New York: Columbia University Press, 1960.

Dilthey, W. *Selected Writings.* Edited by H. P. Rickman. Cambridge: Cambridge University Press, 1976.

Dittmer, Lowell, and Samuel S. Kim, eds. *China's Quest for National Identity.* Ithaca: Cornell University Press, 1993.

Dreyfus, Hubert L., and Paul Rabinow. *Michel Foucault: Beyond Structuralism and Hermeneutics.* 2d ed.; Chicago: University of Chicago Press, 1983.

Duara, Prasenjit. *Culture, Power, and the State: Rural North China, 1900–1942.* Stanford: Stanford University Press, 1988.

Dull, Jack L. "The Evolution of Government in China." In *Heritage of China: Contemporary Perspectives on Chinese Civilization,* edited by Paul S. Ropp. Berkeley: University of California Press, 1990.

Duus, Peter. *Feudalism in Japan.* 2d edition; New York: Alfred A. Knopf, 1976.

Ebrey, Patricia. "The Chinese Family and the Spread of Confucian Values." In *The East Asian Region: Confucian Heritage and Its Modern Adaptation,* edited by Gilbert Rozman. Princeton: Princeton University Press, 1991.

Elvin, Mark. *The Pattern of the Chinese Past: A Social and Economic Interpretation.* Stanford: Stanford University Press, 1973.

Fairbank, John King. *The United States and China.* 4th edition, enlarged; Cambridge: Harvard University Press, 1983.

Feng Yu-lan. *Chung-kuo che-hsüeh-shih hsin-pien* (A New Edition of Chinese Philosophical History). 2 vols. Peking: Jen-min ch'u-pan-she, 1964.

———. *Chung-kuo che-hsüeh-shih shih-liao hsüeh* (A Study of Historical

Sources for the History of Chinese Philosophy). In *San-sung-t'ang ch'üan chi*, vol. 6. 1962; Honan: Ho-nan jen-min ch'u-pan-she, 1989.

Foucault, Michel. *The History of Sexuality*, vol. 1: *An Introduction*. Translated by Robert Hurley. New York: Vintage Books, 1980.

————. *The Order of Things: An Archaeology of the Human Sciences*. New York: Vintage Books, 1970.

Friedman, Edward, Paul G. Pickowicz, and Mark Selden. *Chinese Village, Socialist State*. New Haven: Yale University Press, 1991.

Fung, Yu-lan [Feng Yu-lan]. *A Short History of Chinese Philosophy*. Edited by Derk Bodde. New York: The Free Press, 1948.

Hekman, Susan J. *Hermeneutics and the Sociology of Knowledge*. Cambridge, Eng.: Polity Press, 1986.

Henderson, John B. *The Development and Decline of Chinese Cosmology*. New York: Columbia University Press, 1984.

Hsiao Kung-chuan. *A History of Chinese Political Thought* 1. Translated by F. W. Mote. Princeton: Princeton University Press, 1979.

Hsiung T'ieh-chi and Wang Jui-ming. "Ch'in-tai te feng-chien t'u-ti so-yu-chih" (The Feudal System of Landownership of the Ch'in Dynasty). In *Yün-meng Ch'in-chien yen-chiu*. Peking: Chung-hua shu-chü, 1981.

Hulsewé, A. F. P. *Remnants of Ch'in Law: An annotated translation of the Ch'in legal and administrative rules of the 3rd century B.C. discovered in Yün-meng Prefecture, Hu-pei Province, in 1975*. Leiden: E. J. Brill, 1985.

Kao Ming-shih. "Yün-meng Ch'in-chien yü Ch'in-Han shih yen-chiu: I Jih-pen te yen-chiu ch'eng-kuo wei chung-hsin" (The Ch'in Documents from Yün-meng and the Study of Ch'in-Han History: Taking the Results of Japanese Research as Central). *Shih-huo yüeh-k'an*, new series 11.3 (1981).

Kao Shang-chih. "Ch'in-chien lü-wen chung te 'shou-t'ien'" ("Conferment of Fields" in the Legal Texts of the Ch'in Documents). *Ch'in-Han shih lun-ts'ung* 3. Sian: Shan-hsi jen-min ch'u-pan-she, 1986.

Ko Chao-kuang. *Tao-chiao yü Chung-kuo wen-hua* (Taoism and Chinese Civilization). Chung-kuo wen-hua-shih ts'ung-shu. Shanghai: Shanghai jen-min ch'u-pan-she, 1987.

Kuo Mo-jo. *Nu-li-chih shih-tai* (The Slave-System Era). 1954; Peking: Jen-min ch'u-pan-she, 1973.

Lee, Mabel Ping-hua. *The Economic History of China: With Special Reference to Agriculture*. 1921; New York: Ams Press, 1969.

Legge, James, trans. *The Four Books*. Reprint; Taipei: Culture Book Co., 1979.

————. *The Li Ki*. Sacred Books of the East, vol. 27. Oxford: The Clarendon Press, 1885.

————. *The Yi King*. Sacred Books of the East, vol. 16. 1882; Delhi: Motilal Banarsidass, 1966.

Levenson, Joseph R. "Ill Wind in the Well-Field: The Erosion of the Confucian Ground of Controversy." In *The Confucian Persuasion,* edited by Arthur F. Wright. Stanford: Stanford University Press, 1960.

Li Chih-yung, ed. *Chung-kuo ch'i-kung shih* (A History of Chinese Breath Control). Honan: Ho-nan k'o-hsüeh chi-shu ch'u-pan-she, 1988.

Li Hsüeh-ch'in. *Tung-Chou yü Ch'in-tai wen-ming* (Eastern Chou and Ch'in Dynasty Civilization). Peking: Wen-wu ch'u-pan-she, 1984.

Li Shu. "Chung-kuo she-hui k'o-hsüeh san-shih nien" (Thirty Years of Chinese Social Science). *Li-shih yen-chiu* 11 (1979).

Li Yüan. "Wo-kuo li-shih shang te san tz'u wen-hua wei-chi" (Three Cultural Crises in the History of Our Country). *Pei-fang lun-ts'ung* 1988.3.

Lin, Paul J. *A Translation of Lao Tzu's Tao Te Ching and Wang Pi's Commentary.* Michigan Papers in Chinese Studies, 30. Ann Arbor: Center for Chinese Studies, 1977.

Link, Perry. *Evening Chats in Beijing: Probing China's Predicament.* New York: W. W. Norton and Company, 1992.

Liu Ch'un-fan. "Ch'in chuan-chih chu-i chung-yang chi-ch'üan-chih te ching-chi chi-ch'u" (The Economic Basis for Ch'in's System of Autocratic Centralized Authority). *Ch'in-Han shih lun-ts'ung* 3. Sian: Shan-hsi jen-min ch'u-pan-she, 1986.

Madsen, Richard P. "The Maoist Ethic and the Moral Basis of Political Activism in Rural China." In *Moral Behavior in Chinese Society,* edited by Richard W. Wilson et al. New York: Praeger Publishers, 1981.

March, Andrew L. *The Idea of China: Myth and Theory in Geographic Thought.* New York: Praeger Publishers, 1974.

Marx, Karl, and Friedrich Engels. *The Communist Manifesto.* Edited by Samuel H. Beer. New York: Appleton-Century-Crofts, 1955.

————. *The German Ideology,* parts 1 and 3. Translated by R. Pascal. London: Lawrence and Wishart, 1940.

Min, Tu-ki. *National Polity and Local Power: The Transformation of Late Imperial China.* Edited by Philip A. Kuhn and Timothy Brook. Cambridge: Harvard University Press, 1989.

Munro, Donald J. *The Concept of Man in Early China.* Stanford: Stanford University Press, 1969.

Nakayashiki Hiroshi. *Chūgoku ideorogii ron* (On Chinese Ideology). Tokyo: Keisō shobō, 1983.

Parekh, Bhikhu C. *Marx's Theory of Ideology.* London: Croom Helm, 1982.

Pas, Julian F. "Chuang Tzu's Essays on 'Free Flight into Transcendence' and 'Responsive Rulership.' " *Journal of Chinese Philosophy* 8.4 (1981).

Pilz, Erich. "'Feudalismus' und Theoriebildung in der Volksrepublik China: Zur Debatte der 50er Jahre über die feudale Grundeigentumsform." *Oriens Extremus* 30 (1983–1986).

Potter, Jack M. "Land and Lineage in Traditional China." In *Family and Kinship in Chinese Society*, edited by Maurice Freedman. Stanford: Stanford University Press, 1970.

Pritchard, Earl H. "Thoughts on the Historical Development of the Population of China." *Journal of Asian Studies* 23.1 (1963).

Pye, Lucian W. *Asian Power and Politics: The Cultural Dimensions of Authority*. Cambridge: Harvard University Press, 1985.

Racevskis, Karlis. *Michel Foucault and the Subversion of the Intellect*. Ithaca: Cornell University Press, 1983.

Schwartz, Benjamin. "Some Polarities in Confucian Thought." In *Confucianism and Chinese Civilization*, edited by Arthur F. Wright. Stanford: Stanford University Press, 1964.

———. *The World of Thought in Ancient China*. Cambridge: Harvard University Press, 1985.

Searle, John R. *The Rediscovery of the Mind*. Cambridge: MIT Press, 1992.

Shang Ping-ho (1870–1950). *Li-tai she-hui chuang-k'uang shih* (A History of Social Conditions in Various Ages). No publication data available.

Ting I-hua. "Ch'in Shih-huang te cheng-kang hsüan-yen ho hsin-li chi-lu: Ch'in Shih-huang tung hsün k'o-shih wen-tz'u p'ing-i" (The First Emperor of Ch'in's Statement of His Principles of Government and Psychological Record: A Critical Evaluation of the Language of the Stone Inscriptions from the First Emperor of Ch'in's Eastern Circuits). *Ch'in-ling Ch'in-yung yen-chiu tung-t'ai* 1992.1.

Ts'ao Ke-ch'eng. "Chou-tai ts'un-she t'u-ti chih-tu te yen-pien" (The Evolution of the Village Land System in the Chou Dynasty). *Pei-fang lun-ts'ung* 1984.1.

Tu Cheng-sheng. " 'Pien-hu ch'i-min' te ch'u-hsien chi ch'i li-shih i-i: Pien-hu ch'i-min te yen-chiu chih-i" (The Appearance of the "Registration of Commoner Households" and Its Historical Significance: A Study of the Registration of Commoner Households). *Chung-yang yen-chiu-yüan, Li-shih yü-yen yen-chiu-so chi-k'an* 54.3 (1983).

Tu, Wei-ming. "The Confucian Tradition in Chinese History." In *Heritage of China: Contemporary Perspectives on Chinese Civilization*, edited by Paul S. Ropp. Berkeley: University of California Press, 1990.

Twitchett, Denis. "Problems of Chinese Biography." In *Confucian Personalities*, edited by Arthur F. Wright and Denis Twitchett. Stanford: Stanford University Press, 1962.

Wang, Gungwu. "Feng Tao: An Essay on Confucian Loyalty." In *Confucianism and Chinese Civilization*, edited by Arthur F. Wright. Stanford: Stanford University Press, 1959.

Watson, Burton. *Early Chinese Literature*. New York: Columbia University Press, 1962.

Wright, Arthur F. *Buddhism in Chinese History*. Stanford: Stanford University Press, 1959.

Wu Ch'eng-hsüeh. "Lun wen-hsüeh shang te nan-pei-p'ai yü nan-pei-tsung" (On Northern and Southern Schools and Northern and Southern Sects in Literature). *Chung-shan ta-hsüeh hsüeh-pao (she-hui k'o-hsüeh-pan)* 1991.4.

Wu Hsiao-ch'iang. *"Jih-shu* so chien Ch'in-jen chih sheng-ssu kuan" (Ch'in Views of Life and Death as Seen in the "Book of Days"). *Ch'in-ling Ch'in-yung yen-chiu tung-t'ai* 1992.2.

Wu Shu-p'ing. "Yün-meng Ch'in-chien so fan-ying te Ch'in-tai she-hui chieh-chi chuang-k'uang" (The Class Situation in Ch'in Dynasty Society as Reflected in the Yün-meng Ch'in Documents). In *Yün-meng Ch'in-chien yen-chiu*. Peking: Chung-hua shu-chü, 1981.

Yang K'uan. *Chan-kuo shih* (A History of the Warring States). 2d edition; Shanghai: Shang-hai jen-min ch'u-pan-she, 1980.

Yen Ts'un-hsin. "Feng-chien cheng-chih chih-tu te i ko ken-pen ch'üeh-hsien—tu *Shuo-yüan, chün-tao*" (A Basic Defect in the Feudal Political System—Reading the "Way of the Lord" [Section] of the *Shuo-yüan*). Appendix to Hsieh T'ien-yu, *Chuan-chih chu-i t'ung-chih hsia te ch'en-min hsin-li* (The Psychology of Subjects under Autocratic Rule). Ch'ang-ch'un: Chi-lin wen-shih ch'u-pan-she, 1990.

Yü Ying-shih. "Min-tsu i-shih yü kuo-chia kuan-nien" (National Consciousness and the Concept of the State). *Ming-pao yüeh-k'an* 18.12 (1983).

Yüan Chung-i. "Ts'ung Ch'in Shih-huang ling te k'ao-ku tzu-liao k'an Ch'in wang-ch'ao te yao-i" (Ch'in Dynasty Forced Labor as Viewed through Archeological Evidence from the First Emperor of Ch'in's Tomb). In *Ch'in Shih-huang ling ping-ma-yung po-wu-kuan lun-wen hsüan*, edited by Yüan Chung-i et al. 1983; Sian: Hsi-pei ta-hsüeh ch'u-pan-she, 1989.

INDEX

administrative neglect or indifference, 5, 13–14, 83–85, 126–128; in favor of self-cultivation, 95, 130, 133. *See also* reclusion

agriculture, 69. *See also* estates; land distribution/control; landlords

alchemy, 103

America (colonial), 61

Ames, Roger, 97–98, 130

Anderson, Benedict, 2

aristocracy, 6–8, 35, 38, 74, 80; ancient, 9; civilistic bias, 56–58; distinguished from commoners, 81–83. *See also* great families; literati; *shih-ta-fu*

Augustine, Saint, 98

autocracy (absolutism), 4, 14, 37; "feudal autocracy," 9–12, 16; and restoration under Sui and T'ang, 136–139

avoidance, rule of, 6, 139

Balazs, Etienne, 22, 65–66

Bestor, Theodore, 2, 48

Bodde, Derk, 62, 67

Book of Changes, 90, 92, 105, 133

Buddhism: and detachment, 120–122, 126; and *hsüan-hsüeh*, 110; introduced to China, 112–116; and *Prajñā* schools, 117–119; and reincarnation, 111

bureaucracy: and dominant role in society, 72; expansion of, 27, 83–84; and literati composition, 4–5, 7, 80; privileges of, 66–67; selection of, 42, 55–56, 73–79, 129

calligraphy, 125, 127

camps (fortifications), 42

centralization of authority, 8–10, 12, 14, 37; extent of in medieval China, 45, 50; under T'ang, 138–139; in (Ts'ao) Wei dynasty, 79–80

Central Plain, 2, 25, 43

Chang Chan, 102, 105–106

chang-chü (chapter and verse) scholarship, 88, 114

Chang Chün-mai, 13

Chang Hua, 71, 102–103, 107

Chang Tao-ling, 96

chan-t'ien land system, 63–64; effectiveness evaluated, 65–67

Chao I, 13, 32, 38, 81

Ch'en dynasty, 138

ch'i (substance), 89–91, 100–106, 131

Chia I, 12

Chiang-nan, 1–2, 28, 33; development of, 69–71; as exotic frontier, 26, 52

ABOUT THE AUTHOR

CHARLES HOLCOMBE is associate professor of Chinese history at the University of Northern Iowa. His Ph.D. is from the University of Michigan (1986). Research for the present book took him from Japan to Mainland China, Taiwan, and the Library of Congress. Previous publications include "The Bonds of Empire: Liberty in Early Medieval China," in *The Historian* (54.4 [1992]), and "The Exemplar State: Ideology, Self-Cultivation, and Power in Fourth Century China," in the *Harvard Journal of Asiatic Studies* (49.1 [1989]).

Production Notes

Composition and paging were done in
FrameMaker software on an AGFA AccuSet
Postscript Imagesetter by the design
and production staff of University of
Hawaii Press.

The text typeface is Baskerville
and the display typeface
is Eras.

Offset presswork and binding were done by
The Maple-Vail Book Manufacturing Group.
Text paper is Writers RR Offset, basis 50.